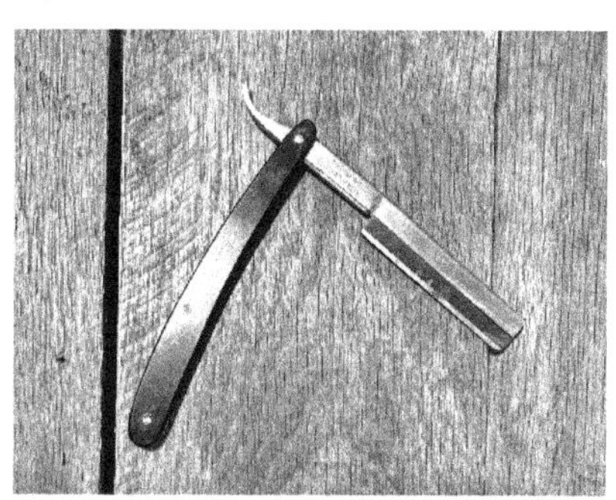

It's only in love and in murder that we still remain sincere.
Friedrich Durrenmatt

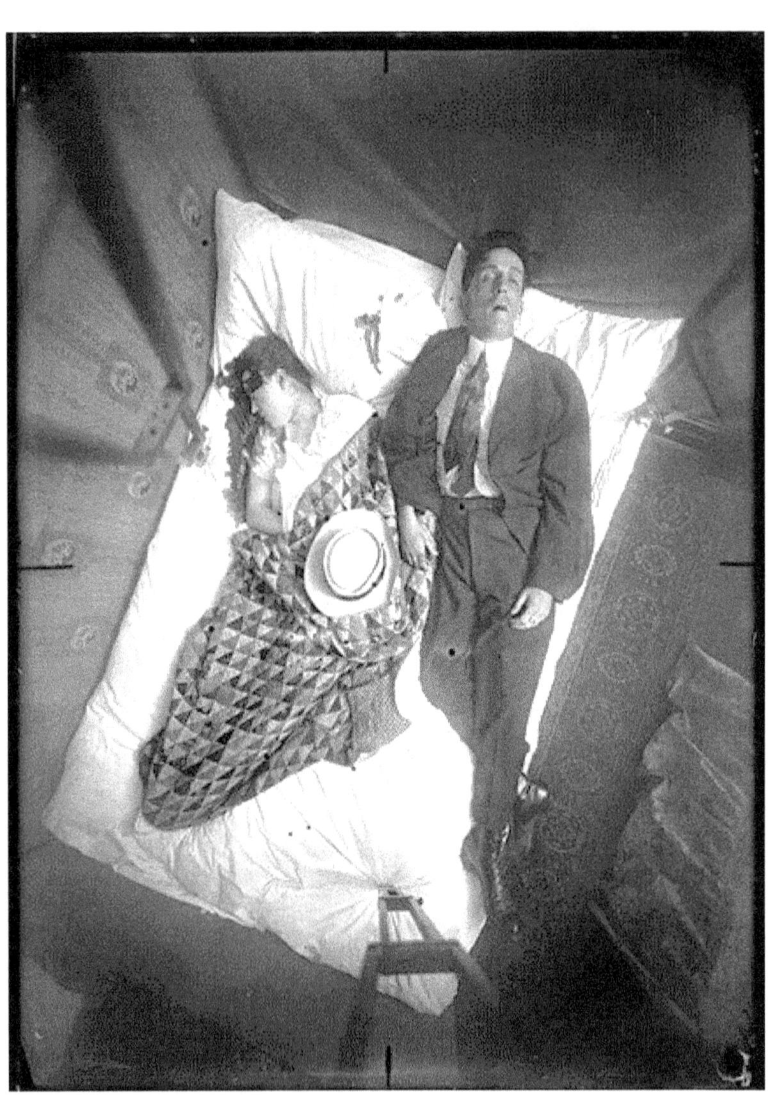

HELL HATH NO FURY

13 MORE SPIRITS OF THE SINISTER & THE SLAIN

BY TROY TAYLOR AND AMANDA R. WOOMER

AN AMERICAN HAUNTINGS INK BOOK

HELL HATH NO FURY 3
13 MORE SPIRITS OF THE SINISTER AND SLAIN

ISBN: 978-1-958589-05-2

Published by American Hauntings Ink
228 South Mauvaisterre Street - Jacksonville Il - 62650
www.americanhauntingsink.com

Cover Design by April Slaughter
Interior Design by Troy Taylor

Printed in the United States of America

TABLE OF CONTENTS

THE SLAIN

INTRODUCTION

"A villain is just a victim whose story hasn't been told yet."

In previous books in this series, I used a long quote from the writer Rudyard Kipling that reminds us that in almost every case, the female of any species is always "much deadlier than the male."

I often wonder what the context was for Kipling's quote. This was a man who championed the colonialism of England in India, who lived in a time of rampant misogyny, and regarded women in general as being only one step higher in importance than the native people that he lived among and wrote about in his books. Was Kipling a man who overlooked the danger of the women who lived in his time, or did he truly consider them dangerous? And was that danger merely because - living in an era designed for the importance of men - they were second-class citizens struggling to be noticed?

Or was Kipling as intelligent as he seemed and knew that women were dangerous simply because they had been overlooked, ignored, and underestimated for so long?

I'd like to think it was the latter, but we'll likely never know. What we do know is that women have rarely been given the respect they deserve, even when it comes to homicide. As writers, researchers, historians, and police officers can assure you - they do deserve respect. Murders committed by women are almost always more terrifying than any man can imagine.

Don't believe me? Think of a horrific case in which a man murders a child. Now, imagine that same murder committed by a woman against a child. And worse yet, what if that child is her own?

Frightened yet? You should be.

Women kill for money, revenge, love, and yes, occasionally, just for pleasure. They have left behind slain lovers, dismembered children, and spirits who refuse to rest. They can be insane, vengeful, and malicious, and their ghosts may continue to demand attention long after their deaths.

They are also the slain - victims who become enduring specters that beg for their stories to be told.

The women within these pages are the lost, disappeared, misguided, spurned, wicked, put-upon, vicious, neglected, misunderstood, sinister, haunted, devious, mistreated, murdered, and spectral - and women you will never forget.

After two books about women who prey on the innocent - and who are sometimes the innocent who are preyed upon - I knew there were more stories to be told.

So, with this third book, I have recruited the talents of Amanda R. Woomer to help me tell more of these stories. Amanda is a passionate advocate for the stories of women, producing an entire series of journals called *The Feminine Macabre*, which allows accounts of the supernatural to be told strictly by women.

Together, we have compiled a new collection of strange tales that may not always tell stories of ghosts and hauntings but are so dark, so wicked, and often so gruesome that they had to be included.

All the stories you are about to read are tales of terror, bloodshed, suffering, death, and murder - and continue to be tales not for the faint of heart or the weak of stomach.

Shakespeare once told us, "Hell hath no fury like a woman scorned..." but honestly, I think that being "scorned" is nothing compared to a woman who is underestimated.

Try that, and you'll pay for it, believe me.

Troy Taylor
Spring 2023

PART ONE
THE SINISTER

"THE RATTLESNAKE'S BLONDE"
BURMAH ADAMS
BY TROY TAYLOR

Wednesday night, August 16, 1933, was a warm one in Los Angeles, but Charles Allen, whom his friends called "Crombie," was in a great mood. He had a date. He'd been friends with Cora Withington for almost a year. The shy, 52-year-old schoolteacher had finally agreed to go to the movies with him.

Crombie took Cora to see the new film Tugboat Annie at Loew's State Theater downtown. The show got out around 9:30 that night.

Knowing how badly Cora wanted to learn to drive, he let her take the wheel of his new Chevrolet coupe. As she approached the stoplight at Third Street and Lafayette Park Place, a car suddenly screeched to a stop next to theirs. A man jumped out of the passenger side with a gun in his hand. He waved it in the face of the couple. "Shell out, sweetheart! And that goes for you, too!" the man cried out.

Crombie hurriedly handed over his watch and the $18 in his wallet. Cora, understandably terrified, started to hand over her purse with shaking hands.

"The next thing I knew," Crombie later said, "there was an explosion - and I felt a sting in my neck."

He didn't realize until moments later that the bullet that nicked his neck was the same bullet that tore through Cora's left eye and exited close to her right one. Blood sprayed across the car's windshield, and the mild-mannered teacher slumped over the steering wheel.

Her purse had snagged on something when she was handing it over. The man shot her for being too slow.

As Crombie reached for Cora, he saw the strangest thing --- the driver of the robber's car was a young woman with platinum blonde hair that was peeking out from under a brown scarf. She was laughing as the car squealed away.

Despite his injury, Crombie memorized the license plate number of the bandit's car. Both victims survived their wounds, but Cora was permanently blinded in both eyes.

The car the bandits were driving didn't belong to them. It was owned by a salesman named Leslie Bartel, who lived about a mile from the scene. He was horrified when he discovered it had been used in the crime.

Earlier that day, while Leslie was chatting with a neighbor, a man and woman drove up and demanded his cash and the key to his car. They left behind a gray Chevrolet coupe that had also been stolen. Leslie noticed that both the man and the woman wore dark horn-rimmed sunglasses, and the woman wore a brown turban-style scarf with platinum blonde hair sticking out at the bottom.

Leslie got his car back the next day. The police had found it abandoned several miles away. On August 22, to identify the man who had shot Crombie and Cora, the police asked Leslie to come in and look at no fewer than 127 suspects they had rounded up from all over the city.

Whomever the man was, he wasn't there.

That same day, a couple who matched the description of the killers robbed seven other people. One of them, Joe Robinson, slowed for a traffic light at Pico Boulevard and Norton Avenue, and as he did, a car pulled up alongside him and forced him off the road. A man, pistol in hand, jumped onto his running board and forced him to hand over $10.

Another man, G.M. Gardner, was held up by the couple when they drove up to his mechanic's garage at San Marino and Vermont. They took $80 from him - his earnings from the week.

On August 26, the couple struck again, robbing several people and grocery stores. The most they got that day was $65 from a carpenter who lived on Occidental Boulevard.

Five days later, on August 31, the pair pulled up to an apartment building at 227 South Western Avenue. As the woman waited in an idling car, the man followed Clarence Lewis into the front door of the building, grabbed him around the chest from behind with one arm, and jammed the muzzle of his pistol to the man's head with the other. "Empty your pockets," he snarled.

But the killer had picked the wrong man. Clarence slipped out of the man's grip, spun around, and punched the man in the jaw. The bandit fired two wild shots as he stumbled back to the car. The blonde woman peeled away.

Only 20 minutes later, though, they struck again. The car stopped at a Safeway grocery store, and while the woman waited with the motor running, the man entered the store and forced manager Jack Hanford into the back room, where he bound and gagged him. He then stuffed the contents of the cash register - about $40 - into his pocket and fled.

These were only a few of the crimes committed by the couple - it would later turn out to be at least a dozen felonies and likely more than 20 - between August 1 and September 1, 1933. In many of the cases, the victims couldn't make a solid identification for one simple reason - they were distracted by the blonde woman's appearance, her apparent thrill about committing the crime, or both.

Mercifully, none of their victims were killed, though this was cold comfort to the residents of Los Angeles - all of whom owned cars. Knowing that the car that stopped next to you at a light might contain the bandits was an unnerving thought.

And that wasn't all that was unnerving. It would be the blonde's laughter as she drove away from the scenes of the crimes that spurred the Los Angeles Police Department to launch the most extensive manhunt the city had seen in several years. A group of police, sheriffs, and lawmakers put together by District Attorney

Buron Fitts used the couple as an example of why extraordinary measures were needed to fight crime. It included a blanket indictment and a $50,000 bond for any person suspected of gang activity - man or woman.

The couple's reign of terror ended on September 6, 1933, when the man was killed in a shootout with police. The blonde was taken into custody, and the police were surprised to find that she was no Bonnie Parker - she was a beautiful, educated, intelligent young woman who had been raised by a loving family.

So, why would 19-year-old Burmah Arline Adams get involved in a violent life of crime? That was simple - she was having fun.

Much to her delight, Burmah soon became a legend. The newspapers were desperate for the kind of sensation that would help them survive the Depression, and when radio broadcasting companies were competing with one another for bigger pieces of a national audience.

Burmah's romantic story landed at just the right time, as the Depression was in full swing. It provided plenty of fodder for the press, who loved the seductive and titillating lives of "female outlaws." Her devil-may-care attitude provided a thrill for readers who'd been beaten down and trampled on by the banks who took their homes, the grocery stores who cut off their credit, and the authorities who never gave them a fair deal.

Burmah's story became one of bloodshed and violence and one that was uniquely Los Angeles during one of the most volatile periods in the city's history.

Burmah Adams grew up in Santa Ana, California, a place famous for the winds that bear its name - winds that crime author Raymond Chandler said could "curl your hair and make your nerves jump and your skin itch." The city is about 30 miles from the Pacific Ocean, and in the 1920s, it was spacious, warm, clean, and surrounded by orange groves.

It was the perfect place to live for Joseph Adams. Joe contracted tuberculosis in 1920 and had a doctor who told him to move west for his health. He reluctantly gave up his job as an accountant in Indianapolis and moved his family to Santa Ana. He already had family in Orange County - a brother and a sister, and an uncle who helped him buy a delivery service for bakeries. Joe rented a house and started working to build up his customer base.

Joe's wife, Pearl, was more excited than her husband about moving to Southern California. She had been born and raised in Elkhart, Indiana, where her family had suffered one tragedy after another. The first was when her younger sister was burned to death after playing with matches in 1905. A few months later, her brother, Elmer, almost died from typhoid. Pearl herself ended up with typhoid in 1910 and scarlet fever a year later. She recovered and was working as a schoolteacher when she met Joe in 1913.

Their daughter, Burmah Arline, was born on January 9, 1914, in Cleveland, Ohio, where Joe sold insurance for a short time. Her mother and father didn't get married for another five years because Joe was still married to another woman in Kansas. The divorce came through in 1919, and Pearl gave birth to another girl, Jo Louraine, in 1924.

In Santa Ana, Burmah, her little sister, and her parents moved several times before finding a house on Birch Street, within walking distance of most conveniences and the girls' schools. Pearl started a home business making candied figs to make money when Joe's deliveries were slow, which became frequent as the Depression gripped the region.

Burmah thrived in her new home. She attended Julia C. Lathrop Junior High School, where she became a favorite of teachers and students alike. Her scores were so good that Burmah skipped a grade back in Indiana, and while young for junior high - she was only 10 - she kept pace with the rest of her class academically and socially. She took part in piano recitals and made the honor roll every semester. She was elected as an officer in the Every Girl's and Boy's Club, won awards for the fastest typing, and was chosen for every dance show put on by the YWCA in conjunction with the school.

Like most children, Burmah likely didn't know about the financial struggles of her parents and the rest of the country. Businesses and banks throughout the state closed their doors in the early 1930s. Investors and depositors lost everything. Farm income in California sank to half of what it had been just a few years earlier. Many property owners lost their homes and farms. Unemployment in the state reached a staggering 28 percent, and nearly a quarter of the population depended on public relief.

But Burmah continued to shine as she moved on to Santa Ana High School. She won a spot in the glee club and stayed on the honor roll. She could be counted on to join every social event sponsored by the junior society of the First Baptist Church, where the Adams family was in the front row on Sunday mornings. She also made a little cash on weekends serving desserts - that her father probably delivered - at wedding receptions.

Burmah's success during her first year in high school was remarkable, considering how the school year had started. One evening in mid-September, a baseball player named Liston Hill accidentally struck her with his car. He rushed her to the hospital, where doctors performed emergency surgery to relieve pressure in her fractured skull. She remained in the hospital for two weeks before she was allowed to go home and finish her recovery. Her classmates brought her flowers, puzzles, and homework for a month before she could return to school.

Years later, one of Burmah's former teachers blamed the accident for her criminal actions. Some of her classmates would say the same, recalling that "after her injury, Burmah's attitude underwent a change until she finally became a different person from the quiet studious girl of her junior high school days."

If there was a change in her personality, though, it didn't stop her from having friends and getting good grades in school. She excelled in English, Spanish, stenography, and geography. She was described as an "unusually intelligent girl who would never do anything untoward, like cheat on a test."

Blanche McDowell, who lived down the street from Burmah, later said that Burmah showed great kindness toward her father, who had a disability. Blanche often pushed her father's wheelchair into the front yard for sun and fresh air. Burmah was one of the few children who ever stopped and talked to him on her way to school.

That kindness would vanish from her life in just a few short years.

In 1929, Joe Adams was in trouble. He worked from early morning until dusk at the bakery, but during the Depression, customers could only afford to pay a fraction of what a loaf of bread cost. Because of that, bakeries could only afford to pay their delivery drivers enough to cover their gasoline and pennies for their labor. If Joe's trucks needed to be repaired, he could count on losing money for the week. It wasn't long before Joe started to show the strain of trying to make ends meet, and the stress caused his rheumatism to flare up.

Even though Burmah had hoped to attend college, she dropped out of high school at the start of her senior year and enrolled in a free cosmetology course that was being offered at the vocational school. It was the quickest and most practical way to make some money. She hadn't had a chance to train for anything else.

After six months of training with her freshly printed cosmetology license in hand, Burmah quickly found work. Her first shop was in Santa Ana, and then she moved to a more upscale salon on Balboa Island. She liked the work, but she craved more of a social life than these quiet neighborhoods had to offer a pretty, unattached young woman. So, she took a job on Wilshire Boulevard in Los Angeles and rented an apartment with some other girls.

But Burmah still couldn't get away from home. Her mother kept dropping in on her, so she decided that if she wanted to be alone, she needed to move farther away. When she heard about a new beauty shop opening in San Francisco, Burmah took a chance and bought a train ticket before her resume had even arrived there in the mail. She was hired on the spot, and Burmah packed up and moved to San Francisco. She wouldn't stay there for long, however.

On March 10, 1933, an earthquake hit the southern part of Los Angeles County. Centered in Long Beach - 20 miles west of Santa Ana - the quake killed 127 people and leveled buildings all over the area. Three people were killed in Santa Ana by falling debris. While her family was safe, Burmah couldn't bear the thought of being so far from her loved ones after such a devastating event, so she immediately quit her job in San Francisco and moved back to L.A. She quickly found a new job at Mildred Juhnke's beauty parlor on South Central Avenue.

Burmah was spending more time with her family, but that wouldn't last either. Her little sister had developed a chronic ear infection requiring a medical specialist, so Joe drove Pearl and Jo to Los Angeles once or twice weekly for treatment. They usually spent the night at Burmah's apartment on South Coronado Street.

Once Jo's condition improved, Burmah drifted along on her own. Working in the beauty parlor daily, she heard a lot of talk from her customers - hardworking clerks, stenographers, wives of wealthy husbands, and others, all with - Burmah felt - more time and money than was good for them. She admired their expensive clothes, jewelry, and shiny new cars. They gossiped about their dates and the swanky hotels, nightclubs, and theaters where they spent their evenings.

Burmah decided she wanted her own piece of the action, but at that point, she hadn't figured out how to get it. "I began to get the fever to go places and see things," she later said.

Soon, she'd have the chance - but I'm not sure it's what she had in mind.

A friend introduced Burmah to Tom White in June 1933. The friend and her date had plans to attend a dinner dance at Sebastian's Cotton Club in Culver City and invited Burmah to go with them. Her date was bringing along a friend named Tom, and while she didn't know him well, she knew he was a "good spender."

Burmah was excited and decided to spend some money she didn't have on a new dress from Bullock's department store.

She also decided to try a new look - one made popular by screen stars like Jean Harlow. She decided to dye her brunette hair platinum blonde.

Sebastian's Cotton Club was one of the premier jazz clubs in Los Angeles. Opened in 1926, it was also one of the first to feature bands made up of exclusively black musicians. It opened late at night and closed early in the morning. If you made it through the night, you'd be served breakfast in the morning.

Burmah was dazzled by the club and by her date that evening. They made a striking couple. Tom was slim with blonde hair and gray eyes. Burmah, a head shorter than her handsome dance partner, had her blonde bob and ocean-blue eyes. He told her he was a stock and bond trader and had inherited a lot of money, allowing him to travel and entertain in style.

But, of course, Tom White wasn't a stock and bond trader - he was something far different, which Burmah would soon find out.

Thomas White was born on July 21, 1897, in Plattsburgh Barracks Post Hospital in Clinton County, New York. His father, Thomas White, Sr., had emigrated from England in 1882 and enlisted in the U.S. Army soon after he arrived.

After being transferred to Fort Omaha, Nebraska, he met a woman named Irene Hamilton, a recent immigrant from Denmark. They were married in 1892 - he was 31, and she was 17. A daughter, Violet Ellen, was born while the couple lived at Fort Omaha. For the next few years, the family moved back and forth between New York and Nebraska. Tom as born in 1897, and in June of the following year, Thomas' regiment was shipped out to Cuba to fight during the Spanish-American War. After the Cuban campaign, the troops returned to Plattsburgh in September 1898.

The Whites never lived in one place for long. The army moved them between New York, Kansas, Nebraska, Washington, Wyoming, and Colorado. In December 1899, while in Detroit, the Whites welcomed a new baby girl, Maud. In 1900, Irene and the children rented a house near Vancouver Barracks, where Thomas was stationed.

Tragedy first visited the family two years later at Fort Russell in Wyoming. Maud developed a terrible case of croup and died in June 1902.

Within a year, the family had moved again to Fort Leavenworth, Kansas, where Thomas was promoted to sergeant major, the highest enlisted rank available. After a short stint in the Philippines, Thomas retired from the military.

And then tragedy returned in 1909 when Irene died. The circumstances of her passing are unknown, but by 1901, Violet and Tom were enrolled in Catholic boarding schools in Denver, where Thomas was working.

It was in Denver where Tom first started finding trouble. In April 1911, he and a friend were caught stealing bicycles from a local grad school. He was committed to the State Industrial School for Boys in Golden, Colorado - a reform school for juvenile offenders.

But it didn't reform Tom White. His first major crime - or at least the first one he was caught - was attempting to rob a drug store in Colorado Springs in August 1916. He and a friend pried open the back door and were helping themselves to the cash in the register when a police officer happened by. The thieves almost escaped but were a little too slow. Tom, giving the alias Frank McDonald, pled guilty in district court, but a few days later, his real name was uncovered, which led to a six-month stint at the Buena Vista Reformatory.

Tom was in and out of Colorado prisons for the next two years. He escaped from Buena Vista in 1916 but was quickly captured. He was back in Buena Vista again In May 1917 on a parole violation, but he walked off the ground while a guard was distracted, with only two months before he was set for release. A year later, he stole a car in Colorado Springs and was arrested again, putting him back behind bars at Buena Vista. After less than a month at this "home away from home," he cut through the bars of his cell and fled with another inmate. They headed west to Salt Lake City, where Tom tried to enlist in the army, hoping to start fresh with a new identity.

But, for unknown reasons, the recruiting office in Utah rejected him for service. So, Tom took a chance by returning to Colorado and tried to sign up for service again in Denver. He was almost successful, but then an honorably discharged inmate from Buena Vista, who was also enlisting, recognized him and alerted the military police. Unfortunately for Tom, he had just turned 21, so a reformatory was no longer an option. He was remanded to the state penitentiary in Canon City, where he remained until 1919.

When Tom was released, he moved west to Los Angeles, where his father and sister now lived. Tom got a job as a mechanic at Detroit Electric's Los Angeles branch on Alvarado Street.

Even with his father and sister keeping a close eye on him, Tom was soon in trouble again. He was arrested for drunkenness in 1924, then for robbery later that year, although those charges didn't stick. He was arrested again in 1927 for liquor violations, but a jury found him not guilty.

But his luck soon ran out. In June 1930, Tom and two accomplices broke into the M.A. Newmark grocery store and stole $700 worth of cigarette cartons. They tried to sell them in Hollywood and were arrested.

Tom was convicted of grand theft and sentenced to serve up to 10 years in prison. He was first sent to San Quentin but was transferred to Folsom after he got into a fight with another inmate and partially disemboweled the man with a homemade knife. The other man had managed to gouge out one of Tom's eyes, which had to be replaced with a glass prosthesis.

Even so, two years later, prison officials deemed Tom "reformed," and he was paroled into the custody of his sister, Violet.

Two months after his release, he met Burmah Adams.

The romance between Burmah and Tom was short, exciting, and ugly. The relationship lasted only months, but that was long enough for Tom to initiate his love-struck girlfriend into a life of crime. He introduced her to cocaine, drugged her drinks, and slapped her around when she didn't behave. At her wedding to Tom, her father couldn't help but notice the big black-and-blue bruise on her forehead. There were also old and new bruises on her arms and throat. Burmah said she'd gotten them "falling down."

Burmah's friends and family reported a complete change in character after she met Tom, and after the couple began committing their wild robberies, the grinning peroxide blonde became a boogeywoman in Los Angeles.

A month into their crime spree, Burmah and Tom got married. On September 1, 1933, the local newspaper called the ceremony "one of the prettiest early fall wedding ceremonies" and described the event's details, which took place at Joe and Pearl's house in Santa Ana.

Burmah wore a formal gown of black satin and carried a corsage of white gardenias. It's doubtful that the couple spent their honeymoon weekend on Catalina Island, as reported, and of course, they didn't move to San Francisco, where Tom was supposed to start working at a stock brokerage firm.

No one - not the family, friends, relatives, or the justice of the peace who performed the wedding - had any idea that the happy couple was sitting at the top of the "most wanted" list in L.A.

But the happy couple would only enjoy wedded bliss for five days. The LAPD had been frantically searching for the man the press had nicknamed the "Rattlesnake Bandit" and his "girl moll."

On the afternoon of September 6, Tom sent Burmah to an auto garage just down the block from their apartment at 236 South Coronado Street. Burmah was supposed to retrieve the car they'd stolen from Leslie Bartell, which had needed a few repairs to make a planned trip up the coast. The alley from the apartment to the garage was an L shape, so Tom could wait around the corner from it, out of sight, while Burmah went to pay the bill and get some gas.

As Burmah approached the garage, she noticed several men hanging around. They were dressed in greasy mechanics overalls but didn't seem to be doing any work. They didn't seem to notice her, so she thought little about their presence.

She drove the car around the turn in the alley, where her husband hopped in, and they continued toward a private garage a few doors down from the apartment. Suddenly, the car stalled. Burmah started it back up again and almost backed into a vehicle that was coming up behind her. The driver swore at her and asked her what she was doing. She then did what he wanted her to - she turned around and glared at the angry driver, giving him a perfect look at her face.

He was one of the men from the garage - a police officer in disguise.

Burmah parked the car, and the couple walked to their apartment building, the Casa del Monte. Tom went upstairs, and Burmah followed, dropping in at her old apartment, where her mother and Jo were staying. They spoke for a few minutes, and then one of the men in the greasy coveralls pushed through the front door.

"Where's your boyfriend?" the man barked at her.

"He's upstairs, I guess," Burmah replied.

The man began to ask her questions about the robberies of the previous weeks, and she went over close to him and begged him quietly not to question her in front of her mother and sister. "I'll tell you anything later," she said. "I don't want my mother to know."

The man agreed. "But she's going to know sooner or later," he shrugged as Burmah choked back tears.

At that moment, she heard a scuffle in the hallway, followed by three pistol shots. Burmah heard a voice call out, "We got him!"

Tom had been confronted in the hallway, but the confrontation was brief. When the men announced they were cops, Tom started shooting. Officers opened fire, killing Tom. His body collapsed onto the hallway floor.

The officer who had been questioning Burmah opened the door, and two more men in coveralls pushed their way inside and told her she needed to leave with them.

One of them spoke to her almost apologetically. "Miss, maybe you'd better not go out this way. His body is lying right there, blocking the way."

"Never mind," Burmah sniffed, "I'll step over him."

As she did, she hurled herself forward, slipped past the officer's hands, and tried to jump from the nearby third-floor window. One of the police officers seized her before she could jump, though, and snapped handcuffs onto her wrists.

"Where's the Chevrolet?" a cop asked.

"I haven't any Chevrolet," Burmah said.

"I just saw you drive away from the filling station with it. What did you do with it?"

"You oughta know," Burmah sneered at him.

Unfortunately for Burmah, the press had a front-row view of the action. The LAPD had an understanding with the major papers that they would call before they raided a particular scene or went to the scene of a crime. This meant that reporters and photographers often came along for arrests and raids.

The press documented the new widow's every move. Her odd, chilly indifference to Tom's corpse was noted when Burmah stepped over his body without emotion. Photos were snapped of her at the morgue and, according to the *Herald-Examiner*, "She haughtily walked into the morgue and posed with icy indifference, then like an actress going into a 'sob scene,' she managed to sniffle a little."

The end of the crime spree didn't end the public's obsession with the case --- it fueled it. No one asked why Tom had committed his crimes or asked his sister questions about his past, but for months after the shootings and Burmah's arrest, the media tried to make sense of a young woman from a "good home" who became an outlaw.

Burmah found herself hounded by reporters while awaiting trial at the L.A. County Jail. During the Depression, female columnists - often called "sob sisters" - became all the rage. People sought escapism, and syndicated newspaper groups sought material to fill their pages. Female reporters like Agnes "Aggie" Underwood became the arbiters of the news when it came to female lawbreakers.

Burmah spoke to Aggie and others, giving her an often-changing version of events as she told one of them, "I am not a bad girl. I was so terrified that I did exactly as he told me to do. That's why I am here in jail."

Whether or not Burmah was under the influence of an abusive man, drugs, or sociopathic tendencies during that hot summer wasn't important to most journalists or newspaper readers. She was the "girl bandit" and bore the brunt of her and Tom's crimes. She was described in one *Examiner* piece:

With a sneering smile on her face, 19-year-old Burmah Adams White, icy blonde bride of the slain Rattlesnake Bandit, is pictured as she appeared in the glaring spotlight of the police shadowbox last night for identification by the bandit's victims.

Eventually, Burmah would be a distant memory, overshadowed by the exploits of Bonnie Parker and the ongoing crimes of other "big-time criminals," but in 1933 and 1934, her story burned white hot across national media. It was even featured in the first full-length episode of the popular radio crime drama, *Calling All Cars* and on other shows. Newspapers printed scores of large photos of her, showing off her petite frame, pretty face, huge blue eyes, and Clara Bow mouth, which she was always careful to accentuate with red lipstick.

Her looks sold newspapers, but so did the mystery behind her motives and how reporters could exploit that mystery. She had no logical reason to commit the crimes that she did, so she was described as a thrill-seeker - "the most dangerous type of criminal." She was even featured alongside other gangster "molls," like John Dillinger's girlfriend, Evelyn "Billie" Frechette.

Burmah's trial in the fall of 1933 also became a sensation, inflated by law enforcement officials who wanted to make an example of her - and make a name for themselves. Both the judge that presided over the trial and the prosecutor had their eyes on higher office, and Burmah was just the ticket they needed to garner votes.

District Attorney Buron Fitts had plans to be governor someday, and he planned to take advantage of the public's horrified interest in Burmah.

A native of Texas and a decorated World War I hero, he was the head of California's American Legion and served as lieutenant governor from 1927-1928. However, he grew bored with this largely ceremonial job and decided to mount a campaign for Los Angeles district attorney. He used the media to promote his candidacy, promising to cleanse the city of gang elements and define himself as a guardian of public morals and civic life.

Fitts appointed his toughest deputy, George "The Hangman" Stahlman, to prosecute Burmah. Fitts, Stahlman, and LAPD chief James "Two-Gun" Davis said they would make an example out of her, making her pay the debt to society that her dead husband couldn't pay.

And they did - with help from Judge Fletcher Bowron. Eager to clear his docket, the judge rushed through her trial, forcing an unprepared lawyer to represent her. Witnesses and victims were crammed together in the courtroom, watching each other's testimony.

There was nothing fair about the trial, so it's no surprise that Burmah was eventually convicted of six counts of robbery, three counts of assault with an intent to commit murder, and one count of attempted robbery.

Of course, those were just the ones they could prove.

Judge Bowron sentenced Burmah to a 30-year prison term. He carefully stated his reasons:

It is not a pleasant duty to send a young person, and particularly a young woman, to the penitentiary. As an individual, I have nothing but heartfelt sympathy and pity for this young woman who is about to be branded a convict. But as a judge, my duty is plain. The penalty that I am about to impose is not retribution, but it is hoped that your case will serve as an object lesson to others.

But Burmah's story was not as cut and dried as the authorities and the press made it out to be. She didn't fit into any of the perpetrator categories that existed at the time. She may have appeared to the public to be living a lifestyle of late nights, cash, and fast cars, but the reality was that she had often worked two jobs to support her parents and younger sister, who needed costly medical treatments that working-class folks during the Depression didn't have the money for - unless they stole it, of course.

Is that an excuse? No, but Burmah was no "underworld girl," as some called her. Even the police soon realized she was no "bandit's moll." She was "a normal girl, a baker's daughter, who had fallen in with a desperate criminal."

Or was she? I doubt many of her, and Tom's victims quickly forgot about her squeal of delight as they roared away from the scene of their crimes. Or the way Burmah laughed when they drove off after shooting a man in the neck and blinding a schoolteacher for the rest of her life. She hadn't seemed like someone under the control of a "desperate criminal" then.

But Burmah's real guilt didn't matter. Legal authorities unilaterally decided that she must be made an example of what could happen to young girls who thought they "knew the world" and weren't careful.

Her trial and conviction may or may not have discouraged young women from falling in love with the wrong man, but it definitely put Los Angeles in the national spotlight as news of her prison sentence ran on the front pages of thousands of newspapers across America.

It soon became clear who benefited from Burmah's case. A ceremony for the police officers who captured her was held by Buron Fitts, Chief Davis, Mayor Frank Shaw, the President of the Police Commission, and other city executives. They were given certificates and promotions while the city received funding for its first felon registration program. The L.A. County Sheriff's Department received the money to install radios in all its cars.

Meanwhile, Judge Bowron used Burmah's case to attack the California State Board of Parole, arguing that the trial judge in each case should fix minimum sentences. The crusade made him a household name, and in 1938, Bowron was elected mayor of Los Angeles.

Fitts went on to prosecute another "outlaw woman" - Nellie May Madison - in 1934. She was accused of murdering her husband. After that, however, Fitts' career slowed and took a nosedive after a Los

Angeles grand jury indicted him for perjury in connection to another case. He was acquitted at trial two years later and even won a third term as district attorney in 1936, but by then, his dreams of statewide office were over.

And then there was Burmah, the "Rattlesnake's Blonde."

On December 6, 1933, she boarded a train to begin serving her sentence at Tehachapi Women's Prison in Kern County. Luckily for Burmah, the newly opened prison focused on rehabilitation instead of punishment - but it took her some time to settle in. The beginning was hard for her. She was still in shock. In less than six months, she'd met Tom, committed a string of crimes, married, became a widow, was arrested, stood trial, and ended up behind bars.

Compounding her shock was the fact that her father died while she was in prison. Joe suffered an attack of appendicitis, waited two weeks to go to the hospital, and died just hours after his surgery. He had little money and no property to leave the family. Pearl went to work on a walnut farm to survive.

In time, Burmah acclimated to prison life and became a model prisoner. She soon styled the hair of fellow inmates like "Tiger Woman" Clara Phillips, who beat her husband's mistress to death with a hammer.

Many people from her past life - including her mother, friends, neighbors, attorneys, former teachers, and employers - wrote letters to the parole board on Burmah's behalf, asking for her early release.

The district attorney's office - as well as Judge Bowron - opposed leniency for Burmah. "This party drove the car," stated one letter in 1934. "White used a revolver, but this party stood or sat in the car during robberies, laughing or smiling, and in such ways showed a hardened and cold-blooded disposition."

But Burmah would earn her freedom long before the 30 years she had been sentenced to serve had passed. She was released from

Tehachapi on December 1, 1941, and went largely unnoticed by the press. They had bigger things - like the attack on Pearl Harbor a few days later - to worry about.

Burmah was not on parole. She had been released from custody with no further obligations. But she was at odds about where to start over. She returned to her family's Santa Ana home for a while but knew she was a burden since her mother barely had enough money to care for herself and Jo. She knew she couldn't stay because she knew how it would hurt her sister - who was doing well in high school - to have the "Rattlesnake's Blonde" in her house.

She quietly went to San Francisco in 1942, becoming the invaluable office manager of lawyer, investor, and developer of Century City - the upscale business district adjacent to the Twentieth Century Fox film lot - Edmond Herrscher.

In 1945, Burmah met a client of Herrscher's, a structural engineer named Alfred Drymond. He was ten years older than Burmah and had a wife and two children. They started an affair, and Alfred rented a new house for her in Walnut Creek, a suburb east of San Francisco.

In 1949, she had one more brush with the law. On her way home one night, she was speeding and crashed into a railroad crossing signal on Main Street in Walnut Grove. She was arrested for drunk driving, but because this was a misdemeanor, she paid a small fine and the costs for the repair of the signal.

She continued to work for Herrscher until the end of 1950. By then, Alfred had obtained a divorce, and the couple got married in Reno, Nevada, with only Jo and a friend of Alfred's in attendance.

The couple eventually moved to the Seattle area, and during the 1950s, Burmah tried unsuccessfully to get a pardon from the state of California. She believed she had done her time, had been rehabilitated, and deserved to be a full-fledged citizen again. California's governor disagreed.

Over the next few years, Burmah and Alfred led a comfortable but isolated life in Washington. Alfred's children no longer spoke to him after he abandoned their mother. They moved into a luxury apartment building that Alfred had helped build that catered to wealthy retirees. They didn't have many friends. There were few people in the building that Burmah felt comfortable socializing with since they were much older than she was. Alfred worked long hours and traveled to Canada and Mexico for work.

Burmah's mother, Pearl, died in Santa Ana in June 1962. For whatever reason, Burmah did not attend the funeral. Jo and her husband scraped together enough money to buy a plot for Pearl at the cemetery where Joe had been laid to rest.

Maybe it was the news of her mother's death, her isolation, or perhaps memories of that fateful summer, but Burmah began drinking heavily around this time. She had always been a hard drinker - a trait she shared with Alfred - but things became much worse in the summer of 1962.

It was also around this time that, according to the few friends she had, Burmah began talking about Tom White and the events of that summer in 1933. One of her friends even said that Burmah told her that Tom had been visiting her at night, standing over her menacingly and saying that he blamed Burmah for his death.

This made Burmah drink even more.

Finally, one fall day that year, Alfred came home from work to discover his wife dead on the living room floor. Since she was only 48 years old, the medical examiner performed an autopsy. She had died from "acute cerebral edema" - swelling of the brain - due to "acute alcoholism." Her blood alcohol level when she died had been nearly four times the legal limit.

Burmah had died on September 6 - the same day that, 29 years earlier, the "Rattlesnake Bandit" Tom White had been shot to death by police in Los Angeles.

"THE TIGER WOMAN"

TONI JO HENRY

BY AMANDA R. WOOMER

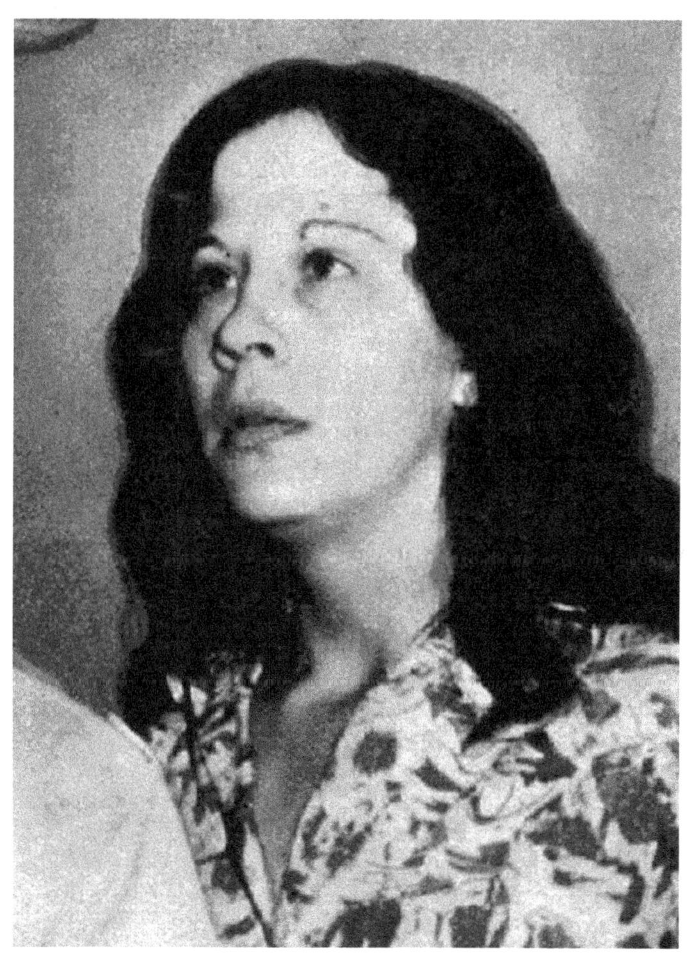

When it comes to convicting and sentencing ruthless criminals, two things can come into play and make the jury and public stop and take notice: sex and beauty. It's not every day that the accused cold-blooded murderer is a beautiful young woman. Still, in the case of Toni Jo Henry, the press described her as the "bad girl of the bayou" and "the Tiger Woman," and the nation was hypnotized by the beautiful 23-year-old woman that went so wrong while so young.

Toni Jo may have grown up to be "the most ornery gal east of the Mississippi," but she was born Annie Beatrice McQuiston. She was the sixth of eight children (seven of whom would reach adulthood), born on January 3, 1916, to Ella Beatrice and James Lesley McQuiston in Shreveport, Louisiana.

Life at the McQuiston home was a bit rocky—James, who worked as a car inspector for the railroad, was known to drink excessively and lash out occasionally. In the early 1920s, Ella was diagnosed with tuberculosis. At this time, little Annie was sent to live with her grandmother. Sadly, Ella wouldn't recover, and she died in 1922 when Annie was only six years old. James remarried shortly after that to a woman named Bertha Lively, and Annie was returned to her father and new stepmother. Almost immediately, Annie wanted to return to her grandmother, and things only got worse. As she got older, she grew to hate her stepmother, and her father would hit her when she lashed out.

She never graduated from grade school. Instead, at just 13 years old, Annie got a job working at a local macaroni factory, though her time would be cut short once her manager learned that tuberculosis was in her family. When James McQuiston learned that Annie had been fired, he beat her.

That day, Annie Beatrice died, and "Toni Jo" was born.

She ran away from home and started working in a local dance hall. Toni Jo quickly realized that she would be required to do more than just dance, and at only 13, she became a prostitute. When Toni tried to leave the dance hall, the owners wouldn't let her. For months, she was trapped there until one day when she managed to escape with a client. She lived with him for several years, working in various brothels in Shreveport's red-light district, and quickly became addicted to cocaine.

By 16, she had worked as a prostitute throughout Shreveport, other parts of Louisiana, and southern Texas, hopping from man to man, never staying long. She was no stranger to local law enforcement as she was arrested multiple times for vagrancy and assault. However, she was never sent to jail because she was still considered a child. But her life seemed to take a turn for the better -- possibly for the first time -- in 1939.

Toni was living and working in Austin, Texas when she met Claude "Cowboy" Henry. He was a boxer with a criminal record. Most recently, he had been charged with the murder of a former San Antonio police officer named Arthur Sinclair–though Cowboy assured Toni Jo that he had fired his gun in self-defense. He was currently out on bail awaiting his trial when he met Toni. Cowboy may have been down on his luck, but he immediately swept Toni off her feet. Originally one of her clients, Cowboy became the only man Toni would ever love, aside from her younger brother. He helped Toni get off drugs and helped her get clean, and on November 25, 1939, the two were married.

The pair honeymooned in southern California, and for a single month of her life, Toni Jo knew true happiness, but all of that changed when Cowboy received a telegram. It instructed him to return to Texas to stand trial for Sinclair's murder immediately. Toni begged Cowboy not to travel to Texas and instead go on the run with her. Despite her pleas, he returned to Texas and was convicted of murdering Arthur Sinclair. His 23-year-old bride watched as her new husband was sentenced to 50 years at the Texas State Penitentiary in Huntsville. According to reports, when the judge convicted Cowboy, Toni Jo stood up and shouted across the courtroom, assuring Cowboy that she would get him out.

Whether Toni believed Cowboy's tales of self-defense and thought she was doing the right thing, or if she was so blinded by love she couldn't think straight does not matter – Cowboy's conviction was the beginning of Toni Jo's downfall.

Cowboy was sent to prison on January 27, 1940, and by February, she had hatched a plan. She convinced two teenagers to break into a gun shop and steal guns and ammunition she would use to break Cowboy out of jail. She recruited an accomplice, a man named Finnon "Arkie" Burks – an army deserter and ex-con who claimed to know the prison's layout. He seemed to be the perfect ally for a prison break. The duo planned on traveling from where they were both staying in Orange, Texas, to Arkansas, where Arkie knew of a bank they could easily rob.

On Valentine's Day, Arkie and Toni found themselves wandering along a dark Louisiana country road in the freezing rain when the headlights of a Ford coupe pulled up behind them. Masquerading as a newlywed couple, they asked the driver for a ride. Unaware of their wicked plan, 41-year-old car salesman John P. Calloway offered the soaking-wet couple a ride.

The journey was quiet as they traveled down the dark road, but outside Jennings, Louisiana, Toni and Arkie pulled their weapons out on Calloway. They robbed him at gunpoint, took his watch and wallet - with only $15 in it -- and ordered him to climb into the car's trunk. The Ford coupe would make a perfect getaway car after breaking Cowboy out of jail.

Toni and Arkie hopped back into the car and continued driving, soon turning onto a narrow dirt road and parking beside a frozen rice field. Calloway was pulled from the trunk and ordered to strip because Toni wanted a change of clothes for Cowboy. With her .32-caliber revolver, she pushed him through a barbed wire fence – the barbs tearing at his bare skin – and ordered him to crawl in front of her. They made their way across the frozen field, and as they reached a rice straw stack, Toni instructed the naked man to kneel before her and say his prayers. At this point, Calloway no doubt realized what was at stake and began begging for his life.

According to Toni, Calloway asked her to let him go – not for his sake but for his family; his daughter was about to graduate from college, and he knew she would want him there. As the man tried to reason with her, she shot him between the eyes, killing him instantly.

Calloway's naked body lay among the rice straw stacks as Toni returned to Arkie, who was clearly shaken. As he sat in the stolen car, Toni hit him with the butt of her revolver because "he turned yellow, like a little rat." The murderous pair sped off with Calloway's watch, cash, and clothes. They made their way to Camden, Arkansas when Arkie grew nervous about what Toni would do for Cowboy – he was comfortable helping to break a man out of jail and even robbing a bank, but he had not signed up for murder. While Toni slept, Arkie took the car and abandoned her, hoping to leave the affair behind him.

But it wouldn't work out that way. Eventually, he'd pay for his betrayal with his life.

It didn't take long for Toni to realize what she had done. She took a bus back to Shreveport using the money she had stolen from Calloway. She first arrived at a local brothel run by an old friend, looking for a place to lay low and figure out what she should do next. Toni decided to stay with her aunt, Emma Holt.

While there, Toni hinted that something had happened. Suspicious of her niece, who was known to have a wild and violent side, Emma tried to contact her brother, Louisiana state police officer George McQuiston. McQuiston was on vacation, though, so Emma brought his colleague, Sergeant Dave Walker, over to her house to speak with her niece. When Walker questioned Toni, the young woman immediately confessed, told him where he could find Calloway's body, and even handed him the murder weapon – the revolver with one bullet fired.

At first, Walker didn't believe the young woman's story – no missing persons were reported, and neither a body nor a car had been found. However, it was odd that an innocent woman would admit to such a heinous crime, so he arrested her and handed her over to the Lake Charles police.

Those officers decided to listen to Toni's story, placed her in the backseat of their car, and drove around until she could point out the rice straw stacks from that fateful night. As the police crossed the frozen field, they were horrified to find Calloway's body right where Toni had left it. Shortly after Calloway's body was found, his Ford coupe was recovered, abandoned in Arkansas with Calloway's clothing inside, as well as cigarette butts with lipstick on them. It wouldn't be long before Arkie would be arrested and charged with murder, as well.

Toni Jo faced a judge and jury on Wednesday, March 27, 1940. The newspapers were obsessed with the sultry brunette with her dazzling smile and wicked ways. Her defense argued that her life was "fatally misdirected from girlhood" and that she was nothing more than a product of her unfortunate circumstances.

Despite the press coverage and attention the trial received, her attorneys were nothing more than tax lawyers and had never worked a criminal case, much less a murder trial. Judge Hood presided at the

Calcasieu Courthouse as Toni reversed her confession and tried to blame Arkie.

The jury didn't believe her story. They deliberated on Friday, March 29, for just six hours, returning with a guilty verdict. At this time, such a verdict in a first-degree murder trial required a death sentence by hanging. Despite this death sentence, according to reports, Toni showed no emotion as the verdict was read.

Toni and her lawyers quickly filed an appeal, claiming that the sensationalized reporting of the country's newspapers had affected the jury. Shockingly, she was granted a new trial.

Her first retrial occurred in February 1941, with Arkie taking the stand to testify against her. The jury took only one hour to deliberate this time before finding her guilty again. Newspapers reported that Toni showed an ounce of emotion for the first time – her lower lip quivered, and she bit her lip as the verdict was read.

Her lawyers appealed once again and won yet again. The third and final trial began on February 3, 1942, under Judge Mark C. Pickrel. Hanging was off the table this time. But this wasn't good news -- the method of execution had changed to electrocution. The jury took less than an hour to declare both Toni Jo and Arkie guilty. When the judge sentenced her to death, it's said that Toni shouted at him, "I ain't afraid of what's comin'!"

Incarcerated at the Lake Charles Prison, the "Tiger Woman's" execution date was set for August 10, 1942. However, her doomed date with "Gruesome Gertie" -- as the state's portable electric chair was dubbed -- was postponed. Her lawyers, though inexperienced with criminal cases, had managed to appeal to the United States Supreme Court. They argued that Louisiana's change of execution method from hanging to electrocution was unconstitutional. Ultimately, the state Supreme Court, Governor Sam H. Jones, and the federal court upheld the sentence, and Toni Jo Henry would finally pay for her crime on November 28, 1942, with her life.

While Toni Jo was known to be a wild prisoner and liked to pick fights during the years of her three trials, she became a model prisoner by the end of her time in prison. She was baptized by the Catholic priest, Father Wayne Richard. She also spent her days with a black and white terrier that had been born in prison, and in her final weeks, she even permitted interviews with the press.

When asked why she killed Calloway, she claimed it was a "thrill slaying" and finally admitted in a sworn statement that she had pulled the trigger, not Arkie, to clear his name and "prevent two lives being given for one." She also expressed her love for Cowboy time and time again and how she hated all men except him. Despite her love for Cowboy and hatred for men, her passions seemed to die down when talking about Calloway. In an unnervingly calm manner, she informed the newspapers:

In the first place, the victim doesn't return to haunt me, I never think of him. I've known all along it would be my life or his. I believe mine is worth as much to me as his was to him. I wonder, though, sometimes, why it's legal now for some fellow to kill me.

Five days before Toni Jo was to face her executioner, the public was shocked to learn that Cowboy had escaped from prison and was on his way to Toni Jo. The police in Lake Charles were informed of his plan to either break Toni out of jail or kidnap the judge that sentenced her. A double guard stood around her cell that day as Cowboy traveled from Texas to Louisiana.

However, just like Toni Jo's attempt to rescue her husband, Cowboy's attempt to save his bride also failed. He was promptly recaptured and sent back to prison in Huntsville, but not before capturing the imagination -- and somehow even the hearts -- of the public. They began to insist that the star-crossed lovers should be able to meet one last time before November 28. The authorities couldn't fulfill a meeting of the two convicts, but they did permit the couple a phone call on Friday, November 27.

For one brief moment, Toni Jo spoke with the only man she had ever loved. She told him:

Get rid of that prison suit, go out the front door. Go straight and try and make something of your life.

Witnesses to the two telephone calls report that Cowboy was emotional and crying while Toni sounded cheerful and relaxed.

On Saturday, November 28, 1942, Toni Jo woke up and refused to read the newspapers. Instead, she spent the morning listening to the radio, reading her Bible, and playing with her terrier.

Only a few hand-selected witnesses were permitted inside the jail to watch the execution. However, a large crowd had gathered outside the jailhouse, some people climbing on cars and barriers hoping to catch one last glimpse of the "Tiger Woman."

Toni Jo donned a simple black dress and a pair of black pumps. She cried as her head was shaved and requested to wear a bright and colorful scarf to hide her baldness.

At 12:05 p.m., she left the condemned cell, admittedly a bit nervous and afraid, though still managing to remain calm. Holding Father Richard's hand, she made her way down the 22 steps from the second floor to the first-floor corridor of the Calcasieu parish jail where "Gruesome Gertie" sat waiting.

At 12:12 p.m., she stood before the portable electric chair as Deputy Sheriff Henry Reid asked her if she had anything to say.

"I think not," were her final words.

She smiled at her executioner before being strapped into the chair. Electrodes were placed on her shaved head and her leg before the leather mask was placed over her face. The switch was thrown, and 2,000 volts of electricity coursed through Toni Jo's body. According to the few witnesses permitted at the execution, her body trembled, and her fists clutched tightly as blue smoke rose from her head.

It took nearly two minutes for her to die, but by 12:15 p.m., the local coroner, Dr. E.L. Clement, and the prison doctor, Dr. H.B. White, pronounced the "Tiger Woman" dead.

Toni Jo Henry was the first and only woman to be executed in Louisiana's electric chair and the second white woman in the state's history, preceded by Mrs. Ida Bonner LeBouef in 1927.

No family claimed Toni Jo's body. Instead, Father Richard and the local funeral home director saw to her burial. Father Richard designed her tombstone, and the funeral home director donated the plot where she would be buried, not wishing to see the beautiful young woman buried in a potter's field. A dozen people attended the funeral, officiated by Father Richard, and all were from the local Catholic church. Father Richard – perhaps Toni's only friend while imprisoned – oversaw her final wishes, ensuring she was buried with her crucifix in her left hand.

Justice was served for John P. Calloway's family, but the specter of Toni Jo Henry lingered over the town of Lake Charles and all who were involved with her trials.

Legends abound of a curse, with tales spreading shortly after Toni's execution. C.V. Pattison, the state prosecutor, and Rabb Fanguy, the deputy jailer, both died of a heart attack. Henry Reid had a stroke while tying his shoes. And district judge Pickrel, who was Toni's final judge, was later charged with manslaughter after killing a person with his car.

And while the jail was demolished in 1956, the Calcasieu courthouse is said to be haunted. There are reports of the smell of burning hair and old-fashioned perfume. The courtroom where all three of Toni's trials took place is located on the second floor, and a woman with shoulder-length black hair has been seen briefly before vanishing. Other rumors claim that the shadow of Toni Jo's body was burned into the wood of the electric chair, and when her body was removed, a small blue orb of light was seen by everyone present rising from the chair.

The woman that was a "prostitute at 13, a drug addict at 16, and a killer at 23" is remembered today as both a beauty and a beast. While her crime was ruthless, it's likely that if she were on trial today, she would not be sentenced to death.

Why the ghost of Toni Jo Henry still haunts the old courthouse will remain a mystery for now. Her victim may not have returned to haunt, but she certainly did.

"THE STARVATION DOCTOR"
LINDA BURFIELD HAZZARD
BY AMANDA R. WOOMER

Fasting, while a controversial approach for weight loss in the medical community, has been part of humanity for thousands of years.

Hippocrates -- the father of medicine -- as well as Plato, Socrates, and Aristotle, all praised the benefits of fasting. It's said that biblical figures such as Jesus Christ, Moses, and the prophet Elijah all fasted for extended periods. Today, many Christians will fast during Lent, and Muslims fast during the month of Ramadan from sunrise to sunset.

Fasting has also been used as a non-violent protest through hunger strikes. Most notably by Mahatma Gandhi, the 1981 Irish hunger strike that ended with 10 participants killing themselves by starvation, several British and American suffragists, and Russian opposition leader Alexei Navalny.

In the early twentieth century, fasting became the newest form of alternative medicine, claiming to cleanse the body of impurities and diseases. It was a concept promoted by author Upton Sinclair, psychic phenomena researcher Hereward Carrington, and quack doctor Linda Burfield Hazzard -- who went on to kill as many as 40 patients through her "fast cure" - and left an indelible mark on American history.

Born on December 18, 1867, in Carver, Minnesota, Linda Laura Burfield was the oldest of seven children born to Susan O'Neil and Montgomery Burfield. Her father was a farmer, and Linda spent her childhood helping to run the house with her mother. When she was 19 years old, she married a man 14 years her senior, Erwin Perry, in 1887. The couple quickly had two children – a son named Rollin, born in August 1889, and a daughter named Nina, born in March 1891.

For a short while, Linda was a faithful wife and mother on their Minnesota farm, but Linda and Erwin eventually became estranged after the first few years of their marriage. Linda accused Erwin of abandoning her in 1898. However, it's more likely that Linda left him when she moved to Minneapolis in 1900, and in 1902, their divorce was finalized.

And it was around this same time that Linda killed her first victim.

Shortly after setting up shop in Minneapolis, Linda began to offer her own fasting program, called the "most beautiful cure." At this time, she believed that sickness and disease were caused not just by overeating but by food in general. If you could rid your body of all the food in your stomach and intestines, you could cleanse your body of anything, even cancer. It was a revolutionary concept not embraced by conventional doctors of the day. Still, Linda's charisma and confidence were enough to convince ailing patients to try her fast cure, and one of those patients was a woman named Gertrude Tozer Young.

Mrs. Young was a 40-year-old woman who had experienced partial paralysis of her left arm and leg after a stroke in 1900. Even though traditional doctors told her she would never have full movement of her left side again, Dr. Linda Perry -- as she was known at the time -- had a different opinion. Despite having no medical training, Linda prescribed Mrs. Young a 40-day fast, assuring her that once the fast was complete, she would have full use of her arm and leg again.

The fast began in October 1902 at Mrs. Young's apartment at 711 Third Avenue South in Minneapolis. In early November, Gertrude was found by a friend sweating, shaking, and vomiting a thick, dark, putrid-smelling substance. Dr. Perry's solution was to open the apartment windows to offer her patient some fresh air -- despite the freezing November temperatures.

Unsatisfied with Dr. Perry's treatment, Gertrude's friend sought the advice of her previous doctor, who had seen Gertrude just a few weeks before her fast began and had described her as "fat as butter" and in good health. He insisted that she break her fast immediately with bone and vegetable broths and soft foods -- the fast, he assured her, would only kill her, not heal her.

However, Gertrude Young was determined to complete the fast, genuinely believing she would be healed at the end of her torture.

She wasn't. Gertrude died on November 18, 1902 - day 39 of her 40-day fast.

Although Linda Perry was responsible for Gertrude Young's death, she was not arrested because, technically, no crime had been committed. Mrs. Young could have broken her fast at any time but instead chose to abstain from food. There was no law against that. Of course, the rings missing from Gertrude's body were never found, which adds a bit of suspicion of foul play.

Despite this setback in her new fasting methodology, Linda continued to take on patients and give lectures. On November 11, 1903, she remarried a man named Samuel Chrisman Hazzard, taking his name. Samuel Hazzard was a West Point graduate who had been charged with forgery, embezzlement, and bigamy when it was revealed he hadn't bothered to divorce his wife before marrying Linda. After serving time in prison, he joined Linda on her mission to convince the public of the healing power of fasting.

By 1906, Linda and Samuel Hazzard had left Minnesota and moved to the state of Washington, where a peculiar loophole allowed practitioners of alternative medicine to get licenses without any medical training.

Dr. Hazzard's dream was to run a sanitarium to help patients undergo her fasting cure. However, it would take years and at least a dozen deaths before she would see her grand sanitarium come to fruition.

It didn't take long for Hazzard to start getting patients for her program in Olalla, Washington, with advertisements that read: "Treats all nervous diseases, women, liquor, habits, vices, and painless childbirth."

Hazzard's patients would fast for days, weeks, and sometimes even months on a fast of tomato or asparagus broth and, occasionally, orange juice. According to traditional medical doctors, this was one-fifth of the nourishment a person would need to live. And yet, some patients managed to survive her treatment and endorsed her. However, dozens were not nearly as lucky.

In 1908, the first wave of victims began with the deaths of Lenora Wilcox, Daisey Maud Haglund -- who fasted for 50 days -- and Ida Wilcox. That same year, two parents living in Seattle were accused of starving their eight-month-old daughter directly under Hazzard's orders. However, the *Omaha Daily Bee* published a woman's success story after she fasted for 62 days with Dr. Hazzard and lived to tell the tale.

In 1909, the untimely deaths of Blanche B. Tindall, Viola Heaton, and Eugene Stanley Wakelin occurred. While in Hazzard's care, Wakelin was found with a bullet in his head, though whether it was suicide or murder is still unknown – the fact that Hazzard had become the administratrix of his estate shortly before his death is suspicious, to say the least.

Hazzard became well-known in the Seattle region–for better or worse–in 1910. The King County Superior Court ordered the State Medical Board to bestow Hazzard with a medical license. However, a handful of people had already died under her supervision, and their friends tried to fight against this decision but were unsuccessful for the time being. Linda Hazzard was now the only person in the state licensed to practice "healing by fasting."

Around this time, a man named Mr. Bede pulled his wife from Hazzard's program. When she started it, she weighed about 140 pounds, and when she was rescued, she was under 100 pounds.

That same year, Maude Whitney and Earl Edward Erdman starved to death. In May 1910, Lewis E. Rader, a state legislator from Washington, died under mysterious circumstances after fasting with Dr. Hazzard for 29 days to cure a stomach issue. While staying at the Outlook Hotel, doctors wanted to examine him to determine whether he was insane. But before they could, Hazzard literally kidnapped him. Eventually, he would die and leave Hazzard the land where she would build her house and a series of cabins that would serve as her sanitarium, Wilderness Heights.

Three more deaths occurred under Hazzard's watchful eye – Frank Southard, C.A. Harrison, and Ivan Flux – before the Williamson sisters arrived.

Dorothea, 37, and Claire, 33, were born in southern India. Their father had died shortly after Claire was born, when Dorothea was only four years old, and their mother died 16 years later, leaving the sisters with a $500,000 fortune -- almost $16 million today. The sisters left from Liverpool in May 1910 to begin a trip around the world, bidding farewell to their childhood nanny, Margaret Conway.

While staying at the Empress Hotel in Victoria, British Columbia, they saw an advertisement for Dr. Hazzard's new sanitarium on the old Rader land. It read:

Wilderness Heights,

Olalla, Wash.

Dr. Linda Burfield Hazzard, Author of Fasting for the Cure of Disease, *Superintendent.*

An institution devoted to applied Natural Therapeutics, specializing upon Fasting and a Scientific Dietary, Superbly located near Seattle on Puget Sound. Fifty acres of grounds with modern spacious buildings. Terms reasonable.

The sisters were immediately intrigued by this exciting new medical treatment. Today, many historians believe the sisters were hypochondriacs. Both of their occupations at this time were listed as "invalid." In early 1911, Dorothea was said to have swollen glands and rheumatic pain, and Claire supposedly had a dropped uterus. The Williamsons had already given up meat and wearing corsets to help cure their ailments and were proponents of various forms of alternative medicine.

The two women decided to venture south to Seattle and meet with Dr. Hazzard. Both sisters only intended to stay for two to three weeks because Claire was preparing to travel to London, and Dorothea was on her way to Australia.

On February 26, 1911, the Williamson sisters met Linda Hazzard for the first time. They were quickly informed that the sanitarium they had read about in the newspaper wasn't quite ready yet, so instead, Hazzard would begin their treatment while they stayed in the Buena Vista apartments on Seattle's Capitol Hill. Treatment costs $60 per patient per month -- reasonable terms, indeed.

When the treatment began, it was merciless. Food consisted of a cup of broth made from canned tomatoes twice a day -- not fresh from the sanitarium's garden as they had been promised. The sisters were subjected to hot water enemas that lasted for hours. They cried out in agony before they would faint, the canvas covering the tub catching them as they fell. Violent massages that resembled beatings were given by Hazzard herself, as she would pummel the sisters on their shoulders and heads, screaming, "Eliminate! Eliminate! Eliminate!"

After just two weeks of treatment, Dorothea could no longer walk. She was experiencing delirium and fainting spells, and yet, the treatment continued.

The two sisters were kept in separate rooms, unable to see or hear one another. What may have been called the "most beautiful treatment" was quickly killing them.

By April 1911, both sisters were emaciated and resembled skeletons with skin pulled tight over their bones. On April 22, 1911, when Wilderness Heights was finally ready, the sisters were transported in separate ambulances to Hazzard's new sanitarium in Olalla – but not before one of the sisters managed to send a telegram to their devoted former nanny, Miss Conway.

While at Wilderness Heights -- or as the locals called it, when patients resembling skeletons were found wandering down the road, "Starvation Heights" -- the abuse that Dorothea and Claire experienced continued. Hazzard informed the sisters they'd be under the care of "Mother Lillie," who turned out to be a farmhand named Frank Lillie, who would bathe Claire in a wash basin in the kitchen and conduct other humiliating tasks for the young heiress.

A young nurse named Miss Esther Cameron, who worked at the sanitarium for two weeks until she was fired after missing a day of work due to illness -- claimed she could feel Claire's backbone while touching her abdomen. Purple spots had begun to appear on her skin, and her lips were pulled taut over her teeth. She cried out in pain when carried to and from her baths. At the start of her fast, Claire weighed 126 pounds; by May 18, she was less than 50 pounds.

On the evening of May 18, 1911, Dorothea was permitted to see her sister as she lay in bed, gasping for air. According to Dorothea's account, she watched as Hazzard walked over to Claire and asked her, "Would you like a treatment, Claire?" The young woman didn't respond. Hazzard placed her hand on Claire's abdomen and pressed down hard. Claire threw her head back and cried out in pain before fainting. Dorothea looked to Hazzard and asked, "Is it all over?" Hazzard simply responded with, "Yes."

That night, Dorothea heard people walking in her sister's room for several hours. Although she believed her sister had died before her very eyes, Claire's official time of death was at 4:00 a.m. on Friday, May 19, 1911 -- two months and 21 days after starting Hazzard's fasting cure.

Shortly thereafter, Hazzard would conduct her own autopsy on Claire in the bathtub, recording that the official cause of death was cirrhosis of the liver -- not starvation. The following morning, her body was laid on an ironing board in the kitchen, with Hazzard informing the staff to speak of Claire's death to no one.

What may have been a tragic case of a woman going too far to reach her ideal health quickly became suspicious.

As soon as the Williamson sisters had begun their treatment, Hazzard took all of their valuables – rings, jewels, clothes, and money adding up to about $6,000, or $188,000 today – and never returned them. The London and New Westminster County Bank of London received a request for all money held and received in the future in the name of Claire Williamson to be forwarded to Linda Laura Hazzard on May 26, 1911, even though Claire had died on May 19th.

When Miss Conway arrived from Australia on June 1, Claire had been dead for several weeks. Dr. Hazzard spoke with her -- while wearing one of Claire's robes -- informing her that Claire had added Hazzard to her will with a yearly gift of $125 to the sanitarium, which would be approximately $4,000 today. She also told the woman that

Claire had made Hazzard the executrix of her estate, and because Dorothea was deemed insane -- by Dr. Hazzard, of course -- she was now the older sister's legal guardian for the rest of her life.

Margaret Conway was unable to remove Dorothea from Starvation Heights for nearly two months after Claire's death. Eventually, Dorothea's uncle, who lived in Tacoma, was able to pay $1,000 -- $31,300 today -- to rescue his niece. When she began Hazzard's fasting cure, she weighed 109 pounds, and by the time she was free, she weighed 61 pounds fully clothed.

It only took a few weeks for the British government and the Williamson family to start seeking justice against Linda Hazzard and Starvation Heights on several accounts -- fraud and forging signatures to manipulate the sisters' wills and checks; an unauthorized autopsy, for which Dorothea sued Hazzard for $25,000; stolen belongings; and most unnervingly, the possibility that Claire's body was exchanged for a healthier looking one at the funeral. According to the women's uncle: "It did not look like Claire. The hair was a lighter brown than hers, and her face and hands were changed."

It was suggested that Hazzard was in cahoots with the Butterworth mortuary, and they had replaced Claire's emaciated skeleton with a healthier body. When Claire's uncle approached the open casket -- the custom of embalming was odd to the Brit -- he informed Hazzard of his concerns. Her only response was to pull him away from the casket. But others would agree that the body laid out at the funeral was not Claire.

As the local authorities finally began investigating the suspicious deaths surrounding Starvation Heights, it was revealed that many of the upper-class victims had left a significant amount of their fortunes to the Hazzards. There were also gold teeth that had been removed from corpses and other valuables that were never recovered from the sanitarium.

Linda Hazzard was arrested on August 5, 1911. Since there was no jail in Kitsap County for women, she remained under constant surveillance at the home of Mrs. W.A. Reid until her court date. What would follow would be considered one of the most notable trials in Washington's history.

On January 16, 1912, under Judge John B. Yakey, Linda Hazzard was put on trial for the first-degree murder of Claire Williamson. The prosecution claimed Hazzard was obsessed with proving her fasting regimen would work but needed a small fortune to build her dream sanitarium. So, she began carefully killing wealthy patients after editing their wills and conducting their autopsies to hide the actual cause of death. The defense denied that Hazzard had any hand in killing anyone. Claire's death was not brought on by lack of food, they claimed, but by a pre-existing condition that would have killed her anyway.

Nearly 90 witnesses were called to the stand, with 67 for the defense alone. Nurses testified, claiming they asked a local osteopath if they should sneak bone broth into the sisters instead of just asparagus broth. The head nurse, Nellie Sherman, was reported saying she "never had a case like this and didn't want another." Conventional doctors testified that Claire would have needed 25 quarts of the asparagus broth daily to survive, not just two cups. The state even suggested that Hazzard's interest in Spiritualism and the occult allowed her to hypnotize the two sisters to do what she instructed them to - though Hazzard claimed this was the "most ridiculous charge of all."

But the star witness for the defense was Dorothea Williamson. She described a day at Starvation Heights, including the amount of food she was given, the torturous enemas she had to endure, and the humiliation of being bathed by a man and fainting on several occasions. She informed the jury that Hazzard had encouraged her to commit suicide multiple times by throwing herself out the window or into a nearby gulley.

Although a nurse named Sarah Robinson, who claimed to be at Claire's deathbed, testified that the sisters were never denied food nor kept apart, the defense's attempt at winning over the jury was thwarted when it was revealed that Hazzard was signaling to the witnesses, trying to bribe the jury, and even had someone break into Dorothea's summer home in Tacoma.

The trial lasted three weeks. Hazzard hated her all-male jury, saying she'd "rather have placed her faith in the hands of a woman jury."

The jury deliberated for 20 hours. During this time, Hazzard said confidently, "They won't hang me – the muscles in my neck are too strong." However, her confidence in her fasting cure wasn't enough to save her from justice.

At 6:35 p.m. on Sunday, February 4, 1912, the jury filed back into the courtroom as everyone – including Linda Hazzard, who nervously bit her lip – waited anxiously to hear the verdict. As the clerk began to read the ruling, the lights went out. The bailiff dramatically struck a match, and Linda Hazzard learned her fate by the dim glow of the tiny flame.

Guilty of manslaughter.

It certainly wasn't first-degree murder like Dorothea Williamson had hoped for, and many suggested that Hazzard was found guilty of manslaughter solely because she was a woman. If she had been a man, it likely would have come back as guilty of first-degree murder.

Hazzard was adamant that a "fasting treatment never killed anyone" – fully convinced that people were not dying of starvation, and she was being targeted for being a successful woman and because of her unorthodox methods.

And when she began to argue against the verdict, Judge Yakey replied: "The verdict was amply supported by the evidence, and a contrary verdict would not have met the ends of justice."

In the darkness of the courtroom, Hazzard's lawyer, Mr. Kelley, asked for the bail to be dropped from $10,000 to $5,000, claiming, "My client is at the end of her resources." Judge Yakey refused.

Several days later, Hazzard was sentenced to hard labor at the Washington State Penitentiary for two to 20 years. She would also have to pay $973 of the $1,570 in cash she had stolen from Dorothea. And perhaps the harshest punishment of all -- her medical license was finally revoked.

Although Dorothea was not present in court when the verdict and sentencing were read, justice was finally served for her sister. The sensationalized trial made headlines across North America, reaching Hawaii and Alaska.

But despite finally being convicted of killing one of her patients, Hazzard refused to change her ways. Samuel Hazzard, Frank Lillie, and Miss Nellie Sherman quickly raised the $10,000 bail, and Hazzard was again out in the world.

Immediately after the trial, Hazzard began her own fast to prove the doctors that had testified against her wrong. They claimed a human couldn't survive for more than 14 days without food and water. She managed to fast for 45 days -- dropping from 142 pounds to 102 -- before breaking her fast with a tablespoon of rice, a teaspoon of olive oil, and six leaves of lettuce.

At this same time, she also appealed to the State Supreme Court. Because of this, the state medical board could not take away her license to practice. She was not officially convicted until their verdict was decided, which would take over a year.

In the meantime, she continued to kill.

During the year and a half that she waited for her appeal request to reach the State Supreme Court, she killed three more patients -- that we know of -- starting with a woman named Mary Bailey. She was the first suspicious death at Starvation Heights since the sensationalized murder trial, catching the attention of the Seattle coroner, Dr. Lewis, who quickly ordered an inquest into Mrs. Bailey's death.

Mrs. Ida J. Anderson was Hazzard's second victim after the trial. She was a teacher whose relatives opposed her going to see Hazzard. She died after just 14 days in Hazzard's care, and an inquest into her death was ordered in March 1913.

A man named Robert Graham – the royal baker to King George and Queen Mary of England – disappeared from the sanitarium in 1913. When authorities questioned Hazzard, she contradicted herself by first saying Mr. Graham was not a patient at Wilderness Heights but simply a guest. Shortly after, she began to insist that he was successfully taking the fast cure. Whether he was a guest or a patient didn't seem to matter -- he was dead, and being a royal baker, he would have also been wealthy.

On August 12, 1913, Hazzard's appeal finally reached the Washington State Supreme Court. They denied her request, saying the lower court "tempered justice with mercy."

This wasn't good enough for Dr. Linda Hazzard, so she appealed again. In fact, she appealed to the State Supreme Court four times and once to the United States Supreme Court, which denied her appeal on Christmas Eve, 1913. Linda Hazzard would pay for what she did to Claire Williamson, serving two to 20 years, working hard labor.

Newspapers around the country on Christmas Eve informed the public that the Starvation Doctor was going to jail amidst ads featuring Santa Claus and Christmas presents.

Hazzard left for the state penitentiary in Walla Walla on December 26 at 3:30 p.m. She didn't wait for the police to escort her – she went willingly. Her friends and supporters flooded the train station -- no doubt adding to Hazzard's sense of martyrdom -- to bid her farewell. She traveled with two friends -- Miss Marion E. Dunbar and Mrs. Mary Edwards. When she arrived in Walla Walla, she was refused admittance because she had arrived before her commitment papers and was told to wait.

For two years, Linda Hazzard served her sentence, all the while thoroughly convinced that she was innocent of any crime and was targeted for being a woman in a male-dominated field. In July 1914, she entered an application to be pardoned, signed by 200 supporters.

On December 26, 1915, Hazzard was released on parole after serving the minimum number of years in her sentence. When she returned home, a crowd greeted her at the train station. She was now more than ever convinced that her work was vital and commenced practice immediately, even though her medical license had been revoked as part of her sentencing.

Hazzard finally got the full pardon that she desperately needed in June 1916, compliments of Governor Ernest Lister.

Shortly after her release and pardon, Linda and Samuel Hazzard left Washington and moved to New Zealand, where Hazzard worked as a dietitian and an osteopath. In 1917, when local authorities discovered that she was working under the title "Doctor," even though her license had been revoked after the 1912 verdict, they fined her £5.

But Linda Hazzard's time in New Zealand was short-lived, and newspapers announced her return to Seattle on October 2, 1919.

In 1920, she finally opened her dream sanitarium with 100 beds available to patients who still came to her for her fasting treatment. Because her medical license had never been reinstated, she called her new sanitarium a "school of health" to get around certain legalities. However, she would continue to argue that her license should be returned to her since she received a full pardon from the governor.

This updated "school of health" continued to follow Hazzard's fasting regimen since she was still considered the "greatest authority on the fast and all-natural curative methods." However, the diet she placed her patients on was a bit more filling than the asparagus broth Claire Williamson was subjected to. It included vegetable soup, honey-sweetened lemonade, a baked potato, and salad.

Under this new diet, not nearly as many people died under Hazzard's supervision, but on January 31, 1924, the starvation sanitarium was put back on the authorities' radar. A man named Victor Johnson, aged 50, died while working with Hazzard. His death made headlines. When asked to produce her license to practice, Hazzard could not do so, and for a short time, the sanitarium was expected to shut down. But just like all the loopholes and bizarre coincidences that allowed Linda Hazzard to start practicing -- much less continue practicing her questionable methods for over a decade -- no one ever came for her, and she continued her work.

Dr. Hazzard added another victim to her ever-growing list the following year -- a man named L.M. Ritter. According to reports, he died while under Hazzard's supervision. According to his autopsy, he had tuberculosis. However, he had also been fasting for 84 days, so there was little doubt that a lack of nourishment hastened his death.

In March 1925, Hazzard was arrested by the local police for practicing medicine without a license. But again, she was released shortly after and returned to her sanitarium.

The craze surrounding Hazzard's healing treatment began to fade after the death of L.M. Ritter. Although her dream sanitarium had over 100 beds for patients, in its final years, she was lucky to have a dozen people filling them.

In 1935, Hazzard's "school of health" burned to the ground and was never rebuilt. She was arrested for the last time on May 6, 1936, when she tried to hide the whereabouts of a man named William Jussila. However, the authorities' official reasoning was that she continued practicing medicine without a license.

Hazzard died in 1938 when she was 70 years old. She had been subjecting herself to her own treatments to restore her failing health.

Ironically, she starved herself to death.

After the death of Linda Hazard, the Pacific Northwest was finally free of the so-called "doctor" who touted the benefits of starving her patients to death. However, the original Starvation Heights was still considered the "most murderous house in Washington's history" – reminding the community of the horrors that transpired within – until it came down in 2021.

Before that, those that visited reported poltergeist activity with chairs piling up in front of the bathroom door. A psychic that visited the house said that the spirits of Hazzard's patients were sitting quietly in the attic, afraid to move. Homeowners reported hearing footsteps, distant screaming, and banging. Local paranormal investigators caught voices on their audio recorders during investigations, and many believed that Linda Hazzard haunted the room where she died.

With the demolition of Starvation Heights, the town of Olalla could finally move on, but some question whether the spirits of Hazzard's victims remain on the land.

While there were more than a dozen documented deaths on the property, it's suspected that she killed as many as 40 people during her time as Dr. Linda Burfield Hazzard.

She was only convicted of one.

Justice may have been served for Claire Williamson, but it wouldn't be surprising to find the rest of her victims - both known and unknown - lingering still on the land where the old sanitarium once stood, desperate to be known, remembered, and avenged.

"SHOEBOX ANNIE"
ANN FRENCH
A.K.A MARY ELLEN SMITH...
MAYBE
BY TROY TAYLOR

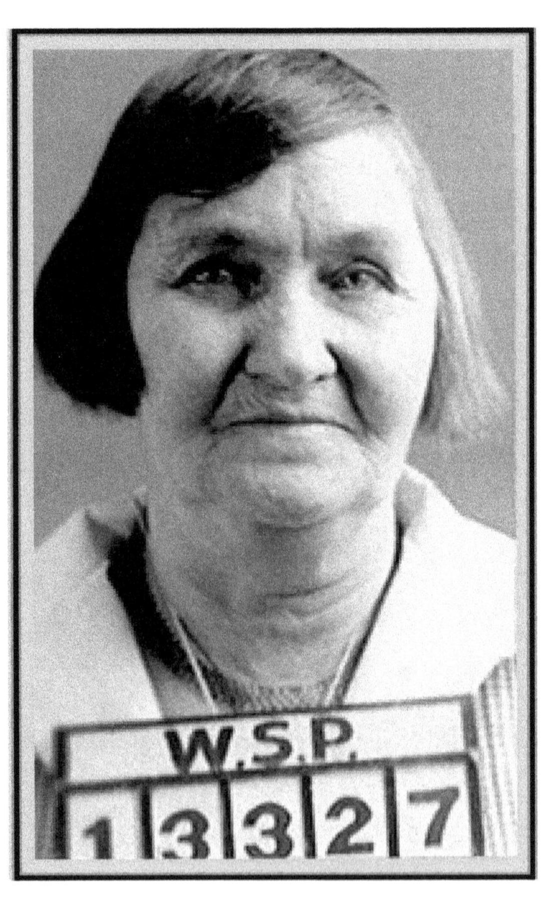

They called her "Shoebox Annie," but it wasn't her name. They called her that because she carried a shoebox around with her and sold soap, shoelaces, and other items out of it - including moonshine. She lived in Goosetown - a working-class neighborhood in Anaconda, Montana - in the 1920s. However, she left such an impression behind that even those growing up decades later avoided the corner of Alder and Commercial Avenue, where her house once stood.

It was the house where she and her son murdered people, boiled the flesh from their bones, and burned what was left.

Annie had a pet magpie whose split tongue allowed it to talk. She sometimes went door-to-door with the bird, selling soap and homemade liquor. The magpie was trained to pick up jewelry off dressers and fly out of the house with it. If you let Annie in, she'd steal things. You could only get rid of her by buying her booze.

Annie's real name was Ann French. Maybe.

It might have also been Mary Ellen Smith. Probably.

In truth, though, no one knows. We only know the names she used when she committed her crimes and went to prison.

We don't know what her name was when she was born or what she called herself when she began teaching her son how to get away with murder. He had a lot of aliases, too - like C.D. Montaine, C.C. Skidmore, De Casto Earl Mayer - but William Donald Mayer was likely the closest to the truth. Or at least that was the one he was using when he realized he was caught and decided to take his own life.

That's the only kind of death that his mother hadn't taught him about.

We must start the story of "Shoebox Annie" later in life when her son - whom we'll call "Mayer" here to make things easier - was already full-grown and well-schooled in the art of crime. Her early life is a complete mystery. We don't know the identity of her son's father, where she came from, her exact age, or much of anything.

Mayer had started his criminal career writing bad checks for his mother and graduated to burglary, at which he didn't excel. He was arrested as a teenager and sent to the Whittier Reform School in California in 1912. He was using the alias C.D. Montaine at the time.

After his parole, the mother and son moved to Montana, where Mayer was soon in trouble again. He was arrested for stealing an automobile in Bozeman in 1917 while using the name C.C. Skidmore and was sent to the Montana State Penitentiary for a stay of between four and nine years.

In 1920, he was paroled but didn't hurry home to his mother this time. When Mayer had been arrested, his girlfriend - a drug addict named Doris Cheney - had been his accomplice. Behind bars, he'd found out that Doris had ratted him out, leading to his arrest. She was now living in Seattle, and Mayer followed her there, delivering a brutal beating that left her unconscious and bleeding but still alive. With that accomplished, he returned to his mother, now living in Anaconda, Montana.

Following his mother's instructions, Mayer connected with a man named Ole Larson, A Norwegian immigrant, and grifter. They sold phony oil stocks, bilked a few merchants with bad checks, and swindled some wealthy women out of their husband's estates. But one day, Mayer learned that Larson had a bank draft for $750, so he invited his friend to his mother's house for a nice, home-cooked meal.

Ole Larson was never seen again.

His bank draft was, in any case. A few days later, Annie forged his name on the check and cashed it.

A short time later, Mayer learned that his old girlfriend, Doris, had gotten married, and her husband had money. He started working his charms on his old flame, who was still strung out on drugs, but hoping to kick her bad habits. Husband or not, the two became friendly again, and Mayer invited her to visit with his mother one night in February 1921.

Like Larson, Doris was never seen again.

But her husband did report her missing, which led to a police investigation. When officers searched Annie's house, they found the missing woman's possessions - luggage, jewelry, even underwear - but not the woman herself. She had simply vanished, and Annie and Mayer claimed to have no knowledge about where she had gone. She went out one night, they told the police, and she never returned.

The only trace of Doris could be found in rumors whispered in the neighborhood. Neighbors were said to have noticed an "offensive smoke" rising from Annie's chimney around the time of the murder. When asked about it, Annie told the neighbors that she was burning some leftover bones from meat she and her son had eaten but didn't want to throw into a garbage can and attract rodents.

But this was only a rumor - it wasn't evidence. Even if detectives had believed it, they couldn't charge Annie and Mayer with murder. They might have killed the woman - and Ole Larson, too - but there was no way to prove it.

But not everyone cared about what they could prove. In April 1921, Doris' mother, Lois Hendricks, traveled from Texas to Anaconda, looking for her missing daughter. She went straight to Annie's house and demanded to know where her daughter was. Annie claimed not to know, but this wasn't good enough for Lois. The disagreement between the two mothers turned into a screaming match and became physical. Lois pulled a pistol from her purse and shot Annie at close range. Two bullets pierced her body, and Lois fled the scene. Annie recovered from her wounds, and she and Mayer wisely chose not to pursue charges against the mother of the woman they'd likely killed.

When Lois Hendricks returned to Texas, she took all her daughter's possessions with her. They had been recovered from Annie's house by the police. Two items weren't included, though - a watch and a diamond ring - but they would turn up later. Mayer used them as gifts for Ruth Hardwick from Oxford, Idaho, whom he later married. After giving them to her, though, he changed his mind about the ring and pawned it in Salt Lake City. The pawnbroker alerted the police, but Annie redeemed it before detectives could get their hands on it.

It was around the time of the Salt Lake City trip that Annie and Mayer made a mistake. They made the trip in a stolen car, which they sold to an Anaconda resident for $365 when they returned. The new owner took the vehicle to a garage for repairs, and the mechanic noticed that the engine numbers had been altered, which meant it was likely stolen. He called the police, who contacted special agents with the Division of Investigation - the earlier incarnation of the FBI - which had automobile theft high on their list of priorities.

After restoring the original motor numbers as part of the investigation, the car was traced to a Salt Lake City woman, Mrs. E.V. Fritz. She told the police her young son had mischievously scratched his initials on the gasoline tank cap. She had varnished it over, but when agents removed the varnish with ether, they found the initials.

The theft and taking the car across state lines violated the National Motor Vehicle Theft Act, which had been pushed through Congress by the Division of Identification's eager young director, J. Edgar Hoover. This put agents on the trail of William Donald Mayer.

It didn't take long for them to track him to Pocatello, Idaho. He was living with a blind woman who was selling soap around town - or so she claimed. She wasn't blind, and she wasn't selling soap. It was "Shoebox Annie," and she was peddling liquor and abortion medications. The police had been told that her son often appeared in town driving several different makes of automobiles.

Officers went to the house where Mayer was living with his mother one evening, and just as they arrived, he was leaving. In one hand, he carried a rifle; in the other was a black bag containing stolen automobile plates, keys for different makes of cars, wire cutters, screwdrivers, and devices for opening locked car doors.

He was arrested on the spot.

Loaded into the backseat of the car, he was taken to police headquarters. One of the federal agents opened the door for him, and he climbed out. Suddenly, he pushed the agent into a nearby police officer and began to run. The agents and cops opened fire, but Mayer didn't slow down. He rounded the corner of a building and disappeared.

From the opposite direction, Annie appeared. She was on her way into the station to try and pay her son's bail. She had heard the gunshots but didn't know they had anything to do with her son until she walked inside. Seeing an attorney that had represented her in a minor case a short time before, she hurried over to him, pushed a package she was carrying into his hands, asked him to keep it for her, and to go to her house and get her car out of the garage.

Oh, and when he did - drive it into a river.

Annie fled the scene while the baffled attorney was still trying to understand what was happening. When he opened the package, he found a bundle of bank bonds, which he promptly turned over to the police. But they were less interested in the bonds than in the car parked in Annie's garage. They quickly returned to the Mayer house and found their garage was hiding more than an automobile.

When they opened the door, their flashlights revealed fresh blood on the floor and along the running board of the car that was parked there. They found a spattered trail and discovered Mayer crammed into the corner of the garage, bleeding profusely. He had been struck by bullets in the shoulder and forearm during his escape. The wounded man returned to the garage, removed the license plates from the car, and tried to alter the engine numbers before his strength failed him.

A search of the house followed, revealing Annie's stash of liquor. She was arrested for bootlegging. They hadn't even had a chance to investigate where the package of bank bonds had come from yet.

By now, news of Mayer's arrest had spread to other law enforcement agencies in the region, and Jerry Murphy, the chief of police in Anaconda, let detectives in Pocatello know about the still missing Doris and what the neighbors claimed had happened to her.

With that information in hand, Pocatello detective Tom Roan went to see Mayer in the hospital. He was recovering from surgery for his gunshot wounds. Detective Roan told him that the cops in Anaconda had discovered the bones of the woman he'd murdered there.

Roan said that Mayer turned white. He also claimed that the wounded man offered him a bribe if he would help him escape.

"I'm not interested in helping you escape," Roan told him. "I want to help solve that murder." The police there had worked on the case day and night and wanted to close it.

But Mayer shook his head. "They can't get my neck," he blurted out. "They can't find the body - or all of it."

The same story was also fed to Annie that night. She was securely behind bars. She listened calmly and denied having anything to do with a murder. But later, according to the jail matron, she woke up screaming, "Oh Donald, Donald, they've found it! They've found it!"

But, once again, none of that was evidence. Nothing he'd done could be linked to a murder. He knew he was going to jail, but he didn't want his mother locked up. He offered a trade - he'd go to Utah voluntarily to face charges for stealing the Fritz car, and he'd plead guilty to stealing the car found in his garage, as long as Annie wasn't prosecuted.

The police and prosecutor took what they could get and agreed to the deal. Mayer was sentenced to spend the next ten years in prison, but he only served two. When he was paroled, officers from Montana were waiting for him. They arrested him for the second automobile theft charge. He'd already pled guilty to this one and was fined $25. Annie paid the fine, and Mayer was again a free man.

Mayer now returned to Oxford, Idaho, to his wife, Ruth, and stayed there until May 1923. That was when the bones of an unidentified woman were found in Montana, and the police announced plans to try and identify them as Doris Cheney, Mayer's missing girlfriend.

He didn't stick around to find out that the body wasn't Doris - he left the state. On his way out of town, he stole an engine from his father-in-law and used the cash to fund what turned out to be a very short trip. Mayer was picked up by the cops in Steamboat Springs, Colorado, who were already looking for him on theft charges in their state.

Mayer was tried again and sentenced to a few years at the Colorado State Penitentiary in Canon City. He was paroled, and this time, it was officers from Idaho who were waiting for him when he walked out of the prison's gates. They were taking him back to Oxford to face theft charges for stealing the engine. However, for the night, they locked him up in the local jail for safekeeping - a jail he wouldn't stay in for long. Late that night, Mayer and several other inmates managed to escape. Using a smuggled tool, they removed the bars from their cells, walked out the back door, and vanished.

Mayer remained on the run until January 1924. He was arrested in Kansas and returned to Pocatello to face the charges brought by his father-in-law. The trial was short and ended with Mayer being acquitted of all charges. Soon, he was back at home with his mother, but he couldn't stay out of trouble.

He soon had the FBI on his back again. Using the name Earl Montaigne, he and an accomplice transported two young women from Colorado to Idaho. One of them was only 17. The other was married and had two small children. Mayer tried to force the underage girl into prostitution, but she refused and threatened to inform the police. Alarmed, he sent her home. He had better luck with the other woman. His threats got her out onto the street, and she soon began turning over her earnings to Mayer - until the FBI charged him with violating the Mann Act, which prohibited taking women across state lines for sexual purposes. For this, he ended up serving three years in Leavenworth. After he was paroled, he moved back in with his mother, now living in Seattle.

And then James Eugene Bassett came to town.

In September 1928, James - a former Navy ensign who now worked in government civil service - arrived in Seattle on his way to the Philippines. He'd been transferred from the East Coast a short time earlier and had been staying in the city with his sister and brother-in-law, Theodore Winters, in Bremerton, the Puget Sound Navy Yard community about 12 miles from Seattle. He was scheduled to leave town on September 10.

James had driven across the country in his blue Chrysler roadster, which he intended to sell before leaving. He placed an advertisement in the newspaper, offering the car for sale, and a man who gave the name De Casto Earl Mayer answered the ad right away. He offered James $1,600 for the vehicle, provided that the two of them could stop by the home of the buyer's "aunt" so that she could take a look at it. James agreed, and arrangements were made to meet on September 5. He allowed the potential buyer to climb behind the wheel for a test drive. James opened the passenger door, climbed inside, and the two men drove away.

It was the last time James Bassett was ever seen.

The next day, James' sister received a telegram saying that her brother had gone to Vancouver with a friend and planned to remain there for several days. She didn't think anything odd about it then, but when James failed to return on September 10 and then failed to report to the ship taking him to the Philippines - she became alarmed. Her husband contacted the police.

It's hard to say if the police would have taken them as seriously as they did without Eugene Levy, a Seattle businessman. On September 11, he reported that he had been menaced by a man who responded to an advertisement similar to the one placed by James Bassett. His description of the man who answered his ad was also very close to the man with whom Bassett had last been seen. Soon, a search was underway for James and the mysterious stranger.

A few days later, a police officer in Oakland, California, pulled over a blue Chrysler roadster that matched the one in which the missing man had been seen. The occupants were De Casto Earl Mayer and his mother, Mary Ellen Smith. They denied knowing James Bassett, even though they had his car. The man produced a bill-of-sale for the vehicle and insisted it had been legitimately purchased.

However, they had difficulty explaining why James Bassett's wristwatch, cuff links, and wallet were also in the car. Those items must have been in the car when they bought it, they told the police, and they hadn't noticed them until now. The pair were arrested and taken to Oakland police headquarters, where the roadster was searched more thoroughly. The police found a rifle, a pistol fitted with a silencer, a gas gun, chloroform, a meat saw, and a pair of tongs suitable for breaking bones.

When questioned about these sinister items, the pair told the police they'd had them for years. There wasn't anything strange about them at all.

The mother and son - "Shoebox Annie" and William Donald Mayer, of course - continued to insist they knew nothing about a missing civil servant, but this didn't stop the Oakland cops from sending them back to Seattle.

By now, an intensive search had started for James Bassett. Every possible clue was followed. Sheriff Claude L. Bannick and a score of deputies searched everywhere within a 20-miles radius of Seattle, assisted by state patrolmen, city detectives, and even the Boy Scouts. Abandoned buildings were scoured, lakes and rivers were dragged, and countless feet tromped through woods and fields. Following a tip, they even dug up the yard of a small house that Mayer had recently rented north of the city - but nothing was found.

The suspects were arraigned on September 25 but continued to maintain their innocence. Constant grilling got the authorities nowhere. When they proposed to force a confession from Annie using "truth serum," her attorney, John F. Dore, protested to the courts, and a judge stopped the interrogation.

Weeks passed, and all efforts to find the body of James Bassett failed. Finally, on December 5 - three months after the civil servant had vanished - King County Prosecutor Ewing D. Colvin charged the prisoners with grand larceny. There was no way to prove they had committed murder.

The trial lasted ten days and ended in convictions. Appeal motions consumed a few more weeks, and then on January 30, 1929, it was decided that Mayer had violated the Washington law that made anyone convicted of three felonies a "habitual criminal." This meant a mandatory life sentence.

Mayer went to Walla Walla Penitentiary for life, while his mother was sent away for an indeterminate time of up to 18 years.

The pair were now safely behind bars - but that's not quite the end of the story of James Bassett.

Mayer returned to court on May 12, pending an appeal to the State Supreme Court. His attorney, Henry Clay Agnew, argued that errors were made during his trial and that his sentence had been prejudiced. The court didn't agree, and Mayer went back to prison.

The newspapers of November 21 announced a surprise to the people of Seattle - Mayer had confessed to James Bassett's murder! After being questioned with a lie detector, Mayer had narrowed down the location of Bassett's body after being caught in a lie replying to "yes" and "no" questions. Bassett was buried, the confession said, in Swedish Cemetery.

The police rushed to the scene and thoroughly searched the graveyard, but nothing was there. No clues, no body, no James Bassett.

And then the real story came out. The police had repeatedly questioned Mayer for seven days in a row, hooked up to a polygraph machine, and hammered with questions about the murder case and the location of Bassett's body. The questions had been relentless, followed by beatings. Finally, exhausted, Mayer agreed to "confess" to killing Bassett if his mother was not charged with murder.

Prosecutor Colvin agreed, and the search took them to the cemetery, where the authorities found nothing.

Mayer reported the beatings and the questioning to his attorney, who went to the judge. A court ruling on the matter rejected Mayer's "confession" and banned further use of the lie detector. The court also rejected the appeal that Mayer's lawyer had filed several months before.

Mayer and Annie were both behind bars. No further efforts were made to find Bassett's remains. Legally, the case was closed.

But it wasn't quite over yet.

On May 4, 1938 - just five days before she was due to be released from prison - Annie made a startling confession to the warden that she and her son had not only murdered James Bassett but three other people, as well.

According to her story, Mayer had lured James to a house they rented in Richmond Highlands, where they planned to "do away with him." After picking up Bassett, he was driven to the house where she was waiting. James had been told that she needed to see the car and would write the check. Annie was sitting on the couch when the two men walked in. An iron rod was hidden in a quilt next to her - just in case.

"When we say we would pay in check, Bassett consented," she told the warden. "He said it was okay with him. I got up from the couch and sat down at the writing desk."

Mayer gave her the hint to step out of the room when James sat down in a chair in front of the fireplace. Mayer stepped up behind him, handed him a blank telegram, and said, "I am going to have your car, and I won't pay you for it. You write this telegram as I say it."

Bassett refused at first, but Mayer threatened to kill him if he didn't. Finally, he scratched out the note to his sister, which Mayer would later send, telling her that James would be gone for a few days.

And then he hit him with the hammer.

James fell out of the chair and out to the floor, landing with a loud thump. Annie came back into the room. She later said she'd heard his body fall, and when she entered the room, he was "gurgling." Mayer stepped forward and hit the man again, shattering his skull.

Annie helped her son drag the body into the bathroom. She removed Bassett's clothing, and Mayer helped her lift the body into the bathtub. Annie then went to work with the meat saw and the tongs, cutting Bassett into pieces and removing his arms, legs, and head.

When Mayer became sick while watching her take the dead man apart, she "gave him an eggnog to keep him up."

Annie cleaned up the blood spattered all over the bathtub and the surrounding walls and then burned all the clothing. After dark, they took the body pieces - minus the head and hands - and drove to a "patch of woods somewhere between Cathcart and Bethell" and dumped them in the brush. The next morning, they took the head and hands to another patch of woods and buried the hands on one side of the road and the head on the other "in an old abandoned woodchuck's hole."

No one knows why Annie suddenly decided to confess to murder. Some say it was a religious conversion. There are rumors of another inmate who used Annie to shorten her own sentence by convincing Annie to come clean. Other stories say that the warden ordered a guard to dress up like a clergyman, telling her that whatever she told him would remain secret.

But no one really knows. What we do know is that Annie abruptly stopped protecting her son for the first time in his life.

Whatever caused her change of heart turned out to be fatal for Mayer.

On May 7, mother and son were taken to Seattle and charged with murder. Mayer, sullen and contemptuous, said that his mother was "crazy" and that her "confession" was a "pack of lies." But Annie continued cooperating with the authorities, even traveling with detectives to show them crime scenes and reenact the murders.

While Mayer claimed he'd had nothing to with any murders, Annie sent detectives out searching for body parts. They combed the areas she described inch by inch but found nothing. That was not, however, going to stop the prosecutor from bringing her and Mayer to trial.

The courtroom was jammed when the trial began on November 28. On the stand, Annie seemed composed as she repeated her confession. It was all the prosecutor had, aside from the belongings of Bassett's that had been found in the car. There was no body, but Prosecutor B. Gray Warner asserted he could prove murder had been committed beyond a reasonable doubt even without a corpse.

During the trial, their life of crime unraveled from the witness stand, and their gruesome deeds were printed in newspapers nationwide.

The state rested its case on December 11, and fearing a death sentence, Mayer tried to deal his way out of a first-degree murder conviction by offering to show the authorities where they had disposed of Bassett's body parts. The prosecutor turned down the offer.

Later that night, Mayer committed suicide. He shoved two paper towels down his throat and then tied a strip of cloth torn from his shirt around his mouth to keep them in place. He lashed his hands together with his belt to keep from removing the gag and stood waiting for the end in the middle of his cell. When he passed out, he fell forward and cut his head open on the corner of his cot.

He was dead within minutes at the age of 44.

Annie became hysterical when she was given the news. She insisted on seeing his body, kissed his cold lips, and begged to know why he had done it.

Mayer had left a note behind. It read:

Dearest Mother,

Words are sometimes meaningless. I am tired and wish to depart from a place wherein is oppression and leave the house to tell of its builder's fate. And, for the place I leave, I shall find another land.

Everything is all right with me, and it will be easier for you in the future.

Lovingly,
Earl

PS. You will receive help. Prefer cremation without box, etc.

Two days later, Annie again offered her guilty plea and was given a life sentence. She served the next 15 years in prison and then was paroled to a state-run nursing home in March 1953. She managed to hang on there for another 13 years and died on March 2, 1966. She was 100 years old.

The body of James Bassett was never found.

"AMERICA'S FIRST FEMALE SERIAL KILLER"

LAVINIA FISHER

BY AMANDA R. WOOMER

With America's obsession with true crime, we have a lot of "firsts" and "fun facts."

The first recorded hanging of a woman? Jane Champion in 1632.

The first woman executed by the United States government? Mary Surratt for conspiracy to assassinate Abraham Lincoln in 1865.

The youngest woman, or, in this case, girl, executed? Hannah Ocuish, at just 12 years old in 1786.

The oldest? Rebecca Nurse, at 71 years old, was hanged during the Salem Witch Trials of 1692.

The last woman hanged by the federal government? Mary Holmes in 1937.

The most suspected victims? Amy Archer-Gilligan, with 50 suspected murders from 1910 to 1917.

The most confirmed victims? Belle Gunness, with at least 14 - likely more -- from 1900 to 1908.

But with all these statistics and "firsts," there is one that has become evasive in recent years -- America's first female serial killer. For generations, that title went to an enigmatic woman named Lavinia Fisher, but today, historians are unsure if she was wicked -- or simply wronged.

Not much is known about Lavinia Fisher. We know she was born in 1793. But aside from that, we have no information on her parents, maiden name, childhood, or where she grew up. It's as if she mysteriously appeared from nothing when she married John Fisher in the early 1800s. The couple began residing just north of Charleston, South Carolina, where they ran an inn.

Charleston in the Antebellum South was a bustling city, only trailing behind New York City, Philadelphia, Baltimore, and Boston in size. By 1810, it had almost 25,000 inhabitants.

At this time, enslaved and free people of color comprised more than half of the population. It was the only city in the South where enslaved individuals outnumbered enslavers.

Aside from a racial divide, there was also an extreme gap between the wealthy and the lower class, with the top 4 percent of the population controlling more than half of the city's wealth. The War of 1812 led to the Panic of 1819, which some historians consider America's first Great Depression. With racial, class and economic tension rising and the fact that Charleston was a trade hub on both land and sea, it became a prime target for thieves -- particularly pirates on the water and highwaymen on the roads.

The term "highwayman" dates to at least 1617, with terms such as "knights of the road" and "gentlemen of the road" romanticizing the thieves into Robin Hood-type characters. In the American West, they were sometimes called "road agents," and in Australia, "bushrangers." No matter what name they went by, highwaymen were known to violently steal goods and money from coaches well into the mid-nineteenth century.

History has left us names that live in both infamy and, occasionally, as folk heroes, like Dick Turpin, who was immortalized in "penny dreadfuls" in the 1800s; Six-String Jack, known for bantering with his executioner and dancing on the gallows before his execution; and even highwaywomen such as Katherine Ferrers.

Highwaymen have appeared in literature and music through the centuries, including the character of Falstaff in Shakespeare's *Henry IV, Part 1,* and the traditional Irish song *Whiskey in the Jar* with its line, "I first produced me pistol, then I drew me rapier. Said, 'Stand and deliver, for you are a bold deceiver.'" We also see highwaymen depicted in *Monty Python's Flying Circus* during the Dennis Moore sketch, Lorena McKennitt's adaption of the 1906 narrative poem *The Highwayman,* and the 1981 children's fantasy novel, *Ronia, the Robber's Daughter* by Astrid Lindgren. But even if these individuals are painted as both villains and heroes in the arts, that does not negate the fact that for centuries in both Europe and America, highwaymen were a threat to anyone traveling along roads without enough protection, particularly surrounding one of wealthiest cities in the American South.

Highwaymen were a great concern for travelers around Charleston. Traders would carry animal hides, cotton, tobacco, and produce on the road into the city and money on the road that led them out. And cunning thieves were happy to steal it all.

Just six miles north of Charleston, John and Lavinia Fisher ran the Six-Mile Wayfarer House, where weary travelers could stop, enjoy a meal, give their horses a chance to rest, and even spend the night in a warm bed.

But, according to legend, the Six-Mile House was also Lavinia Fisher's house of horrors.

Reports at the time claimed that travelers who stopped at the Six-Mile House seemed to vanish and were never seen again. This quickly led to several rumors surrounding the dastardly deeds that must have occurred inside its walls.

The first suggested that Lavinia -- said to be both charming and beautiful -- would invite lone travelers into the inn. While they ate, she would ask them questions to determine whether they had anything valuable to steal. She would offer them a room for the night and a cup of her homemade tea, which was brewed with oleander - a flower that just happened to be poisonous. Once the man was passed out from her toxic tea, John would enter the room and beat them while Lavinia stole their goods and wares.

The second story goes one step further, claiming that the tea would only put the victim to sleep for several hours. Once asleep in bed, Lavinia would pull a hidden lever, and the bed would collapse, dropping the victim into a pit in the basement. Some of the wilder stories even claimed there were spikes in the pit to impale her victims.

While there were whispers among the locals of the Six-Mile House acting as a hideout for highwaymen, both John and Lavinia were popular and respected members of the community, so the authorities never pursued any of these allegations, even though almost all the men reported missing in Charleston were last seen at the Six-Mile House. It didn't take long for a vigilante gang to form in Charleston and head north to take matters into their own hands.

In February 1819, the mob -- made up of an undisclosed number of members -- decided to put an end to the violence along the roadway. They first stopped at the Five-Mile House, an inn that was situated -- you guessed it -- five miles north of the city. They dragged out those inside the inn and set it on fire, burning it to the ground before continuing north. When they arrived at the Six-Mile House, everyone inside cooperated after no doubt smelling the smoke from their sister inn just one mile away. Believing they were successful in their mission, the vigilantes returned to Charleston, leaving behind a young man named David Ross to stand guard and ensure that no highwaymen returned to the Six-Mile House.

The following day, Ross was attacked by two men and dragged in front of the gang of highwaymen. It's said that Ross spotted Lavinia and recognized her as one of the respected pillars of the community. Convinced that she was there to save him from the highwaymen's wrath, he called out to the lone woman for help. In response, she choked him and smashed his head through a nearby window. Miraculously, Ross managed to escape and fled to Charleston, where he informed the authorities of whom he had encountered at the Six-Mile House.

According to stories, only minutes later, a traveler named John Peeples arrived at the inn, looking for a place to spend the night. As always, Lavinia brought him inside, and while he ate, she asked him a series of questions. Once his room was ready, she handed him a cup of her oleander tea, setting her murderous plan in motion. However, unlike her other victims, Peeples hated tea, and he managed to pour it out while Lavinia wasn't looking.

Suddenly concerned about the amount of information he had shared with the woman of the house, he feared he might be robbed. That night, he sat guard in a chair beside the door instead of sleeping in bed. In the middle of the night, he heard a loud noise and saw the bed disappear into the floor. Realizing that his suspicions had been correct, he leaped through the window, hopped on his horse, and fled to Charleston, where he, too, went straight to the authorities.

Or did he?

Like so many pieces of Lavinia Fisher's story, many of the claims about her have been exaggerated into tall tales over the centuries, so it is challenging to track down facts.

It's true that John Peeples arrived at the Six-Mile House shortly after David Ross fled. But he never stayed the night, he never poured out his cup of poisoned tea, and he certainly did not see his bed disappear into a mysterious pit.

Peeples was traveling to Charleston from Georgia. He stopped at the Six-Mile House simply to give his horse water before continuing down the road. Not too far from the inn, he was attacked by nine or ten people, and he was robbed of $40 -- just under $1,000 today -- and "unmercifully beaten." He noted that there had been a woman in the group and was able to identify Lavinia along with her husband, John, and their business partner, William Heyward.

With two positive identifications in such a short amount of time, the authorities finally acted on the suspicions of the neighbors and backcountry folk.

Local authorities and Charleston citizens gathered as many men and muskets as possible and made their way to the Six-Mile Wayfarer House. The highwaymen were initially ready to fight with 10 to 12 muskets and a keg of gunpowder. However, it didn't take long to realize they were out-gunned and out-manned, and John Fisher quickly surrendered.

Although Lavinia's story is rife with exaggerations and lies, one thing remains consistent – John's love for his wife. It's believed that he exited the inn peacefully to protect Lavinia from the authorities' guns and would later reveal the names of every member of his gang in the hopes of saving Lavinia from the gallows.

Six people were arrested- five in the inn and one in town - including John and Lavinia Fisher, William Heyward, Jane Howard, James McElway, and Seth Young.

According to reports at the time, which already had a habit of exaggerating the truth, when the house was searched, officials found the belongings of dozens of travelers as well as a multitude of secret passageways and the bones of up to 100 victims buried under the inn.

Or did they?

In truth, there was no basement for skeletons to be buried, much less secret passages or a pit filled with spikes. And while two bodies were found near the property – a white man possibly shot when the vigilante mob arrived and an African American woman who had been dead for two years – neither was ever connected to the Fishers.

Even so, with Lavinia and John Fisher in prison, the local authorities burned the Six-Mile Wayfarer House to the ground.

At their arraignment, John and Lavinia were charged with common assault and assault with the intent to murder David Ross and highway robbery against John Peeples. Both the Fishers and their fellow gang members pleaded not guilty. Even though their co-

conspirators were released on bail, John and Lavinia were forced to remain locked up for almost an entire year, and it's likely their time behind bars was horrific and unbearable by our standards today.

The Old Jail was the county jail from its construction in 1802 until it closed in 1939. Built on a potter's field of enslaved individuals, it originally stood at four stories with a two-story octagonal tower, but today, there are only three stories thanks to the Charleston Earthquake of 1886. It acted as both a jail and an asylum.

Aside from infamously housing "America's first female serial killer," it also imprisoned pirates, Civil War prisoners of war, and the leader of the attempted 1822 slave revolt, Denmark Vesey.

At the time it was built, it was supposed to imprison 128 inmates, though as many as 300 prisoners were usually crowded behind the walls at one time. Some prisoners were held in cages that were so narrow they couldn't sit down or sleep. The barred windows did nothing to keep out the cold of winter or summer heat, bugs, or vermin. There was no running water, and wood chips on the floor acted as both bed and toilet. Torture was commonplace, as was sexual assault. It was estimated that 10,000 people died from disease, torture, and violence, as well as executions, during its 137-year history.

Lavinia and John's court date was scheduled for a hot day in May 1819. It did not take long for the jury to reject the Fishers' pleas of innocence. Together, they were found guilty of highway robbery against John Peeples, and although it wasn't murder, they were still sentenced to hang since highway robbery was also a capital offense at this time.

Lavinia and John quickly filed an appeal which the judge granted -- but they'd have to stay in prison until January 17, 1820, while they awaited their fate.

Because they were married, John and Lavinia were placed in the same six-by-eight-foot cell. Originally on the lower level, Lavinia managed to use her charm to get them moved to the upper level, where there was significantly less security.

On September 13, 1819, the two attempted to escape from the Charleston jail. Using a makeshift rope constructed from linens found within the prison, they worked with an accomplice to carve a hole beneath their barred window and shimmy down the wall. After their companion and John were safely on the ground, Lavinia moved to follow her husband, but their poorly constructed rope snapped, leaving Lavinia stranded.

For a short time, John hid in the wharf beneath an overturned boat, trying to think of a way to save her, again revealing how much he genuinely loved his wife. He refused to leave her at the cost of his own freedom, which led to him being quickly recaptured and returned to prison. The couple was now placed under much tighter security.

In January, the state's constitutional court again found the Fishers guilty of highway robbery. On February 2, they were officially sentenced to hang. Their execution was set for just two days later -- February 4.

The governor at the time, John Geddes, received a multitude of pleas from the Fishers, their friends, local clergy, and people of Charleston, asking that the execution date be delayed so John and Lavinia could "prepare to meet their God." Governor Geddes agreed, and the Fishers' execution was pushed to February 18.

As their execution date crept closer, John sought comfort from the local Baptist minister, Reverend Richard Furman. It's said that John converted to Christianity in his final days. According to contemporary papers, John "appeared to have a deep and humbling sense of the vileness of his nature and expressed the most sincere penitence for his offenses as a sinner."

While John seemed to find peace, Lavinia grew angry and bitter. During the last two weeks of her life, Lavinia was convinced she would be pardoned –jumping up any time a jailkeeper appeared with a piece of paper in his hands. In her heart, she didn't think the governor would hang a woman, much less a married woman. Legend claims that when she said this to the judge, he replied, "We'll simply hang your husband first."

While she was not the first woman executed in America, she would be the only one executed in South Carolina -- an unusual thing for Charleston's citizens.

On January 28, 1820, the *National Advocate for the Country* wrote:

> *The trial, conviction, and punishment of a* female *for* Highway Robbery *is happily a* very *rare occurrence in any age or country.*

Almost exactly one year from their arrest -- Friday, February 18, 1820 -- the Fishers' execution date arrived, and it's said that neither John nor Lavinia Fisher went to their deaths without a fight.

At 2:00 p.m., the couple was escorted from the jail to a carriage that would carry them less than two miles north to where the gallows had been constructed -- just outside the city center where Line and Meeting Streets intersect. At the sight of the gallows, it's said that John grew pale and pulled Lavinia close, his body trembling.

Legend says that Lavinia insisted on wearing her wedding gown to her execution -- though the fact that the Six-Mile House had been destroyed in the fire along with all of her belongings makes this highly unlikely. Instead, she probably wore a white shift or smock.

Witnesses to the execution claim that Lavinia appeared "unwilling to die" as she was carried up the gallows' steps, kicking, screaming, and cursing the Charleston elite and the governor, whom she blamed for encouraging her conviction. No doubt, she grew tired of waiting for that pardon to arrive.

As Lavinia continued to spit and curse, Reverend Furman read a letter written by John. In the note, John claimed that since he was now a Christian, he could not die for a lie, and he insisted on his innocence, begging the crowd of 2,000 onlookers for mercy. He found none.

Lavinia would not go so quietly. Her final words colorfully echoed through the crowd: "If you have a message you want to send to hell, give it to me; I'll carry it."

As with so many aspects of her life, there are conflicting reports -- of varying degrees of authenticity -- of how Lavinia Fisher met her end. Some claim that after she informed the crowd that she was off to hell, she leaped from the platform, robbing the executioner of his kill. Other stories suggest that the married couple were able to embrace one last time before the trapdoor was sprung beneath them, "launching them into eternity."

Either way, Lavinia - who was only 27 years old -- died without "a struggle or a groan." Her neck instantly broke.

John was not so lucky and struggled for several minutes before strangling to death.

Today, local ghost tour guides claim that Lavinia was buried at either the Circular Congregational Church at 150 Meeting Street or the Unitarian Church at 4 Archdale Street. However, there is no evidence that either location is her final resting place.

A potter's field was located directly next to the jailhouse at this time, and if Lavinia Fisher was buried, it was likely there without any kind of ceremony. We say "if" because several newspapers from the early twentieth century claim that the Charleston Museum put her skeleton on display several times.

If so, perhaps this is why she doesn't rest in peace.

Ghost stories emerged almost immediately after Lavinia was hanged for her alleged crimes. Citizens who walked past the jailhouse claimed to see her face floating behind the bars of what had once been her jail cell.

While there were undoubtedly some unusual things about Lavinia Fisher -- particularly her documented final words -- there are so many missing pieces to her story that it is difficult to see how a woman convicted of highway robbery could become "America's first female serial killer."

However, legends of murder and an evil house with a dark secret are not modern-day fabrications by tour guides looking to scare their audience -- these rumors began in 1830, just ten years after the Fishers' execution.

At this time, a Scotsman named Peter Neilson wrote his memoir, *Six Years' Residence in America*. The Scottish businessman claimed to have witnessed Lavinia's execution, though that was the first of many lies since he lived in America from 1822 to 1828, missing Lavinia's death by two years.

To spice up his book and to entertain his readers a bit more, though, he added to the story, particularly the skeletons in the basement and the seemingly countless murders at the inn. What is considered a contemporary account by some is merely a fabrication by the author, claiming "a great number of skeletons were found" when the inn was searched. In truth, if dozens of skeletons had been found on the premises of the Six-Mile House, it would have been reported in local newspapers. Not to mention, hotel guests would've likely smelled the decaying bodies and reported the odor.

On August 31, 1886, the Charleston earthquake – one of the most powerful and damaging quakes on the East Coast – ripped through the city, killing 60 people and causing $6 million in damages, which is over $189 million today.

One of the buildings destroyed that day was the old jailhouse.

After the earthquake, residents began to see Lavinia in the surrounding neighborhood, including the Unitarian Churchyard just around the corner. It was almost as if the jail's destruction during the earthquake had released her.

The jail was eventually abandoned in 1939, and for 61 years, it remained vacant. In 2000, the American College of Building Arts saved the prison; today, it is part of the "Save America's Treasures" program, and work is being done to restore it. But as with so many buildings rich with history left alone for so long, it seems a few ghosts continue to lurk inside, including Lavinia Fisher.

Footprints were spotted in the dust, even though the building had been vacant for years. The dumbwaiter is heard moving on its own though it is no longer operational. Alarms will go off for no reason. Visitors report a choking sensation and shortness of breath on the main staircase, while others have been grabbed, pushed, and scratched. Multiple apparitions have also been spotted over the years, including a jailer, an enslaved man, and, of course, Lavinia, who is supposedly seen in her bright red and white wedding dress.

But why does Lavinia Fisher haunt the place she spent her final hellish year being tortured and abused?

Some historians are beginning to question if Lavinia Fisher ever had a hand in murdering anyone. One theory that questioned Lavinia's guilt suggests that, at this time, Governor Geddes wanted to establish a naval base in Charleston, and he had his sights set on the Fishers' land. The theory claims that the Fishers were targeted by the local government and subsequently removed so that Governor Geddes could show then-president James Monroe the potential location. Monroe ended up not approving the base at that time. It wasn't built for another 80 years, but even so, there seems to be some truth to this part of the story - the base's old Naval Hospital still stands where the Six-Mile House once stood.

A coincidence? Or verification of the story?

Whether Lavinia Fisher still walks as penitence for the atrocities she committed in life or as a way to reveal that she was innocent all along will never truly be known. What we do know is that she has been wrongfully dubbed "America's first female serial killer," having never been convicted of murdering anyone. She was undoubtedly a cruel woman, actively participating in crimes alongside her husband, robbing and attacking unsuspecting travelers.

But did her crimes require her to pay with her life, only to have her name and afterlife shadowed by superstitions and lies?

Today, "Lovely Lavinia" is a ghost of the woman she once was – the result of urban legends, ghost stories, and hearsay. She's evolved over the last 200 years at the hands of those who would profit off her supposed crimes, reborn with each new book and ghost tour to the point where very little truth -- if any -- remains.

But that doesn't seem to matter.

The Holy City's own Woman in White doesn't seem to be going anywhere any time soon. For better or for worse, Lavinia Fisher – be she wicked or wronged – has avoided hell and will always haunt the memory of Charleston.

“KILLER AT MALABAR FARM”
CELIA ROSE
BY TROY TAYLOR

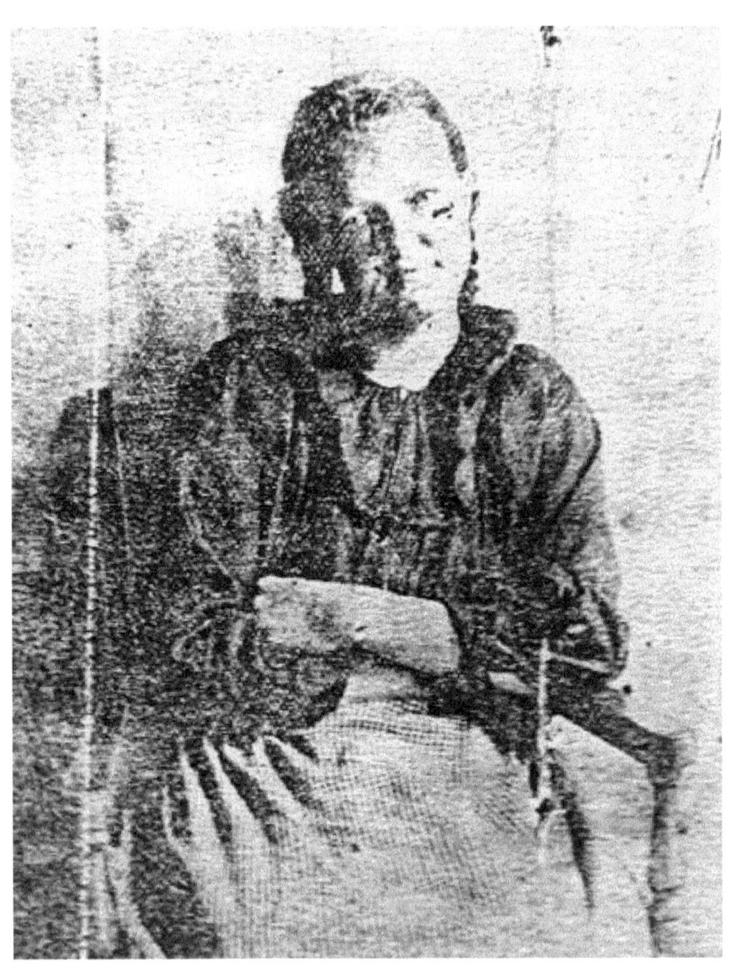

A rainy spring had turned into a wet early summer for the people of Central Ohio in 1896.

Among those who dealt with the poor weather was David Rose, a man half-deaf and mostly crippled from fighting in the Civil War decades before. He was the owner of the Schrack Mill, which he'd bought when his family moved north in 1879. In an age when old water-powered mills were being replaced by gasoline engines, business was slow.

His wife, Rebecca, helped support the family by weaving rugs in the front room of the miller's cottage on the other side of a creek.

Their son, Walter, almost 40, still lived at home and alternated between working for nearby farmers and helping his father at the mill when David's poor health kept him away. He also tended the family's pigs, which they raised for food.

And then there was Ceely. Her given name was "Celia," but living in the foothills of Appalachia, where she'd been born in 1873, had given her a nickname.

The Rose family had lived in central Ohio for more than 16 years but were still considered outsiders, rough around the edges, and a step away from the rest of the community.

But Ceely was even more of an outsider than the rest. Shy and giggly, she was called a girl, but she was 23 years old. She was always thought to be a little slow, faring poorly at the local one-room schoolhouse and never progressing much beyond basic skills. At recess, she either played with the young children or cheered on the boys as they played ball. At home, she was taught the simple tasks of housekeeping, some cooking, and sewing, but nothing as complicated as weaving, like her mother.

Ceely seemed, at best, to be a simpleton to be tolerated or, at worst, an imbecile to be ignored. She was annoying, but she was harmless; everyone thought so.

But they couldn't have been more wrong.

On Tuesday, June 23, David Rose felt well enough to finish some work. He spent the day opening the gates to fill his two millponds, knowing they would flood the mill's basement and turn the waterwheel. By the following day, the mill would be running again. The exertion tired him, but he slept well that night.

On June 24, the family had breakfast together - eggs, slices of bread, bowls of cottage cheese with cherries, and coffee. Some accounts say that Ceely made all of it, while others say she merely helped her mother prepare it. David was hungry and filled two plates. Walter ate a full plate, but Rebecca had only a little. She had awakened that morning with a headache.

Ceely didn't eat anything at all.

Her father encouraged her to eat, and she scooped a little cottage cheese onto her plate and took some eggs, but she never touched it.

When the meal was finished, everyone prepared to get to work. David went to the mill to start grinding a large feed order that he'd received, and Walter took a bucket in search of some black raspberries that he'd heard had ripened at the edge of the woods. Rebecca started on a new rug.

As she was setting up her loom, Rebecca became very thirsty. She asked Ceely to bring her a cup of water. But when Rebecca took a large drink of it, her stomach muscles suddenly cramped and caused her to vomit so violently on the kitchen floor that she collapsed.

Her strange contortions caused Ceely to laugh.

Rebecca tried to get up but began to suffer convulsions and collapsed again. She couldn't stop vomiting. She ordered Ceely to go and get her father at the mill. Ceely ran into the yard, crossed the bridge over the creek, and told David, "mother is puking all over the place."

David hurried back to the house. He got Rebecca into a chair, but stabbing stomach pains made it impossible for her to remain still. She tried to drink more water to fight her intense thirst, but it immediately came back up.

Something was terribly wrong. David went outside to hitch up the horse and buggy. He knew his wife needed a doctor. Their usual family physician, Dr. Budd of Perrysville, was out of town for the week, so he headed over the ridge toward Newville, where a new doctor had recently started seeing patients.

By the time David reached Dr. John McComb's residence, his mouth was parched. He explained his wife's illness to the young doctor, who quickly readied himself to accompany David back to the mill house. As they rushed back up onto the ridge, David's thirst had become maddening. He begged to stop at a farmhouse and ask for some water.

He gulped down the cool liquid, and then, like Rebecca, he began to vomit. His reaction was so violent - and the pains in his stomach so severe - that he fell to the ground. The doctor managed to get David back into the buggy, and he sped towards the Rose home. With some effort - and help from Ceely - he got David into the house and onto the couch in the front parlor.

Just as the older man was settled, someone knocked on the door. It was a neighbor with an emergency - he'd just found Walter up the road by the woods, passed out in a ditch. He had thrown up all over himself.

Dr. McComb went and retrieved Walter and returned him to the house, trying to make him comfortable on a cot in the back parlor. McComb wasn't sure what to do with an entire family seized with vomiting, convulsions, and pain. All of them seemed deathly ill - except for one.

Ceely stood off to the side of the room, wide-eyed, watching everything happening with a tight little smile on her face.

David Rose had been born in 1829, a son in a milling family that moved from New York to southern Ohio. In 1855, he married Rebecca Easter and started his own mill in Pike County, about seven miles east of Sinking Spring. They operated the mill and farmed about seven out of the 80 acres they now own.

In 1856, Rebecca gave birth to a son, John, who died before his first birthday. A second son, Walter, was born in 1857, and a daughter, Julia Ann, was born two years later. The family was starting to flourish - only to be interrupted by the Civil War.

David patriotically enlisted in the Union Army in September 1861. He volunteered as a miller but eventually found himself embroiled in action. His regiment became part of the Ohio Brigade, and they saw fighting along the Mississippi River, at the Battle of Iuka, the Siege of Corinth, and throughout northern Alabama. After a furlough that allowed the men to visit their families in 1864, they were attached to General William T. Sherman during his Atlanta Campaign for the March to the Sea. The regiment was mustered out of service in July 1865.

There's no doubt that David saw some action during the war - he was deafened by cannon fire and had a limp for the rest of his life - but his army record was spotty at best. In April 1863, he deserted but then returned to the regiment two weeks later. In October, illness kept him confined to quarters for weeks, and in May 1864, he was admitted into a hospital in Chattanooga, Tennessee, with "chronic diarrhea." His case was so bad that he was transferred to Nashville two days later and then sent to Maryland for further treatment that lasted a month. He returned to his regiment for a time, only to desert again in November. This time, he didn't return. Regardless, David was honorably discharged in January 1865.

The war wreaked havoc on David's health, as it did to so many survivors. When he applied for disability in 1890, his doctor cited stomach problems, kidney disease, partial deafness in both ears and blindness in one eye.

If his reunion with Rebecca was a happy one, there is no evidence of it. While many families added a baby within a year or so after a soldier's return, David and Rebecca had no other children - until 1873.

Celia Frances Rose was born on March 13, 1873 - eight years after her father's return from the war and 14 years after her parents' previous child, Julia. There were rumors that Ceely was actually Julia's daughter, with the girl's grandparents posing as her parents to prevent embarrassment for Julia. There is no solid evidence of this, but speculation persists.

Nothing is known about Ceely's childhood, but little is known about the other children either. In 1870, both Walter and Julia were attending school, but neither could read or write, which meant their education was limited.

In 1880, the family moved to Richland County, nearly 150 miles away from where they had been living. There is no information as to why they fled southern Ohio, but it may have had something to do with Julia - she mostly disappears from public record. It is known that she married John H. Long in November 1876, had a baby named after his father two years later, and then vanished. There is no death record for Julia, but there is no record of her after that. The Rose family sold their land in 1879 and moved away, buying land and the old mill in another part of the state.

Their new home - the miller's cottage - was built sometime before the Civil War and was a small, square, two-story farmhouse. Inside, the first floor was separated into a front parlor, a back parlor, and a kitchen. A ladder provided the only access to the bedrooms on the second floor. Some steps led down to the cellar. On the west side of the yard was a springhouse, and elsewhere on the land, the Roses kept hogs and had a vegetable and herb garden.

Across the creek was the old Schrack Mill, and above it, on a hill, was the original owner's home. By the time the Roses took over the mill and cottage, George and Angeline Berry lived in the old house with their children. The two houses were in direct sight of each other, only a few hundred yards apart.

The land and mill had been purchased in Rebecca's name, likely to keep David's name off the property so he could file for a disability pension from the army. He was only able to work about six months out of the year, which makes his decision to operate the mill a bit of a puzzle.

But Walter was around to help. When the family moved north, he was 23 years old and seemed to have no plans to move away from his parents. Described as shrewd and with a fiery temper, there is no evidence that Walter planned to marry and start a family of his own. He is another enigma in this baffling story.

With Walter earning money as a farmhand, Rebecca weaving rugs, and David sometimes running the mill, the Roses seemed to be an average rural family, cobbling together a decent though unexciting living as best they could.

But then there was Ceely.

By the time the Roses moved north, it was likely clear that Ceely was "slow." We'd call that "developmentally disabled" today, but in the nineteenth century, she would have been referred to as an "imbecile" or a "moron." She was sent to school but did so poorly that she was not expected to attend every day. One of her teachers later said that she believed Ceely never got above the mental level of a six-year-old. She always played with the smallest children at school, even when she was as old as 20.

As she got older, she became less social and became notorious for childish behavior and pranks, like jumping out from behind doors to scare people. Once when visiting a neighbor's home with her mother, Ceely became fascinated with their new wallpaper, which was printed with bright flowers. Ceely, already in her late teens, crept from flower to flower, kissing each one and giggling.

Oddly, though, she was an avid reader, reading and re-reading every book the Roses owned and every newspaper David brought home. It was said she had a startling recall for the things she read, but her understanding of them was limited - or so most people thought.

Ceely became the subject of many stories in the area. One young woman heard Ceely talking to herself like a small child might do. A mother said that Ceely tried to steal a book that had been delivered to her son from out of their postal box. Another woman said that Ceely was bright enough to know some things were crimes, for her mother often corrected her, but she was not bright enough to understand that she shouldn't do them.

Again - that's what most people thought.

By the middle 1890s, Ceely was a physically mature young woman and big for the time - five feet, seven inches tall, and 190 pounds. But as her body grew and her sex drive was awakened, she had only her child's mind to control them. She learned to do housework, clean and cook, and do needlepoint, but it seemed unlikely she could ever live on her own. She'd never get married or have a husband or a family, but that didn't seem to curb her fascination with boys.

She became obsessed with a neighboring farmer, Clem Herring, who was in his mid-20s. Ceely wrote him a love letter and delivered it while he was plowing in his field. He thanked her and never said another word about it. Clem never spoke about the gushing letter, and Ceely moved on. She delivered another letter to another handsome farmer, Cary Andrews, but he wasn't as kind to her as Clem had been. He laughed in the girl's face and made fun of her, forcing Ceely to find a different approach to romance.

Her next fixation was on Guy Berry, the oldest son of George and Angeline, the next-door neighbors. He was a handsome 16-year-old boy, well-spoken and smart. Ceely could see him when he was at home and when he left the house, so she began following him everywhere. When she approached and tried to speak to him, Guy felt sorry for the slow girl who was often teased for her awkwardness. He was always polite to her and even tried to have conversations with her, merely out of kindness.

This was a treatment that Ceely never expected to get from a young man, and she was soon madly in love with him. One day, she told him they would marry in three years. Guy expressed surprise and said he'd never agreed to any such thing. Ceely told him that he'd better marry her, or she'd marry one of the other three men who were trying to kiss her. "You'll be sorry you didn't take me," Ceely told him.

Guy was becoming frustrated by Ceely's attention and, while not unkind, began trying to avoid her. One morning, his younger brother, Claude, told Ceely that Guy wasn't going to marry her - he had another girl - so Ceely said she'd marry Claude instead. He laughed - he was only 12.

In the late spring of 1896, Guy's patience with the girl wore thin after she began telling everyone in the neighborhood that he had proposed marriage to her. The story quickly spread. Some claimed

Guy had lied to her to save her feelings, while others said it was a cruel joke. We'll never know for sure what really happened, but there have been suggestions that Ceely may have been taken advantage of.

Most farm children knew about sex. They saw what the animals did and lived in close quarters with their parents and older brothers and sisters who were married. Ceely might have been molested - there is an uncomfortable shadow of incest that runs through some versions of this story - by someone, like some of the neighborhood boys or perhaps even Guy Berry.

Whatever happened, Ceely had become convinced they would be married, and she wouldn't stop talking about it.

Ceely's incessant yammering about their impending wedding drove Guy crazy. He appealed to his father for help stopping the gossip, stating that if he could not, Guy would leave home to escape the nonsense.

Angry and irritated, George Berry went down to the mill on June 4, 1896, and told David Rose to control his daughter and keep her away from his son. He pointed out the window to one of Berry's fields, where Guy was trying to plow with a horse team while Ceely was pestering him.

David was angry and embarrassed. He promised to make it stop and walked outside. "Ceely Rose!" he bellowed up the hill. "Get over here right this minute!"

Ceely slowly turned away from Guy and made her way down to the small bridge that crossed the creek. David yelled at her to stop dawdling - he wanted to talk to her. George Berry left as David turned and went back into the mill. Ceely followed him inside.

In the shadows of the dilapidated building, David unleashed his infamous temper. He screamed at her and stomped his foot - she was never to speak to Guy again. She was not to follow him, talk about him, or ever speak his name.

When Ceely was allowed to speak, she begged David not to tell her mother what she had done. David calmed down and told her he'd have no reason to tell Rebecca anything if she behaved. Ceely wept and promised to behave.

But her father didn't keep his word. He told Rebecca everything two days later, which sent Ceely into a rage. When she threatened to do whatever she wanted to do, David told her that as long as he was around, she'd do what she was told.

"You won't be around forever," she sullenly replied.

In the days that followed, Ceely settled down and made more of an effort to help out around the house. David and Rebecca felt the problem with their daughter had been solved, and they could all get past the embarrassing situation she had created.

The spring of 1896 had been a wet one in the neighborhood, and the Roses had started having problems with potato bugs around the house and mill. In mid-May, Walter was sent to the nearby larger town of Mansfield to buy some Rough-on-Rats poison, which was good for killing all kinds of vermin and bugs. The popular concoction of the time used lethal amounts of arsenic mixed with black boot polish to give it an ugly gray color, which prevented accidental ingestion.

Walter bought the poison at Barton's drugstore downtown and then returned home. Rebecca mixed it into a solution and spread it around the outside of the house and mill. She knew the potato bugs would be gone within a day or two. When finished, she put what was left into a kitchen cabinet for storage. Both she and David had stressed to Ceely that she should never mess with the poison. It was dangerous, and even a small amount could kill someone.

Unfortunately, it kept raining, and the potato bugs came back. On June 10, Rebecca decided to mix up more of her solution and reapply it to the house and mill. She went to the kitchen cabinet where she's stored the box of Rough-on-Rats, but it was gone.

She looked everywhere, but the poison had vanished.

It's likely that if the Rose family's usual physician, Dr. Budd, had been the first one at the scene on June 24, the old country doctor might have believed the family's illness was food poisoning or cholera - a tragic misfortune.

But Dr. John McComb, who had first trained as a lawyer before going to medical school - was a new breed of physician. Poison had become a popular murder weapon in recent years, and young doctors like himself had been trained to look for it.

What he saw at the Rose house didn't add up. Three family members were violently ill, while the fourth, Ceely, was obviously fine.

When he asked Ceely is she had eaten breakfast with the rest of the family, she said she had. When he asked if she was in pain, she replied that she was. McCombs was unconvinced. When he asked her if she had prepared the family's breakfast, Rebecca managed to interrupt to say she had made breakfast. When her mother began talking, Ceely stopped speaking.

Soon, neighbors were also on the scene. News of the illness had spread quickly. They were pitching in to help the doctor care for his three patients, all desperate for water. But whenever they drank anything, stomach convulsions forced it back up again.

The severity of the sickness - and the fact that Ceely had no symptoms - convinced Dr. McCombs that something ominous was happening. As soon as the situation was reasonably in hand, he rode back to nearby Newville and wired the offices of Richland County Sheriff James Boals and County Prosecutor Augustus Douglass with his suspicions. Neither man was interested - it sounded like food poisoning, they said. Notify them if anything else develops.

Dr. McComb returned to the Rose house and noticed something unusual in the yard. He looked closer and realized the shapes in the grass were the Roses' chickens - all of them were dead.

He hurried into the house and found more neighbors had come to help. Herbal tea was made from Rebecca's garden, and she could drink some of it. Her symptoms were less severe than those of her husband and son. The two men were so sick they could not sit upright. David was on the sofa in the front parlor, and Walter was resting on a cot in the other.

The next day, family physician Dr. Allen Budd returned to town and took over the case. He had been treating the Rose family for years, mainly dealing with David's various ailments from the war, and wanted to see what was happening for himself. After ruling out other issues, he asked the family about the possibility of poison, but they all dismissed the idea. But they were very sick, and he and Dr. McCombs knew something had to be done. He called several other doctors to consult with them, and all concluded that the family had indeed been poisoned. They began administering iron as an antidote to possible arsenic poisoning, but this was five days later, and Walter and David didn't improve.

David slipped in and out of consciousness, writing in pain as he groaned and cried. The treatments had been too little, too late for him. He died on the night of Tuesday, June 30. No one told Rebecca. They feared the shock of his death might kill her.

Word was sent for the undertaker the next morning, but first, the assembled doctors and County Coroner George W. Baughman needed to perform an autopsy on the dead man.

David's corpse was laid out on boards in the front parlor. Coroner Baughman noticed there were burn-like eruptions around David's mouth. It was believed it had come from the heavy metal content of his vomit, which was common with arsenic poisoning. His stomach and intestines were removed, examined, and placed in jars. An inspection showed that his stomach was severely inflamed - another sign of poisoning.

Once the autopsy was completed, David was turned over to the undertaker for the funeral. The procession for the funeral left the Rose house and marched a mile up the road to where a service was held at the Pleasant Valley Lutheran Church. David was buried after its conclusion in a grave in the churchyard that his neighbors had prepared.

He'd survived the horrors of war but had died of violence in his own home.

The Rose house remained in limbo for the next week. Rebecca made a little progress toward healing while Walter slipped further and further away. Unable to keep water down, he was slowly dying of dehydration. Friends and neighbors continually wet his dried, cracked lips, but there was no way to get water into his system. Finally, he died on July 4.

By this time, residents of the area were in an uproar that the body count had doubled while officials in Mansfield were still doing nothing. A flurry of telegrams and an article in the Mansfield newspaper titled "Grave Suspicions" finally goaded the authorities into action. The attending physicians autopsied Walter and saw the same issues they'd seen with his father's organs - Walter had also been poisoned.

An investigation was soon underway.

County Prosecutor Douglass belatedly realized that he had a mess on his hands. The newspapers were following the Rose case and seizing on every rumor that it would turn into a murder case. Sheriff Boals appeared to have allowed Douglass to head the investigation, carrying out the prosecutor's instructions. He wanted to avoid becoming a target for angry residents the way that Douglass was becoming. The prosecutor's reluctance to take the situation seriously turned it into a scandal, and it would be a detriment to any politician's career if the whole thing went up in flames.

Douglass went to work, directing Boals and his deputies to search the Rose house and the mill for the poison. Ceely - as the only family member who wasn't sick - was already the prime suspect, which was also a concern. Everyone knew the girl was "slow," so it might be hard to prosecute someone who didn't have the mental capacity to plan the crime.

A search of the farm turned up nothing, however. If Ceely had poisoned her family, where was the poison?

Douglass decided to hold a formal inquest at the Valley Hall School. Celia, her mother, and eight others testified at the inquest. Two local residents, unnamed in the newspaper, got so animated in their argument about whether or not Ceely was guilty that it escalated into a brawl. One of them suggested lynching the girl. Douglass calmed things down and asked residents to let the investigation run its course and uncover the truth.

The witness everyone wanted to hear from was, of course, Ceely herself. While she liked being the center of attention, the presence of so many people staring at her caused her to stutter badly when Douglass started asking her questions, especially when he raised his voice.

When he asked the young woman about preparing breakfast, Ceely looked at her mother, who nodded. Ceely then gave a carefully worded reply that sounded rehearsed. When she finished, she looked again at her mother, who nodded approval. Between other questions, though, Douglass kept returning to the breakfast preparation, asking questions in different ways. Each time, Ceely gave the same rehearsed reply, always with Rebecca's approval. Rebecca seemed to have decided that if Ceely was guilty, the girl needed to be protected.

Douglass almost caught her off guard, however. "But, Ceely," he asked her, "why did you put that stuff in the coffee that morning for breakfast?"

"B-B-Because I w-w-wanted to," she stammered, then corrected quickly and said, "But I didn't put it there, though." Even her correction was not a reflection of her innocence. It later emerged that it had not been the coffee poisoned that day but the cottage cheese.

Without a confession from Ceely - and her mother actively hampering the investigation - the authorities could not assemble a winnable case against her. They had motive and opportunity, but the young woman's mental state was questioned, and they had yet to find any physical evidence against her.

But soon, they would. Official tests from David's and Walter's autopsy had returned in the mail from Cleveland. It was discovered that David had not merely succumbed to mild arsenic poisoning - there had been enough in his stomach to kill several people. The results of Walter's test would reveal the same thing.

Prosecutor Douglass now officially had two murders on his hands - but no one knew what to do about it. There was no way to prove who might have given the family poison. Ceely was still the prime suspect, but lawmen - just like people in the area - were divided about whether the girl had done it. Without a confession of some sort, the prosecutor had no idea how to prove that Ceely was a killer.

And Ceely had no plans to confess.

With her mother's health still fragile, Ceely had some time on her hands. Late one morning in mid-July, George and Angeline Berry heard a knock on their door. When George opened it, he found Ceely standing there with a pie in her hands.

"I baked this pie for you and Mrs. Berry," she said, holding it out to him. "But it's only for you two. Guy's not allowed to eat any of this pie, all right?"

Berry uncertainly took the pie, thanked her, and watched her skip away toward the Rose house. George told his wife what Ceely had said, and they immediately decided there was no way they would touch the pie. George went to the back of the house, out of sight of the Rose house, and flung the suspicious pie into the yard.

Later that day, Angeline stepped out the back door to shake out a rug and noticed the remains of Ceely's pie on the ground. There were scores of triangular peck marks in it. She looked up and saw all their chickens lying dead throughout the yard.

Back at home, Ceely wasn't finished with her kitchen projects. One of the regular visitors to the Rose house since the trouble began was Pastor Kramer from the Lutheran Church. He came by once a week to check on things and pray with Rebecca. During one visit, Ceely whipped up a specially seasoned fried chicken for the minister - but when another church member became sick, he skipped his visit that week.

Rebecca, meanwhile, was starting to improve. On some days, she could sit up and visit with guests, and she began to drink some water. Soon, she was eating, too, although the food had to be soft and in small amounts.

One day in July, Dr. Budd told Rebecca that it finally seemed clear that she would survive. He cautioned her that her recovery would be slow, but she would return to feeling normal in time. Rebecca was thrilled and relieved that the danger had passed.

But it hadn't - Ceely had overheard the doctor.

We will never know what conversation passed between Ceely and her mother after the doctor's visit that day but before his emergency return that night. It was likely that Rebecca was making plans for when she was feeling better again. Did she question her daughter about her pursuit of Guy Berry? Did she ask her what happened on the morning the family became sick?

It remains a mystery - but whatever was said, Ceely must have felt that she needed to act. If she saw her mother as an obstacle between Ceely and her life with Guy Berry, then that obstacle had to be removed.

On that afternoon - July 18, 1896 - Rebecca asked her daughter for some bread soaked with milk. Ceely went to the springhouse to bring in some milk and poured some into a bowl for her mother. She sliced off a piece of bread and then carried both items into the front parlor for Rebecca.

Her mother relished the food and ate heartily for the first time in almost a month. She finished the bread and asked Ceely for more. The girl vanished into the kitchen for a few minutes and returned with more bread and milk.

A few bites into the second serving of milk-soaked bread, Rebecca frowned. Something didn't taste right with the second bowl. She paused, then resumed eating. After a few more bites, though, she stopped.

Within the hour, she began to vomit.

Ceely only watched.

A neighbor dropped by, discovered that Rebecca had relapsed, and sent for help. Several other women from the neighborhood hurried to the scene.

At one point, in agony and wracked with pain, Rebecca glared at her daughter. "Ceely, if it's you that's done this, God help you," she gasped.

But Ceely protested that she hadn't done anything.

"Look me in the face and tell me the truth!" Rebecca demanded.

Ceely only smirked and walked silently out of the room.

Dr. Budd was sent for and soon arrived, but he could do nothing for Rebecca, whose condition worsened as the night wore on. While he tried to lessen the stricken woman's pain, he had an urgent telegram sent to Sheriff Boals and Prosecutor Douglass.

When it became clear to Rebecca that she was unlikely to see the dawn, she asked Clem Herring and his mother to write her last will and testament. Amazingly, even after likely knowing that her daughter had poisoned her twice, she still put Ceely in her will. After all the Rose family assets were auctioned off and the bills were paid, Ceely would receive whatever money remained.

At some point during the dark hours of the early morning, Rebecca Rose took her last breath.

The usual postmortem and autopsy were carried out on Rebecca's remains, and the authorities returned to the area for another fruitless search for evidence. To the prosecutor's embarrassment, it looked like he was being outwitted by a girl everyone considered a simpleton.

Ceely seemed indifferent about living in the miller's cottage, but Prosecutor Douglass quickly became aware that residents were beginning to ask how many people would have to die before the law decided to do anything about Ceely.

But not everyone felt that way. John and Jane Ohler were an older couple who lived nearby, and Jane especially refused to believe that a giggling girl like Ceely was capable of premeditated murder. They agreed to take the girl in, and soon, Ceely was spending most of her time reading on the sofa in the Ohler parlor while others around her took care of the household chores.

Douglass needed a new angle for the investigation. He needed something that would appeal to Ceely's emotions - like a friend.

While inspecting the Rose house again for the poison that Ceely seemed to make magically disappear after the murders, Douglass was approached by a neighboring farmer named George Davis. He had a daughter named Tracy, who was a few years younger than Ceely. Tracy had cared for Ceely a few times because she felt sorry for the girl, whom the other children often picked on. Davis offered Tracy's services as a friend who might get Ceely to talk.

Douglass pursued his usual methods first, making the rounds and asking questions, including of Ceely, who remained as stubborn and unhelpful as always. Douglass realized once again that he had to get a confession from Ceely to make a murder charge stick. There were just too many people convinced she wasn't responsible for her actions. They wanted to send the girl to an asylum, but Douglass didn't have that option.

Poisoning takes planning - and planning means premeditated murder. He was convinced she knew what she was doing when she killed her family. He had to figure out a way to prove it.

But he also knew that if he didn't do something soon, some local farmers would take justice into their own hands and lynch the girl.

Finally, Douglass sent word to George Davis to bring Tracy and meet him so that they could discuss the idea of getting a confession from Ceely.

George and his family had known the Roses since they had moved to the area. Their children attended school together, went to church together, and visited together often. They had been good neighbors and had helped out when the illnesses struck but, like many, were uncomfortable with Ceely's lack of symptoms and her apparent lack of concern about what was happening. They had known Ceely for years, and she had visited the Davis farm many times, usually at the invitation of Tracy, who was younger but whom Ceely looked up to.

Ceely knew the other David children, too, including Cora, who was Tracy's younger sister. While at the Rose home, after the family became sick, Cora heard Ceely say something that made her suspicious. Whatever it was - there is no record of what was said - it convinced George that Ceely was guilty, and this put him in touch with the prosecutor.

By 1896, Tracy was 19 years old and worked as a clerk in a Bellville store about 15 miles away. She had heard about the poisonings in newspaper stories but had not been at the Rose home while the family was suffering. She was home to visit one weekend, and George told her he was concerned that without a confession from Ceely, the case might never be solved. He asked his daughter if she'd be willing to try and get an admission from Ceely, and Tracy said she'd do it.

The plan was for Tracy to stay at the Ohler house with Ceely for a few days. The girls would renew their acquaintance and simply talk. Tracy was supposed to start slowly asking questions about the case if Ceely seemed comfortable. When it seemed like she'd reached a point where Ceely was most open, Tracy was to tell the other girl a story - she was to confess that she was in love with a young man, but her parents wouldn't let her see him. She would ask Ceely's advice about what she should do.

Tracy arrived at the Ohler farm soon after Rebecca's funeral. Ceely was delighted to see her, but Tracy pressed for information too fast. She asked Ceely if she had anything to do with that funny business about poison.

Ceely gave her a long, hard stare. "I know how it was done," she replied. "If you don't tell anyone, maybe I'll tell you in a week." That was all she'd say about it at that time.

On July 25, the girls walked around the area and talked for hours. Ceely mentioned once that she had gone to visit Guy Berry. Tracy asked if she had anything else she wanted to talk about, and reassured her that talking would make her feel better. But Ceely said nothing about the murders.

It's unknown if she really went to see Guy. She did visit the old mill and the cottage, and George Berry had instructed his son to feed the Roses' hogs until the auction on August 15, so it's possible.

Tracy led Ceely on another walk past the old Rose house and mill, and as they walked, they passed the cemetery at the Lutheran church. Ceely's family were all buried in a plot of fresh graves next to the road. As they passed, Ceely only glanced indifferently at the turned-over earth and said nothing. Her lack of emotion chilled Tracy.

On the way back to the Ohler farm, they stopped to rest, and Tracy again asked Ceely if there was anything she wanted to talk about. Ceely said she'd think it over and let her know, but she said nothing else.

On July 30, Tracy tried again. They took another long walk, and the route once again led to the cemetery. They stopped and stood next to the Roses' graves. The grass was already starting to grow over David and Walter's graves. Rebecca's grave was still freshly packed. A stone would be placed there after Clem Herring wrapped up the estate business.

Ceely dropped to her knees, folded her hands, and started praying. Tracy was startled momentarily, thinking that Ceely was overcome by guilt.

She wasn't.

Kneeling was how her mother had taught her; she'd prayed that way her whole life. She was only doing what she was supposed to, going through the motions of grief without actually feeling it.

Tracy convinced Ceely to sit down with her and talk. She asked the other girl if she missed her family. Ceely conceded that she missed her mother. Tracy then decided it was time to spin her story for Ceely - the one about the boy she loved but was not allowed to see because of her parents. When she finished, she asked Ceely what she thought Tracy should do about the situation.

Ceely paused for a moment. "I'd kill them," she blurted out. "That's what I did."

Tracy nearly gasped aloud but recovered her nerve. "How'd you do it?" she asked.

Ceely told her that she had put Rough-on-Rats in their food, proudly saying she had "confounded the lawmen" because they had been unable to find the poison. She laughed and said that she was too smart for them - she'd put the poison in a pepper box and hid it under a bush in the yard.

"I guess it's still there," Ceely shrugged. "Want to go and see?"

Tracy did, so they walked down the road to the Rose house. Ceely ran into the yard to the side of the springhouse that faced away from the cottage. She reached under a huge plant and pulled out a metal tin. She opened it up and showed it to Tracy.

"It's empty," Tracy said.

"Yeah, I used the last of it on Maw," Ceely told her, peering more closely into the box. "I thought I got all the stuff out, but there's a little bit left." She held out the tin to Tracy, who could see traces of rat poison in the corners.

"Do you want it?" Ceely asked.

Tracy almost said no but then realized the prosecutor would want it. "Yes, I'll save it as a keepsake," she told the girl.

After getting Ceely back to the Ohler farm - and hopefully telling the couple not to eat anything Ceely might make for them - Tracy made an excuse and hurried home to tell her father what she'd discovered. Together, they took the incriminating pepper tin to Gus Douglass' office.

When they arrived, he had to break some bad news - the tin and confession still weren't enough. Douglass would need a witness to Ceely's confession if he would be able to charge the girl with murder.

So, around August 1 - the exact date isn't clear - Tracy went to revisit Ceely and, this time, lured her out to the Ohler barn to talk, where her father was hiding to listen to the conversation.

Ceely was glad to see her friend and especially glad that Tracy hadn't told anyone what she'd done. She told Tracy about hiding the poison and how her parents had argued after Rebecca couldn't find it when she needed it again. "They never did figure out I took it," she said.

Finally, Tracy asked her who had encouraged her to kill her parents after they didn't allow her to see Guy anymore. Was it her idea? Or was it someone else's? Who told her to kill her family?

Ceely paused for a long moment, staring off into the distance so long that Tracy wondered if she'd heard the question. But then suddenly, Ceely started to speak.

"It was the Devil," she said. "Maw told all about the Bible and the Devil. She said that the Devil would come to you and put bad thoughts in your head, and you had to push him down and not let him do that. After they scolded me so, I guess I didn't want to push him down no more."

Tracy asked her if Guy Berry knew anything about what she was going to do, and Ceely said he didn't. "I told him my folks would be going away soon. I told him the black wagon would come and take them away."

"Black wagon?"

"That black wagon. I told him it would come and get them and go right by his house."

A chill ran down Tracy's spine when she realized Ceely was talking about a funeral hearse. She asked him if Guy had asked her to explain what she meant by that, but Ceely shook her head.

"No, he just told me not to say things like that. I asked him if he got the medicine."

Tracy looked at her. "Medicine? What medicine?"

"He was supposed to get me something that would keep me from getting pregnant," Ceely replied.

Tracy's face burned with embarrassment. Was this another of Ceely's fantasies, or had something been going on that no one suspected?

"Did he get the medicine?" she asked.

Ceely didn't answer and became angry. "All this family trouble ain't none of your business anyhow," she growled at her.

"I was trying to give you someone to talk to," Tracy soothed her. "You know I didn't tell anyone about what you said last week."

Ceely looked at her for a long time. She grudgingly admitted, "I guess you didn't, but you can't tell nobody about this."

Tracy forced a smile. "I promise you that I won't be the one who tells the investigators about all this. Cross my heart," she said and made a motion of crossing her heart.

That satisfied Ceely and she smiled at her friend as if she didn't have a care in the world.

After George and Tracy Davis revealed to Prosecutor Douglass what had been said in the Ohler barn, the wheels of justice slowly began to turn. Ceely was arrested and brought to the Richland County Jail in downtown Mansfield. She was assigned lawyers - Lewis C. Mengert and James M. Reed - who advised her to be careful about what she said to anyone. After being charged, she offered a not-guilty plea and waived her right to a preliminary hearing. She'd wait behind bars for the grand jury to indict her.

Ceely quickly found that she liked the notoriety that came with a murder accusation. She had numerous visitors at the jail - reporters, acquaintances, and the morbidly curious - and they came to see her throughout the rest of August and September. Nearly everyone commented on her politeness, cheerful smile, laughter, and complete lack of guilt for the deaths of her family members.

Investigators talked extensively with Ceely. Either her attorneys failed to tell her to remain silent, or more likely, she ignored them. At one point, she laughed when detectives asked if she'd poisoned the coffee. "I fooled you about that," she said, admitting the poison had been in the cottage cheese.

Ceely also offered a lot of statements to the press about her impending marriage to Guy Berry. His parents, of course, assured the reporters that what she said wasn't true. The press likely should have asked how many things Ceely told them were truthful, but no one did. They spent most of their time writing about her "flirtatious behavior" and how she was "mentally weak, but not insane." One reporter also stated that Ceely was "worried about her folks," but she said she expected to return home soon and everything would be fine.

The comment was presented to show that Ceely could not grasp the enormity of her crime. She told people she spoke to her parents in her dreams, so she knew they were out there somewhere - they weren't really gone.

Was Ceely that delusional, or was it all an act to gain sympathy? If she were insane, the trial would not be allowed to go on, so Dr. George Mitchell was brought in by the prosecution to examine her. He seemed to have little trouble drawing her into a conversation.

It quickly became apparent that she showed no remorse for the murders. In his notes, he stated that Ceely showed little affection for her mother, less for her brother, and none at all for her father.

In his opinion, Ceely was "morally deficient." He did not think she was insane. He wasn't even sure that she was as "slow" as everyone seemed to think she was.

I'd agree with him about that.

Mitchell's report gave Douglas the expert opinion he needed, and he took Ceely Rose's case to the grand jury on September 7. Under questioning, Ceely began to cry, but if Douglass feared that she would gain the jury's sympathy, that fear quickly disappeared. Just seconds after crying, she started laughing at something else in the courtroom. She paid little attention to what was going on.

On Saturday, September 21, 1896, the grand jury returned three indictments against the girl for murder in the first degree.

Jury selection began on October 12, and soon, the trial was ready to begin. W.H. Funke assisted Prosecutor Douglass while Reed and Mengert sat with Ceely at the defense table.

After the jury was sworn in, Douglass offered an opening statement. He described the murders and Ceely's confession. A newspaper reporter noted that the girl showed little interest in the proceedings except for moments when Douglass mentioned her by name, at which point she would cover her face with a handkerchief until he was no longer speaking about her.

Lewis Mengert offered a short opening for the defense, claiming that evidence would show that Ceely was not responsible for the crimes. That would be their entire and sole defense.

The trial continued in the days to come as the prosecution brought in a steady parade of witnesses, that included Coroner George W. Baughman, who spoke of the state of the Roses' bodies. Tracy Davis and her father, George, detailed Ceely's two confessions.

Dr. Budd and Dr. McComb both testified about what they found when called to the Rose home after the poisonings and what they saw during the postmortems. The prosecution also called the doctors who consulted with them to the stand, along with the doctors who tested the stomachs and intestines of the three victims, which were filled with large amounts of arsenic. The state also called George Berry, who testified about going to the mill to speak with David Rose about Ceely - and how the poisonings occurred soon after.

Jane Ohler was also called to the stand. Earlier, she and her husband had been outspoken in their belief in Ceely's innocence. However, it seemed this belief had crumbled during the time Ceely was living in their home.

Next, it was the defense's turn on the stage. Ceely's attorneys started things off by calling a minister, Reverend W.H. Dolbeer, to the stand. He believed Ceely could be taught to do certain things but could not do them on her own. She was not of sound mind, but she was not a raving maniac. Ceely might know it was wrong to commit murder - but he was not convinced she could make that judgment for herself.

A classmate of Ceely's, Lavina Andrews, was also called. She testified about the lack of skills that Ceely possessed, noting that she had learned to sew, but she could not crochet.

On cross-examination, Douglass asked her if she thought the inability to crochet indicated insanity, drawing laughs from the spectators in the courtroom. Lavina admitted that it did not.

One of Ceely's former teachers, Eva Tucker, was also called to testify. She said she considered the girl "silly and not of sound mind." She made it clear that she also felt that Ceely did not understand how terrible the crimes were that she had committed.

Ceely's most recent teacher, Emma Halderman, was next. She spoke about how "peculiar" Ceely's manner was and how she could not memorize even short poems and readings. Douglass poked at her and suggested that perhaps the things she'd given Ceely to remember were too hard. Emma snapped back, "The trouble with her is that she is weak-minded."

As an expert witness, the defense had engaged Dr. E.G. Carpenter, a brain disease specialist from the Newburgh State Hospital for the Insane in Cleveland. He talked about other members of the Rose family who were confirmed with mental illness. None of their names were offered in the newspaper accounts of the trial.

Dr. Carpenter said, "In a person having cousins, uncles, and nephews imbecilic, one should expect to find an idiot." He said that when he examined Ceely, he found her manner strange. She wouldn't look him in the eye and would often laugh and giggle. Her cell was in a very untidy condition. He deduced that the deaths in her family did not bother her much. He concluded that she had deficient mental development.

Anticipating the prosecution's questions, the defense asked Dr. Carpenter if a person could be both an imbecile and have cunning. He replied that it was absolutely possible - an idiot could be bright in some select areas while deficient in others.

During the cross-examination, Dr. Carpenter went into detail about an imbecile's potential level of moral insanity. He said that he thought Ceely could be taught to some degree, but not to the point that she could understand the seriousness of her crimes. He said that when he talked to her, he asked Ceely why she had killed her mother and father.

"I wanted to be the boss in my own house," she said.

A neighbor, Amanda Andrews, said that she had never considered Ceely to be "right," but when cross-examined, admitted that she thought the girl was bright enough to know right from wrong.

Another teacher, Willard Darling, was called to the stand. She said Ceely regularly attended school but was several years behind other students her age. She said she believed the girl to be a "weak-minded imbecile." When cross-examined, she refused to comment on whether she thought Ceely would know that murder was wrong, only that she had a limited idea of right and wrong.

Dr. William Bushnell of Mansfield was next, testifying about his examination of Ceely. He had concluded that she was "of an incompetent mind." He said that she might know that committing a murder was wrong, but due to her condition, she would not have the willpower to resist doing it if that was what she wanted. He added that she might not be a raving lunatic now, but she had the potential to become one.

More doctors followed - Dr. A.H. McCullough and Dr. W.E. Loughridge - and testified that Ceely was insane. On cross-examination, however, Dr. Loughridge allowed that Ceely possessed cunning, and he couldn't rule out the possibility that she had been deceiving him. "Celia Rose has a weak mind," he said, "but a degree of development not known to an idiot."

The defense called more neighbors. Their statements were familiar - Ceely was strange, unable to learn, weak-minded, an imbecile, slow, and, of course, insane. "She jumped out from behind doors and tried to scare people" was a common complaint, as if this was strong evidence of her insanity.

Douglass had a field day with one neighbor's testimony about the doors. He made her step down from the stand and reenact how Ceely had jumped out and scared her. After she performed this, he asked her if she thought this action proved Ceely was insane. The woman fumbled her answer, saying it seemed a little odd for a 23-year-old to be doing it.

Douglass replied. "That's funny. I've jumped out from behind doors to scare people, and no one has ever accused me of insanity." The courtroom roared with laughter.

But behind the scenes, Douglass wasn't making jokes. Witness after witness testified that they thought Celia had serious mental problems and had felt so for years. Douglass had to prove to a jury that this had been a premeditated crime - that Ceely was responsible for her actions. Anything less would result in a verdict of not guilty by reason of insanity.

And the blows kept coming. A neighbor stated that she believed Ceely to be insane. Dr. R.S. Boles testified about treating the family several times, including treating Ceely for diphtheria once. He talked about her peculiar manner, which caused him to believe she was an imbecile and insane.

After a short conference, the defense rested its case. Things were turned back over to the prosecution, who had worked hard to produce rebuttal witnesses, like a neighbor who always felt that while Ceely was foolish and rather silly, she was bright in other ways. He felt she could tell right from wrong, even if she wasn't very smart.

Phebe Herring testified next. "She is not insane by any means," she said firmly. She knew right from wrong. Lorain Wolf, who also lived near the Roses, testified that while Ceely was not of sound mind, she wasn't insane. George Davis returned to the stand to say that he also believed that Ceely understood the distinction between right and wrong. Neighbor Tilman Wiles said the same thing. He had been a customer at David's mill and had spoken to Ceely many times. "I never thought Ceely was weak-minded," he said. "I thought her in great measure to be as sane as other girls."

Coroner Baughman was called back to the stand to talk about the differences between medical and legal insanity. Ceely, he explained, was an imbecile, not an idiot. "An idiot is one who is born weak-minded, totally lacking in reasoning powers, and is not susceptible to education," he told the court. "Imbecility is due to weakening of physical powers and mental powers."

Dr. Budd was also recalled to the stand. He had known Ceely for 16 years and had many chances to talk with her, and he had instructed her about how to care for sick family members in the past. She always did very well, he said. "I never regarded her as insane. I regarded her as silly."

More doctors followed --- all of whom said Ceely was sane. The defense asked one of them if he believed that Ceely was mentally together, and he replied that she was "no worse than the rest of the Rose family."

But of all the doctors who testified, Dr. Samuel Alban dropped what was considered a "bombshell" on the court - by 1896 standards. He told the court, "She is not intellectually insane, she is emotionally insane - she is a sexual pervert."

He said that Ceely had committed the crime because she thought that people stood in the way of her gratification. She was obsessed with Guy Berry. He wouldn't diagnose her as an imbecile or an idiot. He added, "Natural causes may lead to emotional insanity and may be cultivated afterwards. Mental weakness generally follows."

Dr. Alban was trying to connect Ceely's case to what was considered one of the great health problems of the late nineteenth century - masturbation. It was feared, in those days, that too much of it could cause insanity. He was portraying Ceely as an ordinary girl who had a weakness for sexual arousal and subsequently masturbated herself into weak-mindedness. Obviously, by modern medical standards, this is ridiculous, but it was widely accepted at the time.

After more testimony from neighbors, who assured the court they thought Ceely was silly but sane, the prosecution rested its case.

The closing arguments followed, first by William Funke for the prosecution, followed by Lewis Mengert for the defense, then James Reed, then Augustus Douglass with the final word. The closing statements lasted for an entire day.

Of all of them, though, what resonated most for those who attended the trial, was James Reed's closing, in which he argued for Ceely's essential insanity but also pulled in, by implication, the arguments of the state's most sensational witness, Dr. Alban, using his words to support the insanity defense.

The jury began their deliberations on October 20 at 9:00 in the morning. They were only gone for an hour and a half. When they returned, it was with a verdict of not guilty by reason of insanity.

Celia Rose was sent to the Toledo State Hospital for the Insane. On December 17, she became Patient No. 1937. Ceely would spend the rest of her life in one hospital or another. Even though word spread that she had been released in 1897, in truth, she was transferred to the state hospital in Lima, where she ended her days in March 1934. She died from pneumonia at the age of 61. She was buried in the cemetery for unclaimed patients, just south of the hospital.

But this wasn't quite the end of the story of Ceely Rose or the farm where she had murdered her family.

The newspapers would eventually lose interest in Ceely's story once the trial was over and she was safely tucked away in a hospital. She gradually became the subject of legends and scary stories - especially after someone spread a rumor that she'd been released. She was talked about around campfires and used a boogeyman to make sure that children behaved.

And Ceely's story would have likely faded away if not for Louis Bromfield -- the Pulitzer Prize-winning author of the 1920s and a forgotten member of the "Lost Generation" of writers who gained fame in Paris. In time, his writings shifted to writing bestsellers, especially those that could be turned into movies. His novel *The Rains Came* became one of the biggest films of 1938, even winning an Academy Award.

As the clouds of war began to hang over Europe, Louis brought his family home to the United States and ended up in Ohio, looking for the farm of his dreams. In Richland County, he spotted a farmhouse with a sweeping view of a valley. The house was exactly what he wanted, and Louis got out of the car and went up to knock on the door. Clem Herring answered his knock, and Louis made him an offer to buy his house that Clem couldn't refuse.

The Bromfields expanded the house into a sprawling but comfortable 32-room mansion that housed the family, staff, and a constant stream of visitors that ranged from neighboring farms to Indian and European royalty. The place took its name - Malabar Farm - from the Malabar coast of India, which inspired *The Rains Came.* Movie stars were often spotted on the grounds, escaping the stress of Hollywood, and Humphrey Bogart and Lauren Bacall were married there in 1945.

One of his main goals with the farm was to educate people about farming, nature, and the environment. Malabar became part experimental farm, part public attraction, and part hobby farm. Louis broadcast weekly talks about farming from his office that were carried nationwide over the radio, which brought thousands of visitors to the area.

Seeing the interest in the farm, Louis began writing books about agriculture in general and about Malabar in particular. In 1945, he published a memoir called *Pleasant Valley*, which collected history and folklore from around the region, as well as chapters about nature and his plans for revitalizing the farm.

In the book's fourth chapter, Louis told the story of Ceely Rose, as he heard it from people in the neighborhood. Many of the facts are wrong - and Louis never bothered to check them - but the story began to be heard from people outside of the area for the first time.

Louis was so fascinated with the story because when he had purchased the farm from Clem Herring, the Rose house and the site of the old mill came with it. The mill itself was torn down long after the murders, and the foundation stones and beams were used to build the large barn at Malabar Farm.

The Rose house, that small miller's cottage, still stands today across the creek from where the mill once stood. And, depending on whom you ask, Ceely - and perhaps others -- remain at this place still.

Those who have been able to go inside say they've heard mysterious voices. Is one of those voices Ceely herself, or could the tormented spirits of her mother, father, and brother still be crying out for justice so many years after their deaths?

Others have seen Ceely looking out through a window. She spent many hours staring at the adjacent Berry farm when she was alive, watching Gus Berry as he plowed the fields and did his chores. Perhaps now she spends eternity staring out the same window, hoping to get another glimpse of the man that she believed was worth killing for.

And that brings us back around to Ceely's crimes. Was she really the imbecile that the doctors and defense lawyers claimed she was? Unable to tell right from wrong? Or was she more devious than that - a sociopath who knew she was committing murder but just didn't care as long as she got what she wanted?

We will undoubtedly never know for sure, but the questions will continue to haunt us for many years to come.

"FIRST WOMAN IN THE PENNSYLVANIA ELECTRIC CHAIR"

IRENE SCHRADER A.K.A. IRENE SCHROEDER

BY TROY TAYLOR

They started calling them "gun molls" during Prohibition. They were the gangster's "girls" – the women who took care of the outlaws and made sure they ate, treated their wounds, and sometimes waved around their own weapon and often used them to bloody effect.

As the 1920s became the 1930s and the Depression gripped the country, the outlaws and bank robbers became the symbol of the average American's disillusionment with the banks and the government itself. While society crumbled, the outlaws fought back, becoming anti-heroes for a public hungry for change and thirsty for violence. They devoured the newspaper stories, and they swallowed the stories that were broadcast on the radio.

Overlooked by the men were the "molls," who rode in the fast cars' passenger seats, loaded the guns, and spent the cash taken from bank tellers and cash registers along America's highways.

But the women didn't overlook them. They read about them with desperate fascination. John Dillinger had Billie Frechette, Lester "Baby Face Nelson" Gills had his wife, Helen, Harry Pierpont had Mary Kinder, dubbed "Queen of the Gangland," and the list went on.

The "molls" were sexual creatures enjoying freedom, running with gangsters, and basking in a sordid kind of glamour. They weren't cleaning the house, washing clothes, cooking meals, and taking care of a brood of children. When the 1920s had come to an end, the "flapper" went to her symbolic death, but through the "gang girls," she managed to live on - and American women were eating it up.

And then there was Bonnie Parker, one half of a crime duo with her boyfriend, Clyde Barrow. Bonnie was largely responsible for how the "gun molls" would be viewed, and women were fascinated by the idea that Clyde was the one doing all the shooting, but Bonnie seemed to be calling the shots. The humous selfies of the tiny spitfire holding a gun or with a cigar clenched in her teeth became legendary.

But the "moll" portrayed in the press was a far cry from reality. Bonnie only owned a couple of outfits. She didn't look long enough into the future to plan a glamorous wardrobe. They stole enough money to get by for a while, and then they stole again. They weren't ever going to get to settle down. Their crimes were going to lead to either jail or death - and Bonnie knew it. She and Clyde were ambushed on a lonely Louisiana road by six armed lawmen who fired over 100 bullets into their car.

And that's what happened to most of them. When their boyfriends and husbands were captured or killed, the girls usually did time, too. And eventually, their outlaw glamour was long gone, and they faded into history.

But that didn't happen with all the so-called "molls." In rare cases, they really were calling the shots. Bonnie Parker only seemed to be - Irene Schroeder was the real thing. She was a cold-blooded killer who ran the show, dragging her dim-witted husband along with her on a cross-country crime spree that would come to an end in the electric chair.

Irene Crawford was born on February 18, 1909, in Benwood, a middle-of-nowhere hamlet in West Virginia's Marshall County. Her father, Joseph, was a fish salesman, and her mother, Martha, died when Irene was born. She was 47 when she gave birth to her youngest child, Irene. She'd been pregnant for half her life with 12 children, nine of whom survived to become adults.

There was a four-year age difference between Irene and her brother, Tom. As the youngest children, they were close - so close that Tom would become an accomplice to many of his sister's crimes and would break laws on his own. Their older brother, Edward, would also become an outlaw, finally being shot to death by an Osage County, Missouri, sheriff during a prison break in 1931.

Irene grew up tough, which was no surprise considering that she was raised in poverty in West Virginia's northern panhandle, a region squeezed between the neighboring states of Pennsylvania and Ohio. The largest town in the area is Wheeling, which sits on a curve of the Ohio River, pushed up against the base of the Appalachians. The river splits Wheeling into eastern and western halves. In the middle is Wheeling Island, where many wealthy residents built homes in the 1920s. They were the "haves." Most of the others who lived in the region - the farmers, millworkers, and miners - were the "have-nots."

It doesn't take much to guess which category the Crawford family was in.

Irene was only 15 when she married Homer Schrader - she'd later change the spelling to "Schroeder" as an alias - but she declared herself to be 21 on the marriage license. Irene was pregnant, so the wedding hadn't exactly been planned. The baby, a little boy named Donnie, was only 18 months old when Irene had her fill of Homer and took off. The couple never divorced, nor was there ever any attempt at reconciliation. They simply started separate lives.

Irene's new life would be a short one.

When she left Homer, she didn't go far - just three miles or so up the road to Wheeling. In the larger town, she found a furnished room, bleached her hair blonde, and landed a job as a waitress. It was at the diner where she worked that Irene's wild reputation began. She loved attention and loved to make people laugh. She knew she'd never be in the moving pictures, so being a waitress became a poor substitute for it.

She laughed and joked as she served the diner's patrons and soon developed many regular customers, including one man who developed a particular fondness for a woman who must've seemed like a "blonde bombshell" for a quiet, quiet, sheltered churchgoer like Walter Glenn Dague.

Glenn - as he was known - was nine years older than Irene. He grew up around Wheeling, taught Sunday School, and at the age of 21, joined the army during World War I. He served one year as a private in the infantry and returned home in 1918. He moved back in with his parents and got a job at a meat packing plant. In 1920, he married Theresa Hess, and the couple had two sons. Glenn had always been considered a deeply religious man - until he literally ran into Irene.

In 1927, Glenn was working as a used car salesman. On a rainy summer afternoon, he was driving down the street when a young woman darted out from the sidewalk. He couldn't stop his car in time and thumped the girl with his front bumper. She fell but was unhurt, except for some dirt on her waitress uniform and a tear in her stockings.

What happened next depends on whom you believe.

As Irene told the story, Glenn offered to drive her home so she could change clothes and make it to her shift at the diner on time. She later told reporters that she fell in love with him right then and there. No man had ever been so kind to her, and she bemoaned the fact that she'd married Homer and not met a man like Glenn instead.

But her romantic feelings for the car salesman who became one of her best customers at the diner didn't stop her from running off to North Carolina with another man. Eventually, she realized it was Glenn she wanted, though, and returned to Wheeling to find him.

Glenn was thrilled by her return, although friends, family, and fellow church members were shocked when he abandoned his family for a 20-year-old single mother.

In 1929, Glenn left a new job selling insurance and went to work for the Scott Motor Company, a local Chrysler dealership. That job came to an abrupt end, however, when - after a dispute about how much commission he was owed - he stole two cars to make up for what he believed he was due.

He told Irene to pack her things - they were leaving town. They'd be a real family, and Glenn would be a father to four-year-old Donnie. They took off for Toledo, Ohio, but Glenn hadn't thought about how hard it would be to find a new job while on the run from auto theft charges. He was fired from two places after his secret came out, and he applied for a third but was turned down when his prospective employer received a letter that he had "deserted his wife and two children."

So, Glenn and Irene turned to answering magazine ads that promised success and wealth, get-rich-quick schemes that involved the sale of washing machines, silk stockings, and makeup. No surprise - none of them worked out. Irene started taking in laundry and doing odd jobs, but in the end, it wasn't enough. They were still broke, and now they'd been evicted from their apartment.

They went to Pittsburgh next, where Glenn worked as a ditch digger, and Irene once again did laundry. By the summer of 1929, Glenn had lost that job, too. His next one was an assistant to a tree surgeon, which he was dangerously unprepared for. After falling out of a tree, he lost that job, also.

It was then Irene said that Glenn made a decision and told Irene, "If I can't make an honest living, I'll do it another way."

Glenn and Irene didn't want to be criminals. Society had forced them into it. They'd tried to live honest lives, but the world was against them.

Hold on right there.

That's a great story about how their life of crime began. The newspapers and the romance and "true confessions" magazines ate it up, but most of it isn't true.

Both versions of their story start the same way - with Glenn nearly running over Irene in the street - but that's where the similarities end.

Glenn didn't take Irene home to clean herself up for her shift at the diner. He took her to a seedy hotel, where they spent the night together. But that was a problem - the hotel was in Ohio. That meant they'd crossed state lines, which sealed Glenn's fate. He'd violated the Mann Act, a 1910 law that made it a felony to transport a woman or girl across state lines for immoral activity. The law was so vague that law enforcement could even prosecute men when the sex was consensual.

While Glenn may not have understood the consequences of the night in the hotel, Irene definitely did. She used the threat of the Mann Act to extort money from Glenn. It was only when friends and relatives refused to loan him money to pay off the blackmail demands that Glenn agreed to accompany Irene on what became her criminal escapades.

He may not have been a willing participant initially, but with Irene's encouragement, he soon took part in everything she did.

The couple hadn't been driven to a life of crime by their circumstances - they'd chosen a way of life that would lead to danger, violence, and murder.

When the couple arrived in Pittsburgh, they started searching for easy places they could knock over for cash. Their first choice was a filling station located on an isolated road south of the city. They were just missing one thing that all good desperadoes had - guns.

In August, they went into a hardware store and bought two cheap used revolvers. The clerk warned them that they weren't among the best he had, but the pair ignored his warning, thrilled to start their life of crime.

Luckily, during their first job, they discovered that it usually didn't matter if a gun worked or not. As soon as the person behind the cash register saw a weapon, they usually threw up their hands and offered whatever was in the drawer. And that's exactly what happened this time.

When it was over, though, Irene realized they probably needed to test the pistols they'd bought - just in case. They found a quiet spot in the woods, and Glenn tried his gun first. He aimed at a tree trunk and pulled the trigger.

Nothing happened.

Irene's fired once but refused to work again.

They were fortunate the worn-out pieces of metal hadn't exploded in their hands. They obviously needed better guns, but the gas station robbery had only netted them $11. Not knowing what else to do, they went back to the same hardware store and bought two more used handguns.

Unfortunately for their victims, this pair actually worked.

For the next four months, they committed a string of armed robberies across western Pennsylvania, Ohio, and West Virginia, spending most of their time around Pittsburgh since there were so many small towns close to the city where police presence was at a minimum.

They were hitting grocery stores and gas stations, usually one each week. In some cases, innocent suspects were jailed and even convicted for heists that Irene and Glenn committed. One West Virginia man, Frank Howell, received a 15-year sentence for one of their robberies. He spent 14 months behind bars before Irene confessed to the heist.

Of course, Frank Howell wasn't the only innocent person who was suffering because of their crimes - the other was little Donnie, who was sitting in the back seat of the car during nearly all the robberies. Irene insisted that he stay with her, even though the possibility was always there that he could be hurt or even killed if a hold-up went wrong.

And then, of course, there was Irene's brother, Tom, who had hooked up with the pair and helped out with many of their robberies.

In December 1929, Irene decided to spend Christmas at the home of one of her sisters in West Virginia, but the next day, the makeshift gang - one woman, two men, and a little boy - were back on the road.

On December 27, things got ugly for the first time.

For their next robbery, Irene chose a P.H. Butler Grocery store in the Pittsburgh suburb of Butler. At about 11: 45 a.m., while Donnie waited in the car and Tom stood guard outside, Irene and Glenn entered the store. They forced the manager, Wish Angert, into the stockroom at gunpoint. They bound his hands and feet and put tape over his mouth. After stealing the cash from his wallet, Irene also emptied the register, and then they fled the store.

They drove north on the Butler-New Castle Highway - today Route 422 - toward New Castle, planning to cross the state line into Ohio. Unfortunately, though, Wish Angert was found by a customer, and he called the police within minutes of their escape. Irene, Glenn, and Tom had far less of a head start than they thought.

At that time, there was no physical station for the Pennsylvania State Police or the Highway Patrol in New Castle. Instead, officers from both worked out of the Colonial Hotel on East Washington Street. Their office was on the third floor, in the middle of hotel rooms that served as on-duty residence barracks. The hotel owners, John and Mollie Crowl, were so attached to the officers that Mollie called them "her boys."

When word reached the hotel of the P.H. Butler holdup, the state police officers were out on other calls. The only cops available were the highway patrol officers, whose sole job at that time was to enforce traffic laws. The two divisions would merge a few years later, but at that time, the highway patrolmen were mostly stopping speeders and ticketing drivers who ran red lights. They had no choice but to spring into duty on this occasion.

A young corporal named Brady Paul took the call and was told the bandits were likely heading his way. Brady told fellow highway patrolman Ernest Moore to hop in the sidecar of his motorcycle, and together they rode out to the highway, where they set up a roadblock near a farm owned by the Baldwin family.

They stopped several cars, asked for licenses, and sent drivers on their way. Brady knew they were looking for a green car that was carrying a woman and two men, so they were able to easily eliminate any auto that didn't fit that description. It was a tedious job, and Brady wondered if they were looking in the wrong place. The two young men passed the time with good-natured snowball fights as they waited for more cars to come their way.

And then they saw a green Chevrolet coming over a hill, heading in their direction.

Brady immediately saw that the car fit the description of the one they were seeking. One man was driving, and a woman was in the passenger seat. A second man was sitting in the back. But he hadn't planned to see a little boy standing on the front seat between the man and woman - maybe this wasn't the right car after all.

He put up a hand and asked the driver to stop. After the window was rolled down, Brady asked the driver for his license. But the driver didn't hand it over. Instead, the driver opened his door and got out. On the passenger side, the woman did the same and came around the car's hood to where the driver was standing.

Brady Paul again asked the driver if he could see his driver's license. Before the man could reach for his wallet, though, the woman shoved him aside, rushed up to Brady, and rammed the barrel of a pistol into his stomach. She pushed the young officer, walking him backward until his back was against a telephone pole on the edge of the road.

And then she pulled the trigger.

The other patrolman, Ernest Moore, was at the back of the auto, recording the license plate number, when he heard the gunshot. He dropped the clipboard he was carrying and reached for his gun. Before it cleared the holster, the man in the backseat of the car opened fire at him. The window shattered, and two bullets struck him, although neither proved fatal. One clipped the tip of his nose, and the other creased his skull, knocking him unconscious.

Brady Paul, though, was down but not out. Although badly wounded, he opened fire on the car, causing the occupants to scramble for cover. They fired back. Bullets chipped at the telephone pole that Brady was crouched behind. More glass shattered, and the driver went down with a bullet graze to his hip.

Finally, the two men from the car - Glenn and Tom - moved Ernest Moore's body out of the way and roared off down the highway.

Corporal Brady Paul died a short time later at Jameson Memorial Hospital due to his wounds. Irene had just killed her first man, and the "gang" had just graduated from thieves to murderers. As far as the law was concerned, anyone involved in a crime in which someone was killed was guilty of murder, no matter who pulled the trigger.

The manhunt for the killers of Brady Paul had officially begun.

Irene knew the green Chevy needed to go. In New Castle, they slowly cruised the side streets looking for a fast replacement - and then they saw the couple. Ray Horton and his passenger, Elsie Mickum, were just getting into Ray's Chrysler when Glenn and Tom relieved them of it at gunpoint. The bright blue sedan with shiny aluminum wheels was flashier than Irene would have liked, but it got them out of Pennsylvania and into Ohio. From there, they backtracked southeast to Wheeling, where they hid the car and dropped off Tom. He vanished after that, and his whereabouts would baffle the police for years to come.

Before she and Glenn left town in one of the two cars that Glenn had stolen months before, Irene made one last arrangement - she left Donnie in the safe care of her father. She saw how close he'd come to being hurt during the shootout. Irene might have been a lot of things - but she did love her son.

Irene and Glenn had outrun the local police, but it was much tougher to outrun the news wires and bulletins spread across Pennsylvania warning cops to be on the lookout for the pair. The problem for law enforcement was that they had only the barest descriptions of the suspects. Telling officers to watch out for a blonde woman traveling with two men - and now it was only one - didn't give them much to go on. These poor descriptions did result in a flood of tips from the public but were mostly false accusations against innocent people. In one case, a blonde in Salem, Ohio, was almost arrested because she's gone out of town with her husband and son - something her neighbors thought was suspicious. I assume they thought maybe the couple was robbing stores while on vacation. Who knows?

The first real break in the case came from a search of the green Chevrolet when it was finally found. The police discovered children's clothing inside, corroborating Ernest Moore's sighting of a young boy in the car with the killer. A second search of the vehicle found something the first investigators had missed - a small, handwritten receipt from a store in Wheeling. It listed one item - a red scarf. The ticket had a date and amount but no customer name.

State Police Officer Jimmy Brooks, who found the receipt, went to the store and spoke to the sales clerk who sold the scarf. Not only did she remember the sale, but she also knew who'd bought it - Irene Schroeder, who lived in nearby Bellaire, Ohio.

On December 31, Brooks and other officers went to the house in Bellaire. It didn't belong to Irene but to her sister, Ruby Schrader, who had married the brother of Home Schrader, Irene's husband. However, someone else was visiting the home that day - Irene's father, Joe Crawford, and her son, Donnie. Joe told the police that Irene had gone on a trip with her boyfriend and had left Donnie in his care.

As the adults spoke, Donnie watched and listened. According to the officers who were present, the sight of their uniforms sparked an admission from the little boy. "My mommy shot a cop like you!" he proudly announced and even added some sound effects. "Boom! Boom! Boom!" he laughed.

No one else thought it was as funny as he did.

Recognizing the importance of the boy's statement - and probably breaking several laws - the police officers took Donnie into custody. They took the four-year-old out of his family's care, across state lines, and back to Pennsylvania. He was placed in a juvenile detention home operated by a former county detective named Jack Dunlap. Donnie was locked up under heavy guard in case Irene or one of her accomplices came looking for him.

Newspaper reporters ran with this story - not criticizing the cops for their illegal actions -- but fixating on Irene. They mainly focused on her hair and her weight with terms like "heavyset," "big blonde," and "round-faced." May reports claimed she was 30 and a divorcée. They said she'd left her husband to run off with her criminal consort, leaving what they were up to on the road to the imagination of the readers. They were also sure to add that Glenn had abandoned his wife and children for Irene's "earthy wiles."

On the other hand, the press was also building up the heroism of the slain Brady Paul. He was undoubtedly brave when it came to facing down the gang, but stories now made him a martyr, too. Brady had died, they claimed, because he was too gallant to fire at a woman.

Donnie became bait - not just for his mother, but to keep people buying newspapers. Even when there were no new details about the case, editors would fill their front pages with photos of Donnie, the "son of the murderous blonde bandit." In one photo, he posed awkwardly on the lap of a sheriff and smiled for the camera. In another, he posed like a dog. He was being used as a tool - for reporters and lawmen alike. Oddly, though, as important as Donnie's statement had been, Lawrence County District Attorney John Powers announced that Donnie would not be called to testify when his mother was finally caught. He told reporters, "I will not ask an innocent child to take the stand and possibly send his mother to the electric chair."

With a dead police officer, a reward for the killers was posted, and as days passed, it grew larger. By early January 1930, it was up to $3,200, over $50,000 today. While plenty of strangers wanted to collect the money, Irene's clannish family had no interest in helping the cops. They had nothing to say. The only way the police could get any information from them was to question them for hours on end until, out of aggravation or exhaustion, they'd reveal just enough to win their release. Irene's brother John endured six hours of interrogation, only to offer that Irene had been in a shootout with two highway patrolmen, a fact detectives already knew.

In early January, the police arrested friends of Irene and Glenn who had boarded in the same Pittsburgh rooming house they'd stayed in. They were thought to be part of their gang. They weren't and had to be released. A woman believed to be Irene was arrested in Youngstown, Ohio, so Ray Horton and Elise Nickum traveled there hoping to identify the woman who had helped steal their car. They were disappointed to find that the police had nabbed the wrong woman.

On January 8, the newspapers ran their first photographs of Irene and Glenn. Before this, they had only offered descriptions. Irene looked young in her photograph - much younger than readers were prepared for - and she wore an easy, unforced smile. There was now no question about what the bandit couple looked like, which meant that the stakes had just been raised for the duo.

While the police were looking for them, Irene and Glenn were busy robbing stores and service stations to fund a trip out west. After dropping off Donnie, they'd driven south to Parkersburg, West Virginia, where they switched cars and picked up clothing and supplies that an unnamed friend had left for them. Irene decked herself out in men's clothing, hoping to throw off their pursuers.

They crossed the Ohio River into Kentucky, scooted across the southern part of Illinois, and then ended up in St. Louis, Missouri - where they were recognized by a sharp-eyed police officer from the photographs that had now been distributed nationwide.

The officer drew his gun on Glenn, and the two men exchanged shots. The policeman avoided the bullets, but Glenn was hit in the shoulder. Irene threw open her door and, with her own gun in hand, charged at the officer and managed to take his gun away from him. When the cop whistled for backup, the couple fled, again evading arrest.

Glenn's wound turned out not to be serious, so they kept driving. After leaving St. Louis, they continued heading west on U.S. 66 toward their planned destination of California. Glenn had heard there were plenty of jobs in the lettuce fields out there, and he convinced Irene they could start over and leave behind all the mayhem they'd caused back home. Glenn was right about the jobs - but it's hard to imagine Irene being happy living on a farmhand's salary.

They eventually arrived in Arizona, and to confuse any lawmen looking for a man and woman in a car, they picked up hitchhikers as they traveled. One passenger traveled nearly 250 miles with them. When they reached his stop, he filled up their gas tank and gave them whatever money he had left in his pockets.

In Arizona, they stopped for a man who was limping along the side of the road with his foot wrapped in what looked like a bloody bandage. He said his name was Joe Wells, and he'd just been released from the Oklahoma State Penitentiary. But when Irene looked at his foot, she saw that the "bandage" was just an old rag doused with ketchup. Joe had just been using it for sympathy to bum rides.

Irene laughed, and he joined up with the bandits. He ended up staying with them until the end.

The trio stopped in the small town of Florence, Arizona, for gas but then decided to rob the filling station. Irene stayed in the car while Glenn and Joe went inside. While she was waiting at the pump, a deputy sheriff named Joe Chapman drove onto the lot. He came over, made small talk with Irene, and then asked to see her identification.

Instead of showing it to him, Irene blew the horn. To the deputy's surprise, two men came running out of the station, tackled him, and roughly shoved him into the car. They sped off, leaving the highway for back roads. Glenn demanded that Chapman direct them back toward California, but the lawmen took the bandits on a wild ride that looped them back to the town of Chandler, which they'd already passed through.

By now, witnesses had reported Deputy Chapman's abduction and gave the police descriptions of the car in which he'd been taken. When the bandits drove back into Chandler, they were met by three officers with guns drawn.

As Irene gunned the engine, the lawmen jumped out of the way. Joe Wells opened one of the rear doors and pushed Deputy Chapman out of the speeding auto. The officers opened fire, and Irene fired back, clipping Deputy Lee Wright in the shoulder. The bullet punctured an artery, and he went down.

The outlaws drove west until they reached the Gila River at the foot of the Estrella Mountains. Much of the range - then and now - belonged to the Gila River Indian Reservation. It would be on the reservation that Irene, Glenn, and Joe would make their last stand.

Whether they ran out of gas or thought it would be easier to hide in the mountains without it, the trio abandoned their car and waded across the fast-moving river.

They didn't know it yet, but a posse had already been formed to pursue them. The diverse crew included lawmen, citizen volunteers, ranchers, men from the reservation, and Leon Sundust, a local rodeo hero and a member of the Maricopa tribal community. An airplane was sent up to look for signs of the fugitives while the men on the ground pursued them by truck and on horseback.

Soon, the bandits realized they were being chased. They entered a canyon and hid out behind a massive boulder. From here, they opened fire on the posse as they entered the canyon.

Leon Sundust, who had grown up in the area, devised a plan. He and Deputy Jack Carter left the main group of lawmen and picked their way out around the spot where Irene, Glenn, and Joe had holed up. They slowly approached the outlaws from the higher ground behind them.

The fugitives continued to fire at the posse, who shot back, but they were now getting desperate. They'd seen the airplane overhead and were running low on ammunition. The posse, meanwhile, seemed to have plenty. They continued firing at them as they hid behind the boulder. Rock chips flew into the air as bullets ricocheted off their hiding spot. Soon, they were out of ammunition and out of water, too.

Irene, Glenn, and Joe were almost relieved when Leon Sundust and Deputy Carter surprised them from behind and convinced them it was better to surrender than die in the Arizona desert.

The January 14, 1930, capture of "trigger woman" Irene Schroeder and her lover, Glenn Dague, created even more sensational headlines than the original murder and escape. Irene was an actual bandit now. She had once been dismissed as an overweight, peroxide-blonde mother, but now she was a "pretty blonde" while Glenn - never anyone's idea of handsome - was now referred to as Irene's "dapper paramour."

Irene loved the attention and didn't care how the press portrayed her. Immediately after her arrest in the desert, as she was taken away by a deputy sheriff on horseback, she looked directly at a news photographer that was capturing the moment and flashed an expression of both defiance and glee.

Under questioning, Irene first tried to claim she was someone else - Mildred Winthrop. Glenn was, she said, her husband, Albert. Unlike Irene, though, Glenn seemed resigned to his capture. He was quiet and cooperative and offered his real name.

Joe, however, wasn't Joe at all. The stranger who had blindly followed Irene and Glenn into a shootout with a 75-man posse was really Vernon Ackerman. He came from a good - albeit disappointed - family back in Pittsburgh.

All three were arraigned on the day of their arrest. Irene appeared in court wearing a stylish blue ensemble donated by an anonymous woman in Phoenix. Bail was set at $15,000 each, and a hearing was scheduled for January 23. By then, the authorities expected to receive the photos and fingerprints mailed from Pennsylvania so that an official identification of each of them could be made.

But officials back in Pennsylvania had no interest in the bandits being tried in Arizona. A police officer had been killed, and the Lawrence County district attorney wanted to try Irene and Glenn for his murder. Even though Irene still claimed to be someone else, Glenn sullenly accepted the inevitable. Lawrence County detective H. Martin Lee was already on his way with extradition papers that the governor had signed.

Meanwhile, the cops in Arizona were playing their own games with the somewhat dim-witted pair. Maricopa County Sheriff Charles Wright initially refused to let them meet with lawyers, saying, "That isn't our method of dealing with criminals out here." Believe it or not, this was legal for the police at that time. The law provided the right to an attorney for those charged with federal crimes but not those arrested on state charges. That wouldn't be changed until 1963.

Even without legal advice, Irene knew that kidnapping and assault charges in Arizona were much better than murder charges in Pennsylvania. On January 18, to avoid being sent back to Pennsylvania, she confessed to the abduction of Deputy Chapman and assaulting him with the intent to murder. Glenn quickly got on board. The prosecuting attorney recognized the tactic as a ploy to avoid murder charges, and the judge agreed. The guilty plea was rejected.

While Irene was wrangling with the court in Arizona, her father was fighting in Pennsylvania for the return of his grandson. Joe stated that Donnie had been illegally removed from his home and coerced into giving statements about his mother's involvement in a crime. Using money donated by family, neighbors, and friends, Joe hired attorney Benjamin Rosenbloom to demand the return of Donnie or prove why the authorities had the right to detain him. In response, Lawrence County named the boy a material witness and placed him under a $20,000 bond. Joe was forced to end his fight.

On January 27, with extradition papers already on the way to Arizona, Irene and Glenn surprised the court by agreeing to return to Pennsylvania. The group that arrived to take them back was large and well-armed. It included county detective H. Martin Lee, Sheriff Frank Johnston, witness Clarence Evans, New Castle jail matron Minnie McKibbon, Pennsylvania State Police Lieutenant Tom Boetner, Sergeant Edward Bergen, Officer Ernest Moore - who had been in the shootout, and a reporter named Bart Richards.

Adding a woman to the party was of particular interest to the press. Before taking the job as jail matron, Minnie had served as a deputy sheriff under her father, Sheriff William Riddle. She confidently announced that she'd carry a gun while serving as caretaker for Irene. "I always go armed," Minnie told the press. "But usually I can appeal to women prisoners to be reasonable, so there is no need for a weapon."

Minnie would later regret her confidence when called to testify during the trial.

The train ride to Arizona had been long and uncomfortable, and the party had no rest when they arrived. They presented the extradition papers and made plans to return to Pennsylvania immediately with their two prisoners.

The Arizona authorities were happy to see them go. Deputy Lee Wright, who had been injured during the Chandler shootout, was still in the hospital but was expected to recover, so it seemed easier and cheaper to let someone else deal with the expense of their trials.

However, it would only be a matter of days before the Arizona governor would regret this hasty decision.

As the train traveled back east, crowds began to gather at the various stations they passed, hoping to get a glimpse of the bandits they'd read about in the papers. The closer they got to Pennsylvania, the bigger the crowds were. At first, there were hundreds of spectators, but as the train reached Youngstown, Ohio, nearly 10,000 were waiting on the platform. When the train finally arrived in more sparsely populated Lawrence County, it was met with an astonishing 3,500 people. Special railroad officers had to be assigned to handle crowd control.

The authorities carefully orchestrated the removal of the prisoners from the train. When Glenn came down the steps, he was handcuffed to only one man, Detective Peck Lee. On the other hand, Irene was cuffed between two men - Lieutenant Boetner of the state police and Lawrence County Sheriff Frank Johnston. The message was clear. Both the state police and the county sheriff were taking credit for her capture, and it sent a clear message to onlookers, the press, and potential jury members that Irene - the so-called "golden girl," "gun moll," and "blonde bandit" - was a dangerous and slippery killer.

As in Arizona, Sheriff Johnston refused to allow visits from the couple's attorneys - even though they didn't have any in Pennsylvania yet - or even from little Donnie. This didn't seem to dampen Irene's good mood, in any case. She joked, sang songs, ate candy from admirers, and generally seemed to enjoy her time in jail. She was regularly visited by her sisters, who also visited Donnie in the juvenile detention center. She passed along messages for the boy through his aunts.

On the other hand, Glenn spent his days in solitude and kept his thoughts, emotions, and, I'll assume, many regrets to himself.

It took some time, but Irene's sisters eventually got attorney K.H. Powell to represent her. But they made it clear to him that he was only Irene's lawyer, leaving Glenn without representation.

Over the next few days, Irene's defense team grew to include William P. Barnum, a former Ohio judge, Oscar Stevens, Thomas Dickey, and former Pennsylvania state senator Benjamin Jarrett. Although it's not clear who was paying for all of them, the number of attorneys she had seemed fitting in light of all the charges against her - the murder of Brady Paul, assault with deadly intent on Ernest Moore, a shooting and bank robbery in Texas, the kidnapping of Deputy Joe Chapman in Arizona, armed assault in Missouri, and a long string of gas station and grocery store holdups in Pennsylvania, Ohio, and West Virginia. One newspaper described Irene's cavalcade of crimes as "more charges than any woman in history."

On January 27, K.H. Powell was finally allowed to visit her in her cell. When he left the jail, he revealed to reporters that Irene was not in good health. She'd had an operation for appendicitis two years earlier, and it had not healed properly, leaving her in constant pain. Another story made the rounds that Irene had fainted when she was finally allowed a visit from her son, Donnie. Neither story gained much traction - or garnered much sympathy, which was the point - but the defense team was about to face much bigger challenges than her widely ignored illnesses.

On January 29, Maricopa Deputy Sheriff Lee Wright died in a hospital in Mesa, Arizona, from wounds he'd suffered during the gun battle with Irene and Glenn. An angry Governor Phillips demanded that the killers be returned to Arizona.

When told about Wright's death, both Irene and Glenn expressed sympathy. "That's too bad," Irene said, "but we didn't shoot him." Glenn added further explanation, saying that Wright had been "accidentally shot by someone in the posse." They could deny shooting the lawman all they wanted, but they'd each added a second murder to their criminal records.

And more challenges were ahead for the defense attorneys - this time from their client. Whether Irene truly cared about Glenn or simply wanted control of his defense, she refused to continue as a client of Powell and the others unless they also agreed to represent her boyfriend. So, two days after the news about Wright's death, Thomas Dickey went to see Glenn in his cell. He was his first visitor. Glenn's family and friends had abandoned him when his crimes were made public.

It would turn out that Irene and Glenn weren't the only ones with powerful lawyers. Brady Paul's family had hired Frank S. Ruff to assist the prosecutors in the case, led by legal legend Charles J. Margiotti, who had been named as special prosecutor by Pennsylvania Attorney General Cyrus E. Woods.

On January 31, a short preliminary hearing was held. The prosecution called a handful of witnesses. The defense didn't call any. Thomas Dickey believed that if they called witnesses, it would tip off the prosecution to their strategy. Besides that, everyone knew what the outcome of the hearing would be, and they were right - Irene and Glenn would be going to trial, and they'd be held without bail while they awaited their fate. On March 3, a grand jury would meet to determine which crimes the pair would be charged with.

During the weeks between the hearing and the grand jury, the public relentlessly followed everything Irene did behind bars. They wanted to know what she ate, what she read, who came to see her, and how she spent every minute of the day. The papers were happy to oblige them, even when reporting some unexpected news - Irene had turned to religion.

Of course, if you find this hard to believe, you're not alone. Unlike Glenn, who'd had a lifelong affiliation with a church, Irene's newfound faith seemed like a stunt. She began reading the Bible daily and loudly singing hymns that Glenn could hear from his cell.

While Irene and Glenn were waiting behind bars, their attorneys dealt with pressing legal issues. Small towns and big cities alike were coming forward and blaming the gun-toting pair for service station robberies and grocery store holdups, demanding information about the couple's movements while on the run. The city of Cleveland was the most demanding, convinced that Irene and Glenn were responsible for the shooting of a police officer several months earlier. However, the allegations were dropped when the bullets were compared to their guns.

The lawyers also had to decide if the pair had a better chance tried together or separately. And should the trial be held in New Castle, or was it better to seek a new venue? In addition, the Arizona governor was getting impatient. Whether it was true or a ploy to fend off Phillips' efforts to take Irene and Glenn back to Arizona, Sheriff Johnston, and Detective Peck revealed a conversation that backed up Glenn's version of events. When they had been in Arizona as part of the extradition team, a posse member had admitted that Lee Wright had been shot by fellow officers - not by the bandits. Governor Phillips wasn't convinced, but he did offer a compromise - as long as prosecutors in Pennsylvania sought the death penalty for Irene and Glenn, he'd drop the extradition efforts.

Irene and Glenn were now facing the electric chair.

During this time, Glenn's family stayed out of the spotlight by avoiding him altogether, but Irene's family couldn't escape her notoriety. Her son, father, sisters, brother-in-law, and even her estranged husband were all over the newspapers and widely speculated about. Even distant relatives like Ralph W. Holland couldn't avoid the stigma. When he was sent to the West Virginia State Penitentiary for burglary, newspapers identified him as "Irene's cousin." He was, but at least two or three times removed. When her brother, John, was arrested for driving while intoxicated, Irene was mentioned in every news story. There seemed to be no way to avoid the infamy that Irene had caused for the family.

On February 17, 1930, Irene had the dubious honor of turning 21 in jail. Her father and several other family members visited, but it was a tense celebration.

Two days later, a wild rumor spread through town that Irene had escaped from jail and was nowhere to be found. How the story started and spread so quickly was unknown, but law enforcement officials had to scramble to shut it down. The fact that the rumor existed was proof of the level of interest in the case and the community's belief that Irene was a frightening, almost supernatural threat.

Irene did have her supporters. Most of them, especially women's groups, demanded that she be tried in private. They didn't necessarily believe she was innocent, but they didn't want to see her put to death. The decision was, of course, not up to them. When the grand jury convened on March 3, it indicted the couple of charges of murder, manslaughter, assault and battery with intent to kill, and highway robbery.

The pair would also be tried separately, with the prosecuting attorneys choosing which one went first - they chose Irene.

Only seven days later, the trial began with Judge R. Lawrence Hildebrand presiding. A jury was chosen of 10 men and two women.

It was doubtful that anyone believed Irene would be acquitted of the many charges against her. Even her attorneys made it clear that their goal was to keep her out of the electric chair. Under these tense conditions, the trial kicked off, watched with avid interest by the public and the press.

One interesting character after another took the stand. Mattie Jackson, who had been arrested on narcotics charges, had shared a cell with Irene in Arizona. She testified that Irene confessed to the killing of Brady Paul in Pennsylvania. Sheriff Charles Wright followed on the stand and assured the jury that he didn't allow newspapers in the jail, which implied that Mattie could only know details of the murder if she heard them from Irene.

Another Arizona cellmate, Rose Smith, testified about Irene's stories of fleeing Pennsylvania and the shootout with the police officer in St. Louis.

Jail matron Martha McKibbon testified that Irene had smiled after hearing how many bullets had struck Brady Paul. In a more uncomfortable exchange, Martha admitted that the shoulder holster for her pistol had been stolen while she was helping transport Irene back from Arizona. She believed that Irene had taken it.

The prosecution entered bullets into evidence found on sidewalks and under automobile seats. They also called ballistics expert Louis Marr to the stand, who testified that none of the bullets that struck Brady Paul had come from the gun carried by Ernest Moore, undercutting the "friendly fire" theory that was proposed by the defense.

Some of the most gripping testimony came from reporter Ella Kerber Resch, who had published a handwritten document she'd received that was a sensationalized account of Irene's life story. It was published in serial format in her newspaper, the Youngstown Vindicator, and revealed details that bolstered the prosecution's picture of Irene as a cold-blooded trigger woman. Irene later admitted that she'd allowed the story to be published because she needed money for Donnie.

But she hadn't written all of it. It was obvious that the story had been edited and enhanced by someone who knew how to attract readers, but Ella refused to reveal the source of the story. She took the witness stand only after spending several days in jail for her refusal to answer questions.

More than 50 prosecution witnesses testified that Irene either killed Brady Paul, took part in the shootout that led to his death or committed another crime.

On March 18, Irene took the stand in her own defense. She cautiously answered questions, sometimes stumbling in her replies. She did admit, though, that she had been the one who chose Wish Angert's store in Butler, Pennsylvania, to be robbed. But she played into the prosecutor's hands when she confessed that the robbery had "thrilled me for 15 minutes" and that holdups, in general, "tickled" her.

This admission then led the prosecutor to ask if the shooting of Brady Paul had also given her a thrill. "No," she said. "It was all over then."

Even with her own life on the line, Irene tried to shift the blame away from Glenn. She said that Glenn had never fired at Brady Paul - she had. In fact, she fired point-blank into the man's chest but had only done so because she believed that Paul was going to shoot Glenn.

The prosecutor then took Irene on a cross-country trip of her criminal activities, ending in Arizona. In one of her strangest acts of courtroom theater, Irene said that - while describing the shootout in the mountains - she looked up at the sky and saw clouds that seemed to be sending messages. She stated that one cloud looked like an ostrich, and another was "the face of Jesus." She remembered Glenn telling her it was a sign that they should go to Africa and preach the gospel as missionaries.

If Irene was trying to gain the audience's sympathy, she misread the room. Members of the gallery let out a roar of laughter.

Even after being admonished by Judge Hildebrand for the outburst, many failed to keep a straight face.

But Irene wasn't done. She added one last surprise - she was pregnant, she claimed. She expected the baby in about four months. This turned out to be another of Irene's lies.

At this point, Irene's defense team finally decided to announce their planned strategy - Irene was pleading insanity. The prosecution objected, but the judge allowed Irene's lawyers to suggest a psychological justification for her criminal career. They explained that due to a severe head injury when she was 10, Irene had been involuntarily filled with an irresistible impulse to commit criminal acts. As the prosecutors continually interrupted with objections, Irene told the jury about the changes the accident had made to her personality. She even added that she'd attempted suicide several times. Once again, it was a plea for sympathy, and Irene hoped it would help her avoid the death penalty.

During closing arguments, the defense team doubled down on their efforts to offer the jury an alternative version of the shootout, suggesting that Ernest Moore had actually caused Paul's death by hiding and cowering in fear during the gun battle. He'd fired wildly without regard for his fellow officer's safety. They also tried to shock the jury into realizing what it would mean if they recommended the death penalty. They were taken through each excruciating step of the execution, from when the prisoner left her cell to when she was strapped into the electric chair and jolted with lethal electricity.

It was the only time during the trial that the seemingly hardened Irene broke down.

The prosecution used its closing arguments to focus squarely on Irene, even calling the 21-year-old high school dropout the "mastermind of a criminal organization."

The prosecution rested on March 21, and the jury received the case later that evening. It took them less than three hours to reach a verdict.

Irene was found guilty of murder in the first degree, and the penalty was death.

There was a short silent pause in the courtroom, and then the sobbing and screams from Irene's family broke the stillness. Irene accepted the verdict with a blank face. She told her sisters to hush. Her attorneys were already planning to appeal.

Glenn's trial turned out to be far less dramatic. The story of their criminal escapades had already been told, and Glenn's defense was much more straightforward than Irene's. He was presented as a hapless man who had been dominated by his young lover and enticed into committing crimes with her.

This defense was a spectacular failure, and just over a week later, Glenn also received a guilty verdict with a recommended penalty of death.

In July 1930, Judge Hildebrand heard the defense counsels' arguments for a new trial for both Irene and Glenn. A month later, he ruled against them and sentenced both to die in the electric chair on a date chosen by the governor. The lawyers continued to appeal to higher courts, but each upheld the verdicts.

In December, Governor Fisher granted a stay of execution to enable the Board of Pardons to hear arguments about the commutation of the death sentence. Since the board wouldn't meet until January, legal wrangling dragged into 1931.

In February, though, the board refused to commute their sentences, and their execution date was set for just two weeks later, on February 23.

Their only hope was to get Pennsylvania's new governor, Gifford Pinchot, to grant a new stay of execution. A week later, as if Donnie hadn't been exploited enough, Irene's father and several other relatives traveled to Harrisburg to meet with Governor Pinchot. The conversation lasted only a few minutes. The family pleaded for Irene's life - using Donnie as a prop - but the governor explained that his hands were tied by the pardon board. In truth, he knew the case and was unmoved by the meeting and the little boy who would soon lose his mother. He declined the request.

Irene's last night in the Lawrence County Jail was February 20. It was, by all accounts, a peaceful evening. Donnie visited her one last time. "I'm going to die," Irene told him, "but I am not afraid. Be a good boy."

Irene and Glenn both wrote letters detailing their final wishes. Irene wanted to be buried next to Glenn and asked that they have a joint service. She spent the rest of the evening singing religious hymns.

On the morning of February 21, both were awakened to eat breakfast and then taken on a 200-mile drive to the Rockview State Penitentiary near Bellefonte, where Pennsylvania's death chamber was located. The warden met them and described them as being in good spirits.

Reporters overran the small nearby town, and the larger news organizations monopolized all the telephone lines but one - the dedicated line between the prison and the capital, just in case the governor called with a last-minute reprieve.

Plans were finalized. There would be 12 witnesses to the executions, half of whom would be press. They would be sitting right in the death chamber itself. Only a rope divided the spectators from the prisoners and the electric chair into which they'd be seated.

It was the state's policy that executions take place at 7:00 a.m. In the rare event that two prisoners were executed on the same day, the order was determined by their death warrant number. The prisoner with the lower number went first.

Irene was 261, and Glenn was 262.

On the morning of February 23, Irene was awakened at 5:30 AM. She was served breakfast, and then she changed into a gray dress with a white collar and sleeves and a pair of black slippers. A small spot was shaved onto the top of her head for a better electrical connection. She sang gospel songs when the guards arrived at her cell to lead her to the execution chamber.

She shuffled along the empty corridor and stopped at a green door. It was the entrance to the room where the witnesses, warden, and the electric chair waited. The prison's minister and a matron followed her as she passed through the door. Tears streamed from the matron's eyes as Irene sat in the chair and adjusted her posture. Her ankles were secured with leather straps, followed by her wrists, neck, and waist.

The silence of the room was broken by the demonic hum of an electric circuit. More than 2,000 volts surged through Irene's body for three seconds, a humane way to rapidly cease organ function and eliminate the sensation of further pain. A second jolt, at 500 volts, lasted for 57 seconds. This was followed by another 2,000 volts, another 57 seconds at 500 volts, and finally, 2,000 more volts for a final three seconds.

Irene was officially declared dead at 7:05 a.m. The only evidence of the terror of her death was that one black slipper had fallen off her foot during the electrocution.

Eight minutes after Irene's body was removed from the room, Glenn followed her to the other side.

The pair were not buried together. Glenn was taken home to the family plot. The wife he had abandoned petitioned the government for a stone based on his service during the war. The request was granted, and a stone, designated "for the unmarked grave of a World War soldier," arrived on June 29, 1931.

Irene's body was shipped by train to Ohio, where she was buried in an unmarked grave next to her mother. On the way, a railroad employee managed to pry open her coffin and allowed friends to take a look at her corpse.

They wanted to get a glimpse of the very first woman in Pennsylvania to die in the electric chair.

And based on the sensational life she lived of murder, robbery, and assorted mayhem that was splashed across the bloodstained pages of the country's newspapers - who can blame them?

PART TWO
THE SLAIN

"DIANA OF THE DUNES"
ALICE MABLE GRAY
BY TROY TAYLOR

It was a fisherman who reported her first.

He was absently casting his line into the water along the Indiana shoreline of Lake Michigan when he spotted a young woman frolicking naked in the waves. After leaving the water, she danced on the sand like a nymph to dry herself off.

Startled - and perhaps half in love - he told his friends, neighbors, and even his wife about the encounter. The story traveled quickly, even in that isolated area around the lake.

Soon, other fishermen, their curiosity piqued by the nude woman who rose from the waves like a Greek goddess, sought out her stretch of the beach, hoping to see her for themselves. And they did - for the next nine years. The young woman roamed the wild and rugged Indiana dunes region, staying away from people and keeping to herself. She might have lived and died in obscurity had that fisherman not spotted her on that summer afternoon in 1916.

Instead, her legend grew. Newspaper reporters venture from Chicago to see her for themselves. They dubbed her "Diana of the Dunes," a mysterious girl who lived in an abandoned shack and rarely spoke to anyone. She granted interviews to a few visitors but, always gracious, simply said she was a private person who wanted to be left alone.

But "Diana" had a story - a true story, not the myth that was printed and re-printed in books, newspapers, and magazines over the years. After her tragic death, that myth continued to grow and took on a life of its own. Even today, visitors to the Indiana Dunes State Park still catch a glimpse of Diana's ghost as she walks the beach at twilight or swims naked in the waves.

Who was this woman in life?

Folklore of the region states that "Diana of the Dunes" was born Alice Mable Gray, the daughter of a prominent Chicago physician. She was well-educated, traveled widely, and held a secretarial job. But a love affair that ended badly sent her into seclusion in the remote dune country of Northern Indiana. She was said to have arrived in the dunes with only the clothing on her back, a drinking cup, a knife, a spoon, and two guns. After sleeping on the sand for a few nights, she moved into an abandoned fisherman's shack and made furniture out of driftwood.

At first, Alice lived on fish that she caught with nets and wild berries. In time, she sold berries and fruit wine to make money for her essentials. She walked many miles to the small town of Miller for food and library books.

People who came to know her said she was shy but was always kind and courteous. She only wanted to be left alone, but most found it hard to honor this request. She was constantly spied on as she walked the dunes, reading and writing under the sky and stars. Knowing that she swam nude and allowed the sun to dry her on the beach, young men often found excuses to wander past or cast their lines into the water and "accidentally" stumble upon her as she lay in the sun.

In 1920, though, Alice met a man - a mysterious drifter named Paul Wilson. He was described variously in the press accounts of the day as a Texas rattlesnake hunter who read about "Diana" and came north to woo her and as an ex-convict with a police record for armed robbery in Kansas or Michigan.

But whomever he had been, Alice now belonged to him. He was tall, strong, and resourceful, and he improved Alice's shack, sold the extra fish he caught, and created a market for hand-crafted furniture that Alice made. Their finances improved, and Alice was happy, at least for a time.

In June 1922, though, violence entered their lives. Hikers in the dunes discovered the ghastly remains of a man near Alice's shack. He had been strangled to death, and his body partially burned. Paul

Wilson became the chief suspect - he was a stranger and, some said, an ex-convict. Locals claimed he was surly, hot-tempered, and hated trespassers. He was easy to blame for the murder.

When Eugene Frank, a deputy hired to guard nearby dune cottages, confronted Wilson about the murders, a fight broke out. Wilson was shot in the foot, and the butt of a pistol fractured Alice's skull. The police arrested Wilson, and Alice was taken to Mercy Hospital in Gary, where doctors declared her wound fatal.

While the couple was away, their home was vandalized, and Alice's books and furniture were stolen.

Meanwhile, under questioning, Wilson told police that he believed that the murder in the dunes had been committed by an insane, gun-toting hermit named Burke. Burke had a twisted foot, and Wilson claimed he had seen his distinctive footprints near the murder scene.

By then, though, any tracks near where the body had been found had been trampled by police, reporters, and curiosity-seekers. Burke was never found. Was Burke the killer, or was he the unidentified victim? If so, why had he been murdered? And he wasn't, then who was the dead man?

No one ever found out. The body was never identified, and the murder was never solved. Paul Wilson was eventually released and went to find Alice.

She had managed to survive the attack. She was eventually discharged from the hospital but never recovered from her injury. Harassed by morbid sightseers, she and Wilson moved a few miles farther east, vanishing deeper into the wild country.

But progress slowly caught up with them. The shoreline began to be developed, and houses appeared. A new addition of homes called "Ogden Dunes" was built near their second driftwood shack, and Alice and Wilson fled again. They went to Texas, but only for a year. While they were there, Alice was diagnosed with uremic poisoning - the end stage of kidney disease.

On February 11, 1925, Alice died in Wilson's arms. Not long before she died, knowing the end was near, she asked to be cremated and her ashes scattered over the dunes she loved. But the authorities refused to let Wilson make a funeral pyre on the beach, and Alice was buried in Oak Lawn Cemetery in Gary instead. Her grave was in a secret spot, and not even the cemetery's staff was sure of its location. In death, the reclusive woman finally found the privacy she wanted so badly in life.

And, the story concludes, so has her ghost. A century after her death, the spirit of Alice Gray still walks the lonesome sands of the Indiana dunes. Her glistening, baked ghost is still reported emerging from the lake - finally free to spend eternity in the way she desperately wanted to live her life.

Or so the legend says.

This is the legend of "Diana of the Dunes," but, as you'll soon see, the truth of her story is much stranger than the legend.

The years that followed the Great Chicago Fire of 1871 - known as the "Gilded Age" in America and Chicago alike - were likely the most exciting and volatile in the city's history. In the flurry of rebuilding, commerce, and fortune that took place in the late 1870s and into the 1890s, Chicago emerged as a metropolis second only to New York.

On the city's southwest side, home to the great Chicago stockyards, working-class neighborhoods were just beginning to be established. One of the most thriving was Canalport -- now known as the McKinley Park neighborhood -- an area that saw dramatic growth after the Great Fire. Factories and steel mills, brickyards, warehouses, and real estate companies, while immigrants poured into the neighborhoods. Block after block of single-family cottages popped up, each situated close to the next in dutiful order.

One such house, located at 3445 South Hermitage, became the birthplace of Alice Mabel Gray, who would someday be known as "Diana of the Dunes."

Her parents were Ambrose and Sallie Gray, and her sisters, Leonora and Nannie, were much older than Alice at ages 14 and 11. The youngest Gray child, Chester, was born three weeks after Alice's second birthday.

Although most versions of the "Diana of the Dunes" story claim that Alice's father was a wealthy physician, this was not the case. Alice did not leave a privileged background behind when she became a recluse in the Indiana Dunes. This mistake was likely made in the early 1900s when a reporter checked the Chicago city directories and found a doctor named Allen Gray. Because of Alice's obvious education, it was assumed that she came from a wealthy family and that her father was Allen Gray, not "A. Gray," a resident listed in the city directory as a "laborer." That was Alice's father, Ambrose, a man who'd never been what anyone would consider lucky.

Ambrose was born in Fairfield, Connecticut, in 1842. As a boy, he was seriously injured when he was run down by a falling log, which damaged his left eye and left him partially deaf. Freed from farming, he began to apprentice with a spectacle maker named George Staples. When Staples left for Indiana to start a new factory, Ambrose followed.

In 1865, at age 24, Ambrose enlisted in the military during the Civil War and became a private in Company E of the 145th Indiana Regiment. By this time, the war was almost over, and his regiment was sent to Georgia to guard railroad lines before being mustered out in January 1866.

Four months after returning to Indiana, Ambrose married Sallie Gray. Gray was also her maiden name, although they were not related. Sallie had been born in Indiana in 1844, and her parents had come from North Carolina. They were married on April 4, 1866, and had three children who were born in Indiana. The family moved to Chicago in 1873, two years after the Great Fire.

After the Grays settled in Chicago, Ambrose was listed first as an "ironworker" in the city directory and then as a "laborer." What those jobs entailed is unknown. At some point, he began working as a lamplighter. This was during a time when gas lamps lighter the city streets. Ambrose worked along Archer Avenue, the neighborhood road that had been originally constructed to follow the route of the Illinois-Michigan Canal. It was only a few blocks away from his home.

But it was along Archer Avenue that a horrible accident occurred that would have severe and long-term consequences for Ambrose and the rest of the Gray family.

On the afternoon of August 29, 1895, he was working outside of a pharmacy at 3199 Archer Avenue. While filling a gas lamp, a leak caused fuel to pour out onto his clothing, which somehow ignited. His shirt burst into flames, seriously burning his left hand, arm, shoulder, neck, and face.

The druggist on duty at the pharmacy said Ambrose was so severely burned that his skin was hanging off him in shreds. The druggist applied a dressing and sent for Dr. George E. Willard, who had an office nearby. Dr. Willard later noted in a report to the U.S Pension Office: "The destruction of the tissue was so great that he has totally lost the use of his left arm and hand. He also received such a nervous shock as a result of the accident that he was confined to his bed for one year from the date of the receipt of the injury, since which time he has been continuously under my care."

In the year that followed, Ambrose was essentially an invalid. Hideously burned, in great pain, and unable - or unwilling – to leave his bed, household chores fell to Alice and her younger brother, Chester. Their next oldest sibling, Harry, was already 18 and likely living alone, as were the other Gray children. Their father did the only thing he could to provide for his family and filed for an increase to his military pension.

He told the pension board that the burns had caused him "nervous prostration" and that he was "wholly unable" to support his family. Dr. Willard confirmed the dire circumstances. He later filed another request for funds in 1897 but died, at the age of 57, of a cerebral hemorrhage on June 7, 1898, ending his three years of suffering from the effects of his injuries. He was buried in Chicago's Oak Woods Cemetery.

After Ambrose's accident, his wife, Sallie, managed the Gray household affairs. A friend of Sallie's later wrote, "During his sickness and disability, she maintained and kept the family together by hard work, in raising poultry, vegetables, etc." After Ambrose's death, the family continued to seek additional income. In 1900, U.S. Census workers listed Alice as a stenographer, while Chester was listed as working as an "office boy." Meanwhile, Sallie had applied to the U.S. Pension Office for an increase of $2 per month. The process was exhausting, and the results were less than satisfying. On multiple affidavits for the pension board after her husband's death, Sallie detailed her meager finances. Neither she nor her husband owned real estate; they held no stocks, bonds, or investments, and she had no taxable property. She made a living by keeping hens and raising summer vegetables in a backyard garden plot. Chicago neighbors and several from Sallie's childhood home in Indiana sent statements to the pension office, attesting to her marriage and in witness to the truth of her claims. Sadly, the pension board again denied the family's request to increase their monthly stipend. The reason? Ambrose had died without having a medical examination.

In February 1902, Sallie died of pulmonary tuberculosis. She was buried next to her husband. Alice, who was in her fourth year at the University of Chicago then, could not afford the burial. Her sister, Leonora, who had also paid for Ambrose's funeral, purchased a plot for $2, the most inexpensive the cemetery had to offer. Headstones do not mark their graves or those of family members who died in the following years.

That said, it's no surprise that Alice's family later chose not to mark her grave either. Some stories insist, however, that Alice's grave is unmarked because her family "disowned" her, but this isn't true. Descendants who knew Alice maintain that her siblings were very fond of her and spoke of her often.

At age 20 and now on her own in Chicago, Alice moved from the family home to an address on Lake Street. She did well in school. Even though her grades had slipped during her mother's illness, she began earning top marks again the following semester. Given her coursework from that point on, Alice apparently found her favorite field of study and began almost exclusively taking courses in mathematics.

Alice had enrolled at the University of Chicago just six years after the school had opened its doors. Given that her family had little or no income, it seems unlikely that her parents paid her tuition, which was $40 per quarter. She either raised the money on her own through her work or qualified for some sort of scholarship, but either way, Alice enrolled in both undergraduate and graduate studies over a period of 15 years.

During her undergraduate years, from 1897 to 1903, Alice studied German and French. Along with introductory and required courses, she focused on theology, astronomy, and mathematics. Her later courses ranged from geometry to increasingly advanced calculus and advanced theory classes. She often enrolled in multiple math courses each semester. Along with 12 fellow students, Alice was elected to Phi Beta Kappa and was initiated on June 17, 1901. There is no question that Alice was a brilliant young woman.

On March 17, 1903, 31 men and 37 women received diplomas from the University of Chicago. During the ceremony, the university's mathematics department presented its highest academic honor to one student - Alice Mabel Gray. Along with her AB degree, Alice earned an "Honorable Mention for Excellence in Senior College Work." And she was not yet finished with her studies. She had already planned to continue her graduate work in Germany, stopping in our nation's capital along the way.

At the age of 22, seven months after receiving her degree, Alice moved to Washington, D.C., and went to work at the U.S. Naval Observatory (USNO). For the next two years, she worked as a "computer," one of the earliest groups of women hired in this capacity. She had to take the Civil Service Examination to apply for the position. Although no public records exist, she must have scored well because she began her job at the USNO on October 22, 1903. She was "attached to the Division of Meridian Instrument under the direction of William S. Eichelberger for a period of seven months as a computer engaged in general reductions under the direction of editing and printing." This likely meant that she edited tables of numbers for the correctness and looked over page proofs before they were published. After this assignment, she worked as a "miscellaneous computer."

The work was tedious and monotonous, and the observatory listed the computers as "subprofessionals." Work shifts lasted 10 hours each day. Alice spent her hours working on an almanac, figuring routine equations to chart the location of stars. At the time, hand calculations were the only means to obtain results. Each day, Alice worked ten steps of a logarithmic equation, passed her calculations on to another computer, and then worked the same ten steps again, using new sets of numbers each time.

Her pay remained constant during her job term, about $1,200 annually. The pay scale had been set, with little hope of a raise, in 1892.

Despite their mathematical abilities, female computers could not hope to earn a more challenging position at the observatory. Several limitations prevented it, not the least of which was that a senior position required a naval commission, which, by law, women couldn't obtain.

Alice lived within walking distance of the USNO. During her first year, she boarded on U Street in a red brick row house and, in her second year, moved to Wisconsin Avenue, which was closer to the observatory. Very little of Alice's period of employment at the observatory is documented. No official photograph can be found in her employee folder, although other women's files contain their pictures. Observatory computers frequently enjoyed celebratory luncheons for holidays and birthdays. Many photographs of these luncheons still exist, with all the women clearly identified in them. However, Alice is not among them. For whatever reason, she completely avoided photographers during her two-year employment.

She did stand out, though. A notation in her file remarked on her penchant for adopting habits that others found disconcerting for lack of feminine qualities. "Miss Gray... had cut her hair short. She also worked in pants." She was known as a free spirit but had an intense interest in astronomy and wanted to pursue studies in tidal research.

Whether it was boredom or a thirst for more knowledge, Alice became discontented at the USNO. She may have only stayed for as long as she did to save money for her next adventure. In any case, she left Washington, D.C., for Germany in 1906. Records show that she was admitted as a "guest listener" at the prestigious University of Gottingen from the winter semester of 1906 through the summer semester of 1908. The university did not record information about what visiting students studied, but Alice likely focused on mathematics.

A few months after classes ended in 1908, Alice left Germany. Identifying herself as a student, she departed from Liverpool, England, traveling as a second-class passenger on the ship *Kensington.* She arrived in Quebec's Montreal port on September 28.

By October, Alice had already enrolled in graduate studies at the University of Chicago. Of her three classes, two of them were in mathematics. The third was a required course in physical education. During the first eight of the next ten quarters, beginning in the winter of 1909, Alice enrolled in nine mathematics courses, including several seminars. She studied the theory of numbers, algebraic theory, and foundations of pure mathematics.

In 1910, Alice took a lecture class on labor, capital issues, and mathematics. A year later, she studied elementary Italian and enrolled in another mathematics seminar. The seminar marked her last class devoted to studying numbers, which had previously seemed destined to be her life's work.

In the summer quarter of 1911, Alice enrolled only in Beginning Sanskrit and did not return for classes during the fall and winter quarters of 1912. When she registered for classes the following spring, Alice signed up only for philosophy courses - one on Descartes and the other on the "logic of social sciences." Although Alice did not complete the philosophy work, she received high marks in her third course, a political science class called "Population and Standard of Living." It was her last course at the university.

During her last years in college, Alice is said to have worked as an editorial secretary and edited a book, although no record of this exists. In a diary entry dated three years later, she spoke of perhaps editing another book if she had stayed in Chicago. It was this job that she left behind when she disappeared into the Indiana dunes region. She never worked in an office again.

It is unknown where Alice lived or what she did between leaving the university and departing for the Indiana dunes. It is also unknown what caused her life to somehow go off track in the way that it did. She was no stranger to shifting directions. She had changed her life twice before, leaving for Washington, D.C., and then going to Germany, but her abandonment of first mathematics and then civilization itself, seems a very radical change, even for a "free spirit," as she was called at the USNO.

Somewhere along the line, her life had come completely undone.

When Alice Gray left Chicago on a South Shore train in the fall of 1915, she was 34 years old and was intent on finding one thing - solitude. She would find it in the remote regions of the dunes, a place that she likely heard about when she visited her sister Leonora and her family in Michigan City, Indiana.

Determined to disengage from the complications of work and society, she brought a few possessions with her. She had no idea what to expect from her new life. She also had no plans. Alice had no idea how long she would even stay away. At that point, she didn't plan to leave Chicago for the rest of her life.

When Alice stepped off the train at the Wilson stop in Indiana on October 31, 1915, she abandoned her old life. She had been living independently for more than a decade, but even so, making a home in the outdoors, temporary or not, required a far different set of skills than working as a secretary or book editor. When her mother died,

Alice was helpless. She had, at that point, never learned to do anything on her own. It's likely that her stint at the USNO, and her trip to Germany, was to prove to herself that she could make it on her own. Her relatives wanted to help her when she moved to Indiana, but Alice would have none of it. She simply walked away from everyone.

Many writers have proffered various theories as to why Alice left Chicago. Although Alice denied that "a love affair caused me to live this lonesome life," pieces from her diary, excerpted in the Chicago Herald and Examiner in 1918, tell a different story. For a woman who valued her privacy so intensely, it seems odd that Alice would publicly share her thoughts about a man she called only "L" in the newspaper. Whatever the identity of this man, he was apparently a writer for whom she had deep and confusing feelings.

Others say, as did Alice on occasion that she left Chicago because women were second-class citizens in the working world. She was fed up with being undervalued and underpaid. She also expressed disillusionment with her work during a 1916 interview with Honor Fanning, who claimed to be the first female reporter to "penetrate the sanctuary of this modern-world Diana." Alice stated that while working in Chicago, she made little money and did nothing significant in the world. She added, "I had measured myself with the world - and the results were not encouraging. I came here to measure myself with nature."

Another possible explanation comes from one of the first interviews that Alice granted to a Chicago reporter. She stated that she planned to stay for a year because friends told her that she could not live the life of a recluse for even two weeks. She planned to prove them wrong. It seems possible that Alice complained enough to her friends about her situation in Chicago that she was dared to set off on her own, leaving civilization behind as she attempted to commune with nature like Thoreau. Perhaps she set her timetable for one year to prove her mettle to those who doubted she could succeed. It may not have even seemed that risky to her since her sister lived in nearby Michigan City.

Or perhaps it was something else altogether. Maybe it was not heartbreak or unhappiness with her pay and situation that brought Alice to the wilderness. It seems just as possible that deteriorating mental stability could have just as easily been the motivation. We know little of how emotionally affected she was by her childhood, her father's horrible accident, and her year of being bedridden and traumatized. We know very little about Alice's personal life during her college years. We only see her sudden move to Washington, D.C., and then another abrupt move to Germany. We see her strange and sudden disinterest in mathematics, which she had been so focused on for years. We see her disillusionment with the university, her job, her friends, and her life in the city. A stable person doesn't simply throw away their life, move to a remote region, and become a recluse.

During the summer after she arrived in the dunes while speaking with yet another reporter about her search for solitude - by then, an utterly impossible dream thanks to all the attention she had attracted - Alice became hysterical. The interview occurred during her first long day of being besieged by newspapermen who were desperate enough to travel to the region in hopes of finding guides to take them to her isolated cabin. Alice, the reporter wrote, "said sobbingly that she could readily understand why people were driven to suicide."

Her remark might seem to be caused by her frustration over being pursued by reporters, but her diary hints that when she first came to the dunes, the notion of suicide entered her mind. Alice wrote of the day she left the city: "The day I arrived - the day was crowded with thoughts of ending it all."

Soon, though, she fell in love with her new home. She pondered the colors of the landscape, the majesty of the lake, and the beautiful sweeps of sand that made up the dunes. On December 5, 1915, she thought, "What shall I do when I get back?" But by the following Wednesday, she vowed never to return to Chicago. She wrote, "And now a forever sadder and wiser woman - let me forget that acridly chemical atmosphere - even corrosive atmosphere that I knew - now that I am living in the world that belongs to me and to which I belong."

While whatever truly brought Alice to the dunes will forever be unknown, she certainly weathered that first, long winter alone. From October 1915 to midsummer of 1916, she taught herself how to survive in her new home.

Since she had arrived so late in the fall, finding shelter was Alice's most immediate concern. After sleeping outdoors for four days, she moved into an abandoned fisherman's shack. It was "ten feet square and without windows," she said. It was speculated that the shack had once belonged to George "Sandhill" Blagge, a well-known dunes dweller who died just before the winter of 1914. Blagge was a well-liked Civil War veteran and loner with whom neighbors gladly shared an occasional supper. No one was concerned when Alice took over his old shack because no one had ever claimed it.

As if to announce the property transfer, she gave the crude, sand-floored shack a name: Driftwood. She later told a reporter, "Everything I have here, this chair, this cap I wear, these tins, are driftwood, drifted in from the lake - I, too, am driftwood."

During that first cold winter, Alice also used another encampment whenever she could. Known as Sassafras Lodge, it was a teepee owned by naturalists Flora and William D. Richardson, located in a deep hollow of what is now the community of Dune Acres.

In a memoir written by a friend of the Richardsons, Edward C. Howell, Alice is mentioned in an unflattering light as a frequent visitor to their campsite. They discovered her much earlier than newspaper reporters. Howell wrote:

One day we discovered an unkempt, raggedly dressed, snarled hair subterfuge of a young woman had appropriated Sassafras Lodge as her permanent abode. Later, a Chicago Tribune reporter publicized her in a series of articles as "Diana of the Dunes... (We) permitted her to stay provided that on days when we were there, she left it to us. This she usually did. We seldom saw her but saw signs of her, but we could not understand the filth she left. It was a golden rule to always leave the Dunes as you found them... We finally had to ask her to leave because the camp was so filthy and she herself was so unkempt.

On the other hand, around this same time, Mathilda Burton, a local fisherman's wife who claimed to be her nearest neighbor, stated that Alice kept her shack "scrupulously clean." So, who knows what the truth is?

Life in the dunes forced Alice to learn skills that she never dreamed of living in the city -- avoiding sunburn, staying warm in the winter, obtaining food and supplies, and finding stray goods to furnish her cabin with. Basic needs - including food and, for Alice, books - forced her to walk to towns like Chesterton, Miller, Porter, Bailleytown, Furnessville, and Michigan City.

In her diary, she described some of her immediate challenges. Because she feared that intruders would steal her meager belongings, she kept a close guard on them. She collected pine boughs and added them to her oilcloth and blanket bedding to help block the cold that seeped up from the sand under the cabin. Alice knocked on local doors, hoping to buy bread, milk, and eggs from the residents.

A 1916 newspaper article claimed that Alice, in pursuit of food, became quite a hunter, based on the number of trophies that hung on a line outside of her cabin. The reporter described her marksmanship: "During all the bright nights the wild ducks remain out on Lake Michigan. At dawn they come flying in to seek the little salt marshes as their feeding ground. Miss Gray is ready at the last ridge and as the birds come over, she pops them right and left."

Many of the local families shared food and company with Alice. She visited many families in Bailleytown on Saturdays, picking up bread and cookies or getting help from a neighbor to lay a pattern on material for a skirt. Agnes Larson, a lifetime resident of the region, recalled Alice's taste for coffee and Swedish rye bread. Another longtime resident, Hazel Blythe, said Alice bought baked goods from her grandmother, Anna Larson. Her aunt, Ethel Larson, a librarian, used to say that Alice "was a very intelligent lady, read a lot, and checked out large armloads of books." Hazel Blythe noted her family's opinion was that "a lot of things written about 'Diana' were not true."

Accounts of Alice's personal appearance also vary, mainly depending on the season. In her first years in the dunes, newspaper accounts and those who met her say that she typically wore simple skirts or rumpled dresses. It was reported that she favored wearing black, but it was likely the same black outfit worn over and over again. By all accounts, she wore her dark hair short, or "bobbed," as it was called then, a style that remained the same throughout her years in the dunes. She told a fisherman's wife that she cut her own hair, judging its length by her shadow on the sand. She didn't possess a mirror, so she was unaware of how she appeared to others. She apparently offended the Richardson group with her appearance, but they were not the only ones. There would be many reports of her disheveled appearance, grimy face, and wild hair in the years to come.

Newspaper accounts drew attention to her choices of clothing. They claimed she never wore shoes or stockings in the summer but wore big boots in the winter. In warmer weather, she wore a light dress with a "ragged waist" over it and, in winter, the same ragged waist over a short, coarse skirt and a little cap - likely the same cap that Alice mentioned as one of her "driftwood" possessions. Another description of her winter attire told of "heavy mackinaw socks, such as lumberjacks wear," a man's cap, a gray wool skirt, and a knee-length coat.

To the people of Northern Indiana, Alice was becoming something of a legend, and this was before the newspaper reporters discovered her. All kinds of stories circulated about Alice walking great distances. She was reported to have walked for miles at a time - among the dunes, from the dunes into one town or another, and all along the beach, including from her cabin to her sister's house in Michigan City.

Those who knew the eccentric woman found her not only sane and friendly but also fascinating because of the wide range of topics she could discuss. Her voice is said to have a remarkable quality and added to these encounters. It was variously described as "deep," "pleasant," and "lilting." A niece later recalled that "her speaking voice was beautiful."

Vivid oral recollections of Alice Gray are valuable and few. In most cases, the primary sources used to develop her story are newspaper stories of the era, a good many of which are filled with bad reporting and the tall tales spread by locals. These stories are mingled with the stories of those who met her or whose families passed along their first-hand accounts of Alice to the next generation. Thanks to this, it's often hard to tell the difference between fact and fiction. But by combining some of the more coherent newspaper articles with the recollections of the locals, some things about Alice become clearer.

In the early years, she didn't live the life of a hermit, but she didn't seek attention either. Her actions seemed to be guided by what she had to do to survive. Her silence and reclusiveness were caused by her own need for self-discovery and her passion for nature, which she chose to live within.

It does not seem far-fetched that Alice swam naked in Lake Michigan. Although legend has it that she did so at the first sign of ice melting on the lake and continued to do so until ice returned the next winter, she discounted the stories of her winter plunges. She told a reporter, "Just don't imagine that I spend my days and nights up here going bathing -- I did go in yesterday, but I'd like to see myself going in right now with the frost still in the air - climbing hills to gaze at views and wiggling my toes before the fire. Far from it."

It's a matter of practicality that Alice bathed in the lake -- twice daily, morning and evening, or so the rumors went -- when temperatures allowed for it. And if she did so without any clothing, as the fishermen claimed, she kept the few clothes she owned dry. Keep in mind that the area where Alice lived was generally uninhabited, and since locals or vacationers did not usually visit it, her behavior was not strange in any way. Only after Alice was discovered did fishermen put her on their regular route, and even then, it was often with sightseers aboard who were hoping to see the "mermaid." Later accounts do say that she eventually put on a swimming suit, no doubt because the encroachment of civilization spoiled the notion that her location could be considered remote.

Before that time, though, I'd like to think that she really didn't care what people thought. This independent, strong-willed woman obviously cared little for the attitudes of society. She had come to the dunes because she wanted to do so, and if she wanted to swim naked in her own little corner of the world, then she certainly had the right to do so.

Alice had found peace along the shoreline of Lake Michigan, her slice of the undeveloped, wild country - but that peace was not meant to last.

In the summer of 1916, amid one of the worst heat waves in years and as the world teetered into the Great War, the newspapers found something to distract their readers from all the bad news filling their pages daily.

They found a diversion named Alice Gray, the so-called "Diana of the Dunes," and Alice's life would never be the same again.

Nine months after Alice had settled into the dunes, a flurry of newspaper stories belatedly announced her presence. Although lacking background material, the first glimpses of Alice appeared with all the sensationalism the reporters could muster. Accounts of a lonely nymph living in the wild dunes of the lake thrilled readers in Chicago, Indiana, and northward into Michigan. Even after all these years, bits and pieces of these early romantic portrayals are alive and well in the legends of Alice Gray.

Initially, her identity was a mystery. Newspapers printed their guesses, speculating that she might be Elizabeth Wilkins, a former University of Chicago instructor, or Wilhelmina Wilkins, an unrelated heiress from Walla Walla, Washington, who had disappeared two years before. These women, and perhaps others who had gone missing, gained renewed attention in Alice's story.

While several "hermits" had wandered into the region over the years, Alice attracted so much attention because she was younger, female, and an unlikely candidate for such a rugged existence. Those who came before her were older men with colorful backgrounds, mostly loners who kept to themselves. They had also given up on society for one reason or another, but to these crusty old fellows, eking out an existence was second nature.

On the other hand, Alice seemed refined, educated, and unlikely to make a serious attempt at living in the dunes. But she had done it for nearly nine months by the time the newspaper discovered her. How had she done it? And was her life in the wilderness going to continue? Reporters kept close tabs on her - at least in the beginning and more sporadically as time passed. That is until an incident in the summer of 1922 dramatically changed the relationship between Alice and the press.

The first writers that reported Alice's life in the dunes in 1916 focused more on selling newspapers than presenting the truth. Words like "recluse," "nymph," and "mermaid" often appeared in their writings. A short time later, thanks to the creativity of some unknown editor, Alice became "Diana of the Dunes."

Before that, she was labeled the "Mysterious Nymph of the Sand Dunes." The reference to "nymph" came, at least in part, from her reported habit of bathing naked in the lake. This was discovered by fishermen who were content to keep their distance but apparently loved telling the story of what they had seen. Newspapers were tipped off to the story by some fisherman's wife. On July 21, 1916, several rival reporters visited Alice, and their accounts appeared in print the next day.

The *Lake County Times*, an Indiana newspaper, offered a titillating story: "Twice daily, according to fishermen, the nymph of the dunes, whose name is unknown, takes her plunge like a goddess of the wave." Two days later, the same newspaper slightly changed its tone: "Of course, it's all right to call her a beautiful nymph and tell of the gleam of her white glistening skin as she bathes like Venus in the waters and all that, but the fact remains that she's 40 and brown as a berry and tolerably husky."

Alice was neither beautiful nor yet the age of 40. She was 35, unconcerned about her appearance, and fiercely independent. She had no interest in being the "goddess of the waves." Adding to the mystique, she confounded people by speaking with them intelligently and - especially with reporters - with great emotion. While steadfastly guarding her privacy, Alice felt comfortable talking with locals when she walked into town, none of whom threatened her. If anything, she was a curiosity. Both children and adults followed her into stores or the library just to get a glimpse of the unusual woman they had heard about from friends or read in the newspaper.

Ironically, a Chicago reporter, one of the first to interview her, seemed cautious of the information Alice shared, and with good reason. She lied about her history - for the first time but certainly not the last. During the interview, Alice claimed that she had moved to the dunes because a doctor had failed to treat her eyes, and she could no longer work. There is no evidence that she ever had trouble with her vision. She also told him that although her mail arrived addressed to "A.M. Gray," the name was fictitious.

Based on this interview, though, the reporter feared that Alice was slightly insane. She was alternately described as a "nymph," "recluse," "young woman," and a "girl" who was both "hostile" and "hysterical," pacing back and forth on the beach as they talked. At the same time, Alice's obvious intelligence came through, despite the often-frenzied behavior that he took note of. The reporter took liberty in describing her background, using her supposed pseudonym, and placing it in quotation marks. He wrote:

"Miss Gray" is a young woman of apparently English descent. Judging from her conversation, she has a broad classical and general

education. Her skin is brown, despite her assertions that she is living in the wild because of ill health, she has the appearance of one who has never been ill in her life... She is intensely temperamental. Angry moments were followed by laughter...

The reporter concluded as many others have done since, "Altogether, the 'nymph of the dunes' is a mysterious person."

A story in the *Lake County Times* had no question about Alice's state of mind. The reporter stated, "She can converse fluently on any subject, and her speech indicates past refinement and culture until an unsteady brain led her into her odd illusions."

Alice hid for a while in the dunes on the first day that the reporters arrived. Realizing that they didn't intend to give up, she appeared before them one by one. Their questions, often aimed directly at her sanity, sent Alice into a whirlwind of doubts about how she was leading her life. Several articles, all printed on July 26, suggested that after her notoriety arrived, she faltered, reconsidering her idea of staying in the dunes. Several of them, like the Michigan City Dispatch, even claimed "Diana of the Dunes May Go Back to Life," but it was unclear if reporters had even discussed this with her. Another story claimed, "Diana of the Dunes Flees her Habitation," with an account from someone who allegedly saw her at the train station on her way back to Chicago.

The reports made it sound like Alice was considering two options: Returning to city life or moving to another, more isolated spot along Lake Michigan. No matter how conflicted she might have been, Alice chose a third option - to stay right where she was, living in the same cabin, swimming on the same shoreline, and following the same paths to town. Certainly, she knew the publicity would become perhaps more than she could stand, but she must have hoped, even assumed, that it would die down after a while. She likely also stayed because she had made friends there in the dunes, folks that she relied on - for bread and salt, for brief visits over coffee in a warm kitchen, for books, and for sturdier shelter when the cold weather became unbearable. The small circle of acquaintances helped her survive a lonely life. It might have been just too outrageous for her to consider walking away from a life she had carved from the lake, the sand, and the elements.

And there is no question, too, that Alice's love for the dunes was a powerful influence on her decision to stay where she was. She was passionate about the place. She wrote, "I love the great silent darkness up there; the silence that lives in the noise of the winds and water, the darkness that finds itself in the fleeting, eternal waves of those reaches of waste sand; the only reality of life for me is there."

Oddly, Alice's passion for the dunes brought her back to Chicago on April 6, 1917. She was a featured speaker at a town hall meeting at Fullerton Hall in the Art Institute of Chicago. An association of outdoor enthusiasts, mainly from Chicago, called the Prairie Club, had organized to preserve the Indiana Dunes and turn them into a state park. Alice was invited to speak at the meeting about her experiences living in the dunes and to describe the environmental wonders she had encountered. By that time, she had survived in the wilderness for 18 months. She was seen as a testament to living in nature's healing, protective powers. For her speech, Alice read an essay she had written that urged Chicagoans to lead the fight against further industrial development of the dunes. She was interviewed and photographed for the *Chicago Daily News* - but the story and photographs never ran.

On the same day the Fullerton Hall meeting was announced, the United States declared its intention to enter the Great War. Overshadowed by this news, Alice received only a small, one-paragraph mention in the corner of the paper's front page, buried alongside the full text of President Woodrow Wilson's war message and below a banner headline that read, "War Declared!"

But it wasn't war that would change the remainder of Alice's life - it was Paul Wilson.

Paul was born on June 25, 1892, in Michigan City, Indiana. Growing up, he and his family lived on Douglas Street, and he later went to work with his father at the Haskell and Barker Car Company. Paul worked as a "stenciler" and his father as a "riveter." It's hard to follow his history from that point, but there are reports that he served in the army. Paul later claimed that he lived for a while in Pennsylvania. Some say he served jail time there, but his father denied it. Paul also once alleged that he had been a rattlesnake hunter in Texas and, another time, that he was a prizefighter. There's no record of any of those jobs.

In any case, Paul was 26 years old when he found himself back in Indiana. He might have heard about the odd woman called "Diana of the Dunes," and, as a man who liked to tell tall tales about his own past, Paul may have sought out Alice based on local gossip, admiring her independence. In a 1922 interview with a reporter, he spoke of meeting her by chance. When they first encountered each other, he was roaming the beach near Alice's cabin about 10 miles from Michigan City.

We know a few things about Paul Wilson and his relationship with Alice Gray. He was a remarkably tall man with a short, fiery temper. Like Alice, he shunned societal constraints and rules - an attitude that made them kindred spirits of a sort. He was 11 years younger than Alice and was not as well educated as she was, although his imagination was sharp. Words often used to describe the dunes region - trackless, wild, untamed - also seemed to define Paul Wilson. His attraction to the dunes was driven more by a sense of its lawlessness rather than any poetic interest in its natural wonders. He was a drifter who only found a reason to stop wandering when he met Alice Gray.

During the seven years Alice and Paul lived together, they relied on each other, complemented each other's survival skills, and remained loyal to one another in difficult, sometimes terrible, circumstances. For his part, Paul dedicated himself to protecting Alice from the outside world and met their needs any way he could - whether through honest trades such as fishing, furniture-making, boat-building, or through petty thievery. The press sometimes referred to him as Alice's "caveman." By most accounts, he adored her. The fact that she welcomed him into her private world - and allowed him to stay - took the public entirely by surprise.

According to Paul's meandering story, he had returned to Indiana to try and get a job in the Gary steel mills. By chance, he left the train at what he thought was Gary, but it was the Wilson train stop instead. Seeing the lake and feeling tired and dirty, Paul decided to swim. He dropped his belongings on the beach and enjoyed a refreshing nighttime dip in the water, only to discover afterward that someone had stolen his clothes. In the darkness, Paul said, he thought he had tracked down the thief, but he mistakenly nabbed "Diana" as she entered her shack. After a hasty explanation, they walked back to the beach and had a long talk. He worked for a while at a nearby steel mill and then moved in with Alice - just about the time he was arrested.

It was the couple's first separation - and likely their only one - when Paul served a six-month sentence in late 1918 for stealing from a few nearby cottages. He stole articles of women's clothing, including a winter coat, along with food and guns. The path of his footprints, visible in the wet sand, marked the trail from the scene of the last theft directly to Alice's shack. Although the case against him was compelling, Alice vehemently declared his innocence in a later recounting of the incident. She told a reporter, "When those two men charged him with stealing, with only a bit of wrist movement, he could have laid them both away, but he knew that would prejudice the neighbors against me. So, he took the punishment for my sake."

What Alice left out was that during the manhunt, Paul was shot in the right leg by Elmer Johnson, whose cottage had been burglarized, making it pretty obvious that he had been the one who'd broken in.

Paul began serving his sentence at the work farm in Putnamville, Indiana, in December 1918. The previous winter had been the coldest on record for the region, but January through March 1919 was comparatively mild, except for a brief period of snow and high winds. Perhaps because Alice had experienced the harsh winter of the year before --- so cold and miserable that lake commerce was closed due to blizzard conditions and buried local communities under several feet of snow - she sought temporary refuge during the early months of 1919 with Charles and Hulda Johnson. They lived along the Old Chicago Road, about a mile south of her cabin.

Many years later, the couple's daughter, Irene, spoke about living with Alice that winter. She was a house guest for about six weeks, and they got along with her well, for the most part. Alice entertained the children by creating wonderful hand-shadow pictures and plays on the wall. She might have stayed longer with the Johnsons that winter, but a surprising behavior that seemed out of character for the Alice they knew caused her sudden and premature departure.

Paul wrote Alice letters from prison, which she received at the Johnson home. One afternoon, Alice, Irene, and her mother were in the kitchen, and while Mrs. Johnson was busy at the stove, Alice began reading a personal letter that had arrived in the day's mail.

Suddenly, Alice let out an agonizing shriek and cried, "And I thought he believed in free love!"

The outburst disturbed Hilda Johnson, a devout Lutheran. She was appalled by the very idea and upset by the lack of discretion and the intensity of Alice's mournful cry and strange reaction. With little hesitation, Irene later recalled, her mother turned from the stove and said, "Miss Gray, I believe it's time for you to return to your home."

Irene was too young at the time to understand the meaning behind the words that were uttered by Alice that day, but they became more apparent to her in time. Although she assumed that the letter's writer was Paul Wilson, it seems possible that it wasn't. Many still believe Alice escaped to the dunes three years before because of a doomed love affair. Her outcry over the letter occurred in the late winter of 1918 after public attention had been paid to Wilson as her companion. Could her former lover have written the letter, upset over Alice's affair with Paul? We'll never know.

Alice moved out of the Johnson house, but the family continued their neighborly relationship with her. She often bought bread, eggs, and blueberries from the Johnsons. She also continued to pick up mail sent to their house, although the volume of mail eventually slowed to a trickle. Initially, she picked up small checks in payment for book editing work that she had done before leaving Chicago. Along with letters from Paul during his stint in jail, she also received a few notes from old friends and family members, but that was all.

After Paul's release from the penal farm, he immediately returned to Alice. At some point, they pulled up stakes at Driftwood and moved west to a location just past Miller Beach, in the area now known as Ogden Dunes. Whether they built their own shack or co-opted another abandoned one is unknown.

They named their new abode "Wren's Nest," and their daily life remained essentially unchanged. Paul caught fish, gathered wood, foraged for berries, and took on repair jobs for extra money. It has been mentioned that, on rare occasions, the couple took sightseers out on their fishing boat. Paul relied on Alice to visit town for food and supplies because he seldom journeyed away from the beach. What he didn't know about the dunes, Alice taught him. He soon knew every inch of the dunes, stretching from Ogden Dunes to Michigan City. He became an expert guide and claimed he could "tramp the dunes with his eyes shut."

The same year Alice and Paul moved to their new home, a Boy Scout camp was erected east of their shack. The campers used two sturdy rowboats Paul built for them, but their interactions were mostly limited. The lack of contact was enforced by a Scout rule that banned the boys from visiting Wren's Nest. Apparently, the scout leaders were aware of Alice's penchant for nude bathing.

The Scouts were ordered to stay out of their camp, but Alice and Paul allegedly didn't stay out of theirs. It was said that food was always missing from the camp's supply larder. Despite such claims, after the petty theft charge for which he was jailed, Paul stayed out of trouble - until the summer of 1922, when a violent incident in the dunes proved just how precarious their position in the dunes had become.

Alice and Paul vanished from the public eye for the next two years. It would not be until the disturbing summer of 1922, when the neighborly charm of the dunes was shattered, that Alice and Paul would return to the newspapers. In June, a gruesome death in the dunes near Waverly Beach attracted eager reporters, and they looked desperately for clues and culprits - notably "Diana" and her "caveman."

Despite any real evidence, newspaper headlines around the region boldly linked the dunes' most notorious couple to the bloody crime. The stories outraged Alice, while the unfolding events physically and emotionally battered her–this period of publicity - more than any other - haunted Alice to the end of her life.

The story began on Thursday, June 8, 1922. While hiking in the dunes, a Chicago college student stumbled onto a horrific scene. He found the charred body of a man lying across a blackened pile of burned logs. The body was badly decomposed and unidentifiable. A front-page story in the Valparaiso newspaper described in graphic detail what the young man found:

This stranger turned a gastly (sic) white to see laying in the center of the charred log remains, the human bones of a man with the arms sticking straight above his head. All the clothing had been burned up, the flesh completely consumed, and maggots and worms were working on the remains.

Porter County's coroner and sheriff's deputies searched the area for clues but uncovered little information. They deduced that the victim had died about ten days before the body was discovered. Belongings found at the scene - a suitcase with some food inside, new clothing, and a few dollars in cash - were more baffling than helpful. The suitcase was marked with the name "Anderson," yet purchase receipts for the clothing were marked with another name. The only items mentioned in the newspaper reports were a discarded jar, which had been used to carry gasoline, and a rifle found near the man's head. However, local legend has added camping gear, a radio, and a blood-soaked newspaper to the scene over time. Was it an accident? Suicide? Murder? The evidence was there to make all three scenarios possible, but murder quickly became the focus of the investigation.

At least eight Indiana newspapers reprinted, in full or part, a story that ran in the *Chicago Herald Examiner* soon after. It appeared under the original front-page headline that stated, "Diana of the Dunes Being Sought in Slaying Mystery." The article said that the dead man had been found near "Driftwood" and that a fisherman reported Paul "recently was seen putting ashore at Waverly Beach, a short distance from where the body was found." Police searchers, the article went on to say, "sped through the tractless wastes of the dunes all of yesterday seeking 'Diana of the Dunes' and her cave man."

As the newspapers explained it, Paul and Alice became prime suspects for questioning, primarily due to Paul's reportedly hot temper. Things became more worrisome when it was noted that the couple had not been seen around town lately. Had Paul killed her, too? Or had they both disappeared because they had been involved in the murder? The fact that Alice had been living in the dunes for seven years by this time and yet was still seen with suspicion by her neighbors indicates that people were still wary about her motives for living among them, even after all that time.

Alice was angered by what she considered a betrayal by people she considered "friends." She gave a statement to the Gary, Indiana newspaper. The article read:

"Diana of the Dunes," the strange woman who has been a familiar figure among the dunes since 1916 when she left her studies at the University of Chicago to take up a half-barbaric life in the sand hills, was located late yesterday and denied all knowledge of the man's death. Authorities started a search for her when it was found that neither she nor her husband, Paul Wilson, had been seen for several weeks.

She made the following statement to reporters: "I have long been considered the romantic property of the press, and I have been given a lot of undesirable notoriety. I have refused to profit by it, but I see no reason for mentioning my name, or that of my husband, in this investigation. My husband is not an ex-convict, as has been reported.

The article in the Valparaiso newspaper made the earlier mentioned Chicago article sound ridiculous - but that didn't stop the rumor and speculation. Technically, Paul Wilson was an ex-convict, and the paper never clarified why Alice and Paul had disappeared from the dunes before the body was discovered, but this still didn't mean they were connected to the crime. Even so, various reporters continued to insinuate there was a connection. The reporters claimed they knew something about it, even if they weren't directly involved.

In reality, the burned body was discovered at least five miles east of Alice's former shack, Driftwood, and during questioning by the sheriff, Alice and Paul apparently accounted for their whereabouts the previous week by producing a diary of their activities, particularly during the time of the alleged murder. The newspapers, though, unable to give up a good story, did not make note of their alibi.

Even when it became known, it didn't end the rumors. Many claimed that Alice and Paul had been seen in the vicinity of the crime, and one of those who spoke the loudest was Elmer Johnson, the man whose cottage Paul Wilson had burglarized a few years before and had, in turn, shot Wilson in the leg. Apparently, he still had an ax to grind against Alice's "caveman."

On June 11, authorities stated that they had identified the dead man as a 19-year-old bank clerk and vaudeville actor based on information obtained from his brother. The next day, though, the "victim" came forward to proclaim that he was very much alive.

A local taxi driver added more mystery to the case by claiming that near the time of the supposed murder, he drove a woman from a South Shore train stop to a place in the dunes near the site. She seemed anxious when he picked her up, and she asked him to wait for her. When she returned 45 minutes later, she was hysterical - so distraught that the driver suggested he take her to a doctor. She refused his offer and boarded a train back to Chicago. Could this mystery woman be the murderer? According to the newspapers, Chicago detectives were given her description, but she was never found.

In the meantime, hostility was simmering between the Chicago press and the local authorities. Porter County's coroner and sheriff had immediately buried the victim in a wooden box in the sand at the site of his death - meaning to keep his interment intact until the crime was solved. However, within a few days, Chicago reporters brought a doctor to the dunes. They exhumed the body late that night, but only after shaking off a rival reporter during an automobile chase through town. The reporters snatched the jawbone and portions of the skull from the body and took them to the city. A deputy coroner in Chicago conducted an unofficial postmortem, paid for by the newspaper.

Outraged, Porter County's coroner threatened a lawsuit, but it was never filed, perhaps because of the investigative good news that came from the underhanded tactics. Based on additional clues obtained from the height, weight, and jaw measurements, along with the victim's dental structure, the local sheriff could discount the more random claims, suspects, and evidence - and eventually, the involvement of Alice and Paul in the death.

Even so, as the newspapers reported each breaking theory, Alice and Paul continued to be linked to the mystery. Paul's criminal record and reckless relationships with other dunes dwellers surfaced in stories designed to cast a pall over his character and stir up sensationalistic talk. As the weeks passed, Paul's alleged misdeeds and imaginary alibis that he never actually claimed continued to spread.

Disgusted and upset, Alice and Paul tried to debunk the claims made against them. Their actions, though, only added more chaos to the case. They visited Eugene Frank, a deputy sheriff, fisherman, and a hired watchman for many of the cottages along the lake. He had a history of spreading rumors about the couple and even led excursions for sightseers from Chicago who wanted to see Alice's house. Paul had often warned him to stay away from Wren's Nest, especially when he wasn't around, but these warnings never curbed Frank's money-making tours.

Adding to Paul's anger, Frank told beach residents that Paul habitually robbed fishing nets and cottages. One of his cronies, Elmer Johnson, who had shot Paul several years earlier, was convinced by Frank to tell the sheriff that Paul had been seen in the vicinity where the burned body had been found - a blatant lie that was meant to cast suspicion on Wilson.

On the evening of June 14, 1922, Paul and Alice decided to confront Frank. Whether they knew to expect violence or not, their attempt to quell the rumors only managed to bring them more problems. If Alice ever publicly recounted what happened that night, her story never made it into print. Paul's vivid recollections, though, received plenty of newspaper ink:

When we arrived at the fish house of Frank's on the beach, I rapped on the door and knew at once that he had been drinking. He started to yell, called my wife a rat and myself vile names. When he pushed me back, I stepped off the porch and he reached in the fish house and got his gun.

My wife stayed on the porch, and on the porch again he told me to throw up my hands which I did, and he shot me in the foot. My wife, seeing this, stepped up and he hit her at my feet and when I tried to pick her up Frank told me to straighten up or he would kill me.

He then had his son go get a rifle and the other son a horse and then he marched up to the pavilion where he called the police patrol.

Eugene Frank recalled the incident differently. According to his version of that night, Wilson came to his cabin looking for trouble, and as soon as he answered the door, Wilson grabbed him, and Alice started hitting him. He said he struck Alice and shot Wilson, but only in self-defense.

By all other accounts, Frank was merciless to Alice that night. Paul Wilson offered the most vivid description of her wound: "If I had gone there with the intention of having trouble, I would have carried my gun, knowing that Frank's shack is covered with them. I went there unarmed. He struck my wife with the butt of his gun, caving in her skull as big as half my hand, and I haven't a damn small hand."

Frank had little interest in the couple's injuries, which were bleeding profusely. He hitched up his horse and made them walk, as best they could, wounded and in the dark, to the Miller police station, along a two-mile stretch of beach. Paul later stated, "When I tried to go to my wife's assistance, Frank threatened to shoot her. He made us walk 20 feet apart."

At the Gary jail, Paul received superficial treatment for his gunshot wound and, along with Frank, endured several hours of questioning about the incident. Alice was rushed to Mercy Hospital in Gary, where she underwent emergency surgery for a severe skull depression. She remained bedridden for several weeks - which was the beginning of the end of her life in the dunes.

While Alice was in surgery, Paul was still talking at the Gary police station. He related a story about a strange man that he felt sure was somehow connected to the murder that had taken place. Despite knowing Paul's proclivity for storytelling, the authorities embarked on a manhunt in the dunes to find the man - a fellow named Thomas Burke, who had allegedly threatened Alice and Paul, telling them he was going to kill them. Paul managed to convince the authorities that Burke could have murdered the burned man found on the beach. Evidence of this never materialized, however.

And as if things weren't bad enough already, looters ransacked the couple's home during the short time Paul was in custody. Clothes, furniture, and books disappeared, but the worst insult for Alice was the theft of several manuscripts she had been working on. A Gary newspaper blamed the theft on "Chicago reporters, curiosity-seekers and alleged thieves" who helped themselves to "practically everything of value."

The place was so badly destroyed that Paul couldn't even sleep there. He went to the nearby Boy Scout camp to spend the night, and while he was there, Wren's Nest was ransacked again, even though there had been nothing left to steal.

The sheriff charged Eugene Frank with shooting Paul with the intention to kill him, and Paul was charged with assault and battery. Originally scheduled for a grand jury on June 21, it was postponed until June 29 because Alice was still in the hospital.

But no trial ever took place. Alice and Paul did not attend the initial hearing, claiming they had never been notified about the date. Two years later, Eugene Frank was killed in a horseback riding accident, and a grand jury never heard the case.

As the terrible summer of 1922 came to an end, Alice - likely with her head still wrapped in bandages and feeling weak -- traveled to Hammond, Indiana. She was looking for an attorney, vowing to sue the Chicago newspapers for libel. Two years would pass, though, before she acted on her plans for "revenge" against the press.

In the meantime, the region was busy with the new roads that were being built. In November 1923, the new Dunes Highway was opened to great fanfare after three years of construction. Long parades of motor cars, a band playing patriotic music, banners, speeches by public officials from Illinois, Indiana, and Michigan, a bronze plaque, and receptions dedicated to the "greatest highway in the United States" marked its opening. Thousands from as many as 12 different states attended the celebration and jammed the highway for days afterward.

Another project was also underway, excavating the main channel at Burns Ditch, connecting the Little Calumet River and Lake Michigan. The machinery and materials for the project were unloaded and stored at Dune Park, near where Alice had first lived when she arrived in the dunes eight years before.

During all the construction and commotion, Alice and Paul sharply felt the threat of progress as they attempted to return to their simple life in the dunes. The press had left them alone since the events surrounding the murder, but in late 1923, they found something else to write about them - Paul was again in the public glare. He was arrested for fishing without a license and fined $24.

One week after the new highway opened, Gary's newspaper announced that "Diana of the Dunes and her mate" had fled from their shack, although they had been planning the trip for a while. The couple left the dunes in a 20-foot open boat fashioned from scrap, bound for Texas with near-freezing temperatures in the forecast. They planned a route down the Mississippi River.

Alice and Paul blamed their departure on the encroaching civilization. The dunes region was quickly growing in popularity, and new roads from Chicago brought more tourists and encouraged the building of sturdy, permanent homes in beachfront communities. Their shack was no longer private, and a developer decided it should be torn down. The developer, Samuel Reck, was creating a beachfront community in Ogden Dunes, where "fine suburban homes" would be built. Alice and Paul had been squatting on his property. He was happy to send them on their way to Texas.

The departure from the dunes had been a long time coming. Since the murder accusations, followed by the physical and emotional trauma of her head injury, Alice had lost most of the idealism and spirit that had guided her through earlier tough times. Simply put, she just wasn't herself anymore. It was noticeable to those who knew her and had followed her adventures in the dunes. As one reporter noted, "To the observer who sees Diana these days with the physical eye only, much of the romance in connection with her determination to leave the comforts of home and school and live a lonely life in the hills and vales of northern Indiana has departed."

No one knows why, but Alice and Paul's "escape plan" never worked out. Six months after leaving the Indiana dunes, they returned to Wren's Nest. Fortunately, Samuel Reck had not gotten around to demolishing it as he had planned. He didn't fight them when they moved back in.

Despite the looming construction, Paul's boat-building project, and their subsequent trip away from the dunes, Alice's anger over the news stories that linked her and Paul to the murder two years before had not dissipated. In fact, it had festered. She spent most of the summer engaged in writing, preparing a libel suit against some of the Chicago newspapers that she felt had done the most wrong to her.

After eight years of sensational headlines, on June 10, 1924, Alice finally fought back against the press. With the help of a young attorney, Alice, and Paul filed a libel suit against the Chicago Evening

American Publishing Co. in the U.S. District Court in Hammond, Indiana. The lawsuit stated that the articles in the company's Chicago newspapers contained false and malicious libel and defamatory statements reflecting on the couple's character. It was reported at the time that they sought damages from the publishing company in the amount of $100,000.

But, just as Alice never got the chance to have her say in court against Eugene Frank, she never got the chance to face her newspaper adversaries either - the court case ended abruptly with the death of "Diana of the Dunes."

Bad weather hammered Wren's Nest on Sunday, February 8, 1925. The winds shifted and blew, and the already cold temperatures dropped even further. Rain and snow were predicted for the hours after dark. Ice had formed along the shoreline of Lake Michigan. Amid yet another difficult winter, Alice lay seriously ill in her makeshift bed. She had been confined there for nearly a week, refusing medical treatment. At some point late that night, she slipped into a coma.

Frantic, Paul finally left Alice's side to go for help. He knocked on the bedroom window of developer Samuel Reck, the nearest neighbor with a car, and asked him to fetch a doctor. Reck dressed immediately and went to Gary, where he picked up Dr. DeLong. The sand was so frozen that he drove his car down the beach and took the doctor directly to the shack, saving him the precious time required for trekking across the dunes.

The doctor diagnosed Alice with uremic poisoning caused by kidney failure and treated her with hot water bags and stimulants. Despite his best efforts, she never regained consciousness.

Reck and DeLong returned to Gary for more medicine, but it didn't help. After several more hours of bedside vigil, Alice Mabel

Gray died on the morning of Monday, February 9, just before dawn. She was only 44 years old.

The news spread quickly. Within two days, newspapers across the United States reported her death with variations of the stories printed in dunes-area and Chicago newspapers. The headlines ranged from the straightforward "Diana Dead" to the romantic "Diana of the Dunes is Dead, Dancing in Moonlight on Sands of Shore at End." Even the *New York Times* published a six-paragraph article on Alice's life and death under the headline, "Diana of the Dunes Dies of Privations: Chicago Woman Who Took Up the Primitive Life in 1916 Refused Hospital Aid."

Almost every news account featured two simultaneously tragic and romantic notions. In one example, a headline printed in Syracuse, New York, read, "College Honor Student, Who Led Cave Girl Life, Dies in Giant Mate's Arms." This helped set the foundation for the ghost stories that grew after Alice's death. Her one fervent wish, often expressed to Paul while she was living -- or so he claimed -- was that she wanted to be cremated and her ashes scattered on the majestic sand dune known as Mount Tom, the highest in the region. But cremation was unusual then, expensive, and only available at some inconvenient distance from the dunes. Paul had no money but attempted to follow her wishes by building a funeral pyre on Mount Tom - until Samuel Reck convinced him to let Alice's family take care of the funeral plans. Ultimately, they took over planning the arrangements and refused to allow Alice's body to be cremated.

One local newspaper article bluntly said, "Diana of the Dunes is to be buried quietly and 'horribly respectably' late today from a little undertaking parlor in the sooty city of Gary."

The funeral gained a lot of attention from the public, but predictably, newspaper accounts of it vary wildly. Just one story reported that schoolchildren brought flowers to place on her grave, but the fact that Paul was carrying a gun was consistent in every account.

As her body lay in a parlor in the Williams & Marshall Funeral Home in Gary, a crowd of curious people gathered outside while a smaller group of family and friends sat on benches inside the chapel. Reck sat next to a visibly grieving Paul, who was otherwise alone in the back of the room.

The funeral began at 2:00 p.m. and was presided over by Reverend James Foster, rector of the Christ Episcopalian Church. It was a short service, and Paul joined them as those in attendance made their way forward to see Alice's body before the casket was closed for burial. At the sight of her, he began to wail in grief, drawing the pistol from his pocket and waving it in the air. Two people said he yelled a threat, but everyone else heard something different. What they heard was, "Diana, I'll get that damned newspaperman!"

The pall of accusation had hovered over Alice and Paul for two long years, Alice's "revenge" only stymied by her death. Paul - acutely aware that the news coverage of the 1922 murder had devastated Alice and had broken her spirit and her health - was filled with resentment. To make matters worse, he was frustrated and angry over being unable to fulfill her wish to be cremated in the dunes. As it happened, he didn't see her buried in the Gary cemetery either.

Still waving the gun, Paul pointed it at Chester Dunn, Alice's nephew, who had paid for the funeral and signed the death certificate. Someone called the police. Although sobbing, Paul surrendered passively when officers arrived. He was taken to the Gary police station and held for a short time. Once Alice was laid to rest at Oak Hill Cemetery, Paul was released.

The memory of Alice and their failed plans to leave the dunes region and go to Texas haunted him. He supposed he could go without her but simply couldn't leave. He was literally lost without Alice.

But Reck left him little choice. He liked the man, but Paul had to make some sort of move. Just days after Alice's funeral, he gave Paul a gentle push. He told reporters, "We agreed that a good revenge on the curious would be to burn down the shack and remove all traces of it. When he agreed, I carried out the destruction of the shack at once, having no desire to harbor a wild man on the property."

The death of Alice Gray did not end the public's interest in Paul Wilson. For at least six years after her death, newspapers continued to report on his penchant for thievery, his gun-toting ways, and his marriage - in an actual courthouse, this time - to Henrietta Martindale Hyessa. It was evident to everyone that Alice had provided the stability Paul needed in his life, and he was lost without her.

The Michigan City police first arrested him in the spring of 1926 for shooting at a South Shores conductor after he jumped off the train. The conductor said that Paul was upset because the train was forced to pass through a stop where he had meant to disembark. Paul, who admitted being on the train but denied using his gun, told the police that two men were arguing near the train and they had fired the shots, but no one believed his story. Authorities who looked for Paul after the train episode found him "in the hut of an Indian squaw living in the dunes... about four miles west of Michigan City." The "Indian squaw" was Henrietta Hyessa, a white, Wisconsin-born woman who had inherited dunes property.

Henrietta, like Alice, was another well-educated woman who found Wilson appealing. She was an alumna of Smith College and had also done some graduate work at the University of Chicago in 1915 and 1916. While there, she became with Jens Jensen, a noted landscape architect and Prairie Club member. It was Jensen who inspired her to pursue her family property near the Indiana dunes. She had arrived in the region two years before to inspect it and, in

1924, was listed in a local phone directory as the owner of Solomon's Seal Lodge.

In the year that followed the train incident, Paul and Henrietta experienced several changes and difficulties. Less than a week after Paul's arrest, they were married in the Porter County court clerk's office in Valparaiso on May 1, 1926. At the time, he was out of jail on a $2,000 bond paid in part with money from Henrietta's mortgaged property.

Less than ten months later, on March 14, 1927, Henrietta asked Porter County authorities to arrest Paul and place him under a peace bond because he meant to harm himself and also threatened her life and the life of her daughter, Bonno, a seven-year-old child born out of wedlock to Henrietta. She told the Michigan City police that Paul had become angry when she could not "meet his demands for money." After several days of hiding, the police found Paul at a sanitarium in Michigan City. He had gone to see Henrietta, who was a patient there -- and the reason for that is unknown, but not that surprising -- and he was arrested carrying a .38-caliber revolver.

Earlier that day, at Henrietta's request, a Porter County judge withdrew the bond his wife had posted for his release on the earlier charges. He could not raise additional cash and was held at the Michigan City jail after being arrested at the hospital for carrying a concealed weapon. It was later reported that he ate an entire box of sulphur match heads in an unsuccessful suicide attempt during that first night behind bars.

A week later, on March 21, 1927, Wilson was sentenced to one year in jail.

Less than three years later, on November 17, 1930, he was back in court on burglary charges for seven break-ins, including theft from the Pine Township Farm Bureau. Henrietta again posted bond, and he was released.

By this time, Paul and Henrietta's family had grown, thanks to the birth of two children. No doubt at Paul's insistence, they named their first daughter, born in 1928, Diana. The couple's second daughter, Henrietta, was born in 1929.

Just before the new year in 1930, the Wilsons were devastated by losing their home in an unexplained fire. Luckily, no one was home, but by the time the neighbors arrived on the scene, the fire was out of control, and nothing could be saved. Anything that Paul might have had that once belonged to Alice Gray - books, diaries, or manuscripts - they were undoubtedly destroyed in the blaze.

One week after the fire, Paul was arrested again while still out on bail. This time, the charge was reckless driving in connection to an automobile accident that sent three men who were "badly battered" to the Michigan City hospital. A news report stated that Paul was injured but was arrested anyway. There was no mention as to the extent of his injuries.

On February 5, 1931, Paul was sentenced on the burglary charges and sent to the Indiana State Prison for a term of one to five years. He spent two years in jail and was released on January 26, 1933.

At some time, and for reasons unknown, the Wilson family moved to California. The next time Paul Wilson's name was mentioned in a newspaper story, it was to report his death. The story had a common theme - "An unidentified white man, believed to have been approximately 55 years old, was found dead on the floor of a lonely desert cabin about a mile north of Freeman Junction Sunday afternoon."

The dead man was identified the next day as Paul G. Wilson of Freeman Junction, California. On the death certificate, Paul is listed as a "transient." He died of a ruptured aortic aneurysm on "about

October 25, 1941." Although Henrietta was named as Paul's wife, the record also indicated he was divorced.

Little was known about Paul Wilson's life - and just as little about his death. Much of his existence remains a mystery, with only newspaper reports to go by.

And one such newspaper report about Paul helped to create a mystery that still haunts the Indiana Dunes today - the mystery of Alice's ghost.

One of the first articles written about Paul after Alice's death appeared about two months later, in the early summer of 1925. Shared by newspapers all over the country, the story ran a full page and featured the headline "Haunted by the Spirit of 'Diana of the Dunes.'"

According to the story, Paul sat and waited at the foot of Mount Tom, hoping for the arrival of his beloved Alice as she walked beneath a rising moon. The soft waves of Lake Michigan provided background music for his vigil while an evening breeze brushed across the sand hills. Before long, a ghostly figure appeared, moving from the dune ridge to the water's edge. Garbed in a white, billowy veil, she moaned sorrowfully as she drifted along the beach. The vision was that of Diana, the writer insisted, whether her ghost was real or she was merely a figment of Wilson's imagination. She visited a bereft Paul because he suffered from "the deepest grief a heart may know–the knowledge of a failure to keep faith with a loved one who is dead." He mourned at Mount Tom because he could not cremate her body and spread her ashes from its great height, as he had promised he would do.

What else could Diana do but haunt the dunes she loved so much?

In time, like the stories of Alice Gray as "Diana of the Dunes," the story of her ghost took on a life of its own. Just as their ancestors were fascinated with the stories of the "wild woman" who lived among the dunes, locals in Northern Indiana became enthralled with the stories that her ghost still refuses to rest. For many years, such tales have circulated, stating that "Diana of the Dunes" still swims in the cold waters of Lake Michigan at night and that her naked ghost is still sometimes spotted on the beach near where the old cabin once stood.

Are such stories truth or fiction?

Who can say? We know that Alice's story is as important now as it was in the 1920s. She still represents a part of history that many of us have forgotten about the natural world of the Indiana dunes - the battle to keep civilization from encroaching on the natural world.

Alice's story is also one about the battle she fought within herself. She left Chicago on a journey to rediscover herself in the remote sand dunes of Indiana. Was her journey successful and her motives pure? Perhaps not. Did she disappear because of questions about her own sanity? Was she mentally ill? Was she heartbroken? Or was she merely a formidable woman in a time dominated by men who wanted to prove her mettle by living alone in the wilderness?

The story of Alice's life, her passion and pain -- and the collapse of that life started by her assault and crushed skull - survives as the story of a woman with thwarted dreams but with the dogged determination to survive and not to give in when both man and nature squared off against her.

Alice sought solitude but finally only found the peace she wanted after death - or did she? In her lifetime, she lived on her own terms, accomplished what she set out to do, and lived her life to the extent that she wanted to live it.

Does her ghost remain behind because of something she was unable to accomplish? Perhaps, but more likely - if her ghost really does haunt the beaches of Lake Michigan - she has stayed in our world because she loved her life so fiercely that she has simply refused to let it go.

"THE BATHTUB VICTIM" OCEANA "OCEY" SNEAD

BY AMANDA R. WOOMER

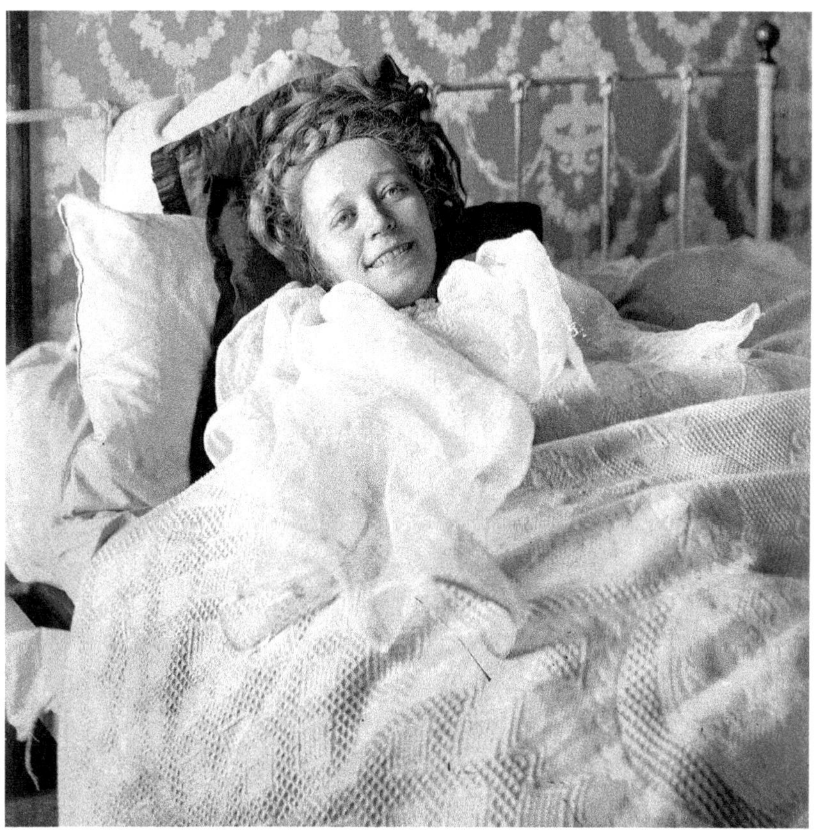

In December 1909, what the newspapers called "the most infamous crime in New Jersey" made headlines after the brutal murder of a young woman.

But it was the story behind the crime that was so baffling - and so chilling. The killers were a trio of women who would come to be called the "Sisters in Black," Their victim was their own flesh and blood -- a 24-year-old woman named Oceana Wardlaw Martin Snead, who had seemingly drowned in a bathtub.

Everyone knew Oceana by the familiar nickname of "Ocey," and her early years were unremarkable -- so unremarkable that we don't know much about her life until her death.

Born on September 20, 1885, likely in New York City, Ocey was part of one of the most respected families in the south, which traced its roots back to before the American Revolution. The honorable Wardlaw family consisted of five children, the most notable -- and intricately entwined -- being Caroline (Wardlaw Martin), Mary (Wardlaw Snead), and Virginia (Wardlaw). Both Caroline and Virginia were educators in New York and the South, though Caroline was eventually removed from her position due to unhinged behavior. Virginia was the headmistress of Soule College in Murfreesboro, Tennessee.

All three of the sisters were considered "queer," according to a former student, and liked to dress all in black, complete with thick black veils that concealed their faces, making it difficult to discern which sister they were addressing.

Ocey was the only daughter of Caroline Belle Wardlaw and a Civil War veteran named Colonel Robert Maxwell Martin, who had fought for the Confederacy. She was the second of two children. Her older brother, Hugh, was born in 1881 and, sadly, died in 1888.

Not much is known about Hugh's untimely death. However, we know he fell down a long flight of stairs when he was only seven. He sustained a number of injuries and eventually succumbed to a brain fever several days later. Caroline received $22,000 since she had thought to take out a life insurance policy just before the boy's death. This policy was worth more than $690,000 by today's standards.

Hugh's tragic death could be considered the beginning of the end for Ocey Snead.

Around 1900, Virginia and her mother were deeded the Montgomery Female Academy in Christiansburg, Virginia. Before this time, Virginia was headmistress of Soule College in Tennessee and worked as a teacher at Montgomery Female Academy in Virginia. Once the school was under Virginia and her mother's control, they renamed it Montgomery Female College, refurbished the dorm rooms, and updated the curriculum. Despite being a spinster, Virginia was extremely successful, happily teaching her students and running both schools with ease. All that changed, though, when her sisters arrived.

Shortly before the deed of Montgomery Female Academy changed hands, Virginia's older sister, Mary, had arrived at Soule College with her sons John, Fletcher, and Albert and began to cause problems. But everything took a turn for the worse when Caroline appeared at the school in 1901.

In January 1901, Colonel Martin died just shy of his 61st birthday, leaving Caroline a widow who needed to tend to her 15-year-old daughter, Ocey. Colonel Martin's will had left Ocey with $100,000, though it quickly disappeared once she and Caroline moved to Tennessee. Caroline was, given $10,000 from his life insurance policy.

Caroline arrived at the school and quickly took over Virginia's role as headmistress, making rash decisions that would eventually drive her and her sisters from Soule College.

Ocey was enrolled at the school and was described by her fellow students as "odd." Some historians believe that Ocey had inherited the peculiarities shown by her mother and aunts. Others think she was the victim of the three sisters' abuse her entire life, leading her to ostracize herself from others and keep to herself.

By 1903, Caroline, Mary, and Virginia were asked to leave Soule College. Together, the three traveled to be with their mother in Christiansburg and took over the Montgomery Female College. Without discussing anything with Virginia or their mother, Caroline changed the curriculum and moved students to different classrooms without any logical explanation. She also raised suspicion among the students and staff when she began locking some of the doors with three padlocks.

This time, Ocey did not enroll in school but decided to live with Mary. Clearly, she still did not fit in with other girls her age. Whatever the reason may be as to why Ocey was seen as strange among her classmates, the behavior of her mother and aunts certainly did not help her assimilate with the other young ladies of the school.

There were whispers among the students about the three older women – dressed head to toe in black gowns, capes, and veils – roaming the halls silently in the middle of the night like phantoms. Some students claimed to have awoken at night to find the three sisters standing around their bed, chanting. Rumors even spread to the town, claiming the three sisters were conducting secret rituals in the nearby Sunset Cemetery at the grave of their brother, John.

By 1906, Ocey was 21 years old and still an outsider among the girls at the school. The Montgomery Female College was starting to fall into disrepair, teachers were leaving, and the three sisters had gotten a bad reputation within the community.

Desperate to keep their business going, Caroline sought out her oldest nephew, John B. Wardlaw Snead, and insisted that he teach at the school. However, John's wife, Anna, begged him not to leave her and their two-year-old son. For a short time, John refused his aunt and even called the police to escort her from his house. However, it seems Caroline, and her two sisters, had an inexplicable power over the other members of their family, and a few weeks later, she returned, and John left with her.

For several months, Anna held onto the hope that John would return to his family and sent him letters, begging him to do so. But there was little hope of him breaking the spell his mother and aunts had on him, and he never returned home. Eventually, Anna was placed in a sanitarium, and their son, John B. Wardlaw Snead, Jr., died at just 18 years old.

John's time at the Montgomery Female College with the three sisters was anything but a happy family reunion. Desperate to return to his family but unable to break away from the control of his mother and aunts, John's spirits quickly dwindled. There are reports that he tried to commit suicide multiple times in the few months he was in their company.

While on a train with Caroline, he fell off the train car. When questioned, Caroline -- and even John himself -- insisted it was an accident. However, the brakeman who had witnessed it all was confident that he had just seen a suicide attempt.

Shortly after falling from the train, John was found inside an open cistern and rescued just in time. Virginia explained that he had been measuring the water supply for the school when he must have slipped in.

Less than a week later, tragedy struck the Wardlaw family once again in the early morning hours of March 3, 1906.

It's said that around 8:00 a.m., John was trying to light the fireplace in his room from the oil of his lamp. Some lamp oil must have fallen onto his clothes, immediately igniting. John began screaming and thrashing around on the ground, summoning Virginia, who raised the alarm. The doctor was called and did everything he could to ease John's pain, but by 2:00 that afternoon, John had succumbed to first-degree burns.

The three sisters insisted it was an accident and not another suicide attempt. If it had been deemed a suicide, the insurance company might have been able to refuse to pay out John's $12,000 policy. Luckily for his mother and aunts, John's death was determined an accident, and they -- not his wife -- were given the large amount of money for this life.

Around this time, John's younger brother, Fletcher Wardlaw Snead, was married to Vashti Gordan McLaurine, the sister of John's wife, Anna. The couple lived in Giles, Tennessee, about 500 miles away from the three sisters' school in Christiansburg. One day, Caroline Martin arrived on Fletcher's doorstep, insisting he come with her. When he asked her what the problem was, she told him there were some issues with the family property. Without asking any more questions, Fletcher promptly left with his aunt, leaving behind Vashti and their six-year-old son, Robert.

According to reports, Caroline and Fletcher stopped in Chattanooga because Fletcher had fallen ill. When Vashti heard her husband was sick, she traveled nearly 150 miles to be with him. But when she arrived at the boarding house, Caroline refused to let her in to see her husband. Vashti returned home but refused to stay away. She soon traveled back to Chattanooga with the intent to be with her husband, but by the time she arrived, she learned that Fletcher was gone – he had been moved from boarding house to boarding house all over the area, and then he and his aunt had left. No doubt heartbroken, Vashti returned to Giles County. Eventually, she would file for a divorce.

Within that same year, Fletcher and Ocey would be married. And that's when things get strange - according to Fletcher, he and Ocey were married no less than three times!

The first wedding was secretly held in 1906 with just the two of them while in Cincinnati, Ohio. They were afraid that because Fletcher had already been married once before, the three sisters would not approve of Ocey marrying him.

The second wedding occurred in Murfreesboro, Tennessee, after the family had discovered the young couple's relationship. Once Caroline (Ocey's mother), Mary (Fletcher's mother), and Virginia were convinced, the couple held a ceremony surrounded by friends and family.

The third wedding occurred in January 1908 when the couple moved north to New York City. Since they were first cousins, they wanted to ensure their marriage was still legal, so they conducted a third and final ceremony.

Ocey welcomed her first child with Fletcher – a little girl named Mary Alberta – on February 9, 1908. Sadly, tragedy would continue to haunt the Wardlaw family, and little Mary Alberta died just a few days later on February 12.

Several months after Ocey and Fletcher left for New York, the three sisters followed. By 1908, the school they had been running had fallen into ruin, they were out of money, and they believed they could find their fortune in New York with Fletcher and Ocey -- and they weren't entirely wrong.

In March 1909, while Ocey was pregnant with their second child, Fletcher lost his job and left New York without any explanation. No reasons were ever given, and even after Ocey's death made headlines, Fletcher claimed that he left his pregnant wife for "strictly personal reasons." Eventually, he would be found in St. Catherines, Ontario, where he lived under an alias. Some believe that Fletcher realized that he was worth more dead than alive with a $24,000 life insurance policy, so he left the family, making it appear as if he was dead. However, when the three sisters went to cash in his policy, the insurance company refused because there was no evidence of Fletcher's death.

Five months pregnant, abandoned by her husband, and left in the care of three peculiar and controlling women, it's said that Ocey fell ill. During her pregnancy, Dr. William R. Pettit tended to her. He insisted she suffered from depression, "general weakness," and malnutrition. He ordered that the sisters provide Ocey with fresh air, a restorative diet, and medicine to sustain both Ocey and her unborn child, and yet, every time he visited them, he found his orders for Ocey's care were not being followed. The young woman continued to grow weaker.

Dr. Pettit's patience was growing thin with the three sisters – they weren't cooperating with him, nor were they paying him for his work.

In the summer of 1909, a neighbor named Ethel Moore came to help assist Ocey in her labor. According to Ethel, Ocey appeared weak, and when the three sisters were out of the room, Ocey confided to her friend that her mother and aunts were trying to starve her to death. Whenever they returned to the room and sensed Ocey's suspicion, they would drug her to silence her.

David Pollock Snead was born on August 2, 1909, but the child was sickly and malnourished. The three sisters took the boy from Ocey and quickly brought him to St. Christopher's Hospital in Brooklyn. Eventually, he would be sent to a nearby orphanage, dying just 11 months later.

The sisters quickly replaced Dr. Pettit with a second physician, Dr. Cornelius R. Love. He simply considered Ocey to be recovering from childbirth and diagnosed her with anemia and "general run down." He prescribed her eggs and milk and left believing she would fully recover. However, when he returned to check on Ocey again, he found her dazed and accused the women of drugging her.

As Ocey continued to recover from childbirth, Dr. Love returned secretly to check on her well-being. Sneaking in through a window, Love tried to give Ocey some food, but Virginia walked in on him in Ocey's room and immediately threw Love out of the house. Dr. Love promptly went to a lawyer to try and help Ocey, only to be told that nothing could be done.

Several months later, the three sisters called on Dr. Pettit once more, bringing him back to their home to check on Ocey. There were two things the doctor noticed from the last time he had seen Ocey Snead -- she was no longer pregnant, though there was no baby in the household, and she was even weaker than before.

Virginia went to Pettit and ordered him to tell Ocey that she was dying and that she should make a will. Instead, Pettit brought in a nurse to care for Ocey and help bring her back to health. Not surprisingly, the nurse lasted for just one day before she, too, was thrown out by the sisters.

When Pettit approached the three sisters about the $100 bill still owed to him, they offered him $1,000 in Ocey's will in exchange. Pettit refused and decided to go to the police.

Ocey's doctor was convinced that she was somehow hypnotized by Virginia, what he called "some hypnotic influence." She was clearly drugged with what he believed to be opium or chloroform, though it would later be revealed it was morphine, initially to help Ocey with post-partum pain. When Pettit spoke with the police, he told them, "She (Ocey) seemed depressed and indeed afraid of those about her."

Shortly after reporting the three sisters to the police, Dr. Pettit returned to the family home to check on Ocey one more time. He found an abandoned house. All four women were gone.

The three sisters moved Ocey to a small house in the Flatlands neighborhood in Brooklyn in September 1909. The neighbors would eventually call the place the "house of mystery."

One day, Virginia, dressed in her signature gown and veil, visited the office of New York City attorney, Julian T. Carabba, asking if he could help a dying woman amend her last will. Carabba refused to change anything in the will without Ocey's written consent, so Virginia allowed him to visit Ocey for the update. As he tried to work with Ocey, who was all but 80 pounds at this time, he noticed the three sisters standing around the bed, chanting and praying as if Ocey had already died. Carabba insisted that Ocey didn't need a lawyer but a doctor and some food. The women claimed that they couldn't afford either of those things. Carabba was quick to help. He offered to write the three sisters a check for some food for Ocey. For the first time since he arrived, the sisters left the room searching for a pen.

The moment the three sisters left the room, Ocey spoke. She told Carabba in a weak, raspy voice that she knew she was dying. Ocey was convinced that Virginia was somehow hypnotizing her. She quickly pulled a piece of paper out from under her pillow. It was her actual will. In it, she left everything to her grandmother, named Carabba the executor of the estate, and begged him to take care of her son, David. That was the last time Carabba would see Ocey Snead.

As Carabba left Ocey's room, the three sisters offered him two of Ocey's life insurance policies worth $7,000 to make them the beneficiaries of Ocey's estate and not their mother. Carabba refused – no doubt Ocey's will was weighing heavily in his pocket – as the sisters walked him out of the house. They never contacted him again, and when he tried to visit Ocey, she had once again vanished.

The three sisters would appear once more, but this time in East Orange, New Jersey. On November 14, Virginia picked up the keys to a small house at 89 East 14th Street. It was later noted that Virginia specifically asked the realtor about the size of the bathtub.

A detail that was later revealed to the police.

Caroline, Mary, and Virginia moved into the house and brought Ocey with them, though it could barely be considered a home. There was no heat and no gas to cook on the stove. There were no curtains on the windows, and the paint on the façade was chipping. The furniture consisted of one cot, a rug, one chair whose missing legs had been replaced by a soap box, and a barrel that acted as a table. The only food in the house was oranges, cereal, and some evaporated milk.

It was November 24, the night before Thanksgiving, when Dr. Charles E. Teeter was summoned to the house in East Orange by Virginia to provide a certificate of health. At first, the doctor insisted on coming the following day because it was late at night. However, Virginia was insistent, and Teeter eventually gave in. When he arrived at the house, he examined Ocey and assured her that she was thin from malnourishment and prone to bronchitis but otherwise in good health. Once she began getting something substantial to eat, she would be just fine. He signed off on her certificate of good health and left.

From November 27 until November 29, Virginia was supposedly the only one in the house with Ocey –something that would come back to haunt her once the police became involved.

One witness at the trial admitted to seeing a "mysterious-looking woman dressed in black" visit the home the day before Ocey was found. Many believe this mystery woman was Ocey's very own mother. Other witnesses reported that on November 28, the second floor was illuminated, and they could see people moving around. This was a rarity because the house was usually dark and quiet.

No one knows for sure what happened on the second floor of 89 East 14th Street on November 29.

That Monday, around 4:30 p.m., Virginia Wardlaw called the police, asking for the local coroner. When the police informed her that there was no county coroner, she told them there had been an accident in her home. The police sent deputy county physician Dr. Herbert M. Simmons to the family home, and he was quickly led upstairs through the cold, dark house to the only bathroom.

Ocey's naked body was lying in the tub. Her head tilted slightly under the faucet. While the bathtub was not full – reports claim that there was only a foot of water or just enough to cover her nostrils – it appeared to be a relatively simple case of suicide. Her nightgown was placed on the floor next to the tub with a suicide note pinned to it. The note read:

Last year my little daughter died. Other near and dear kindred, too, have gone to Heaven. I long to go there too. I have been ill and weak a very long time now. Death will be a blessed relief to me in my sufferings. When you read this, I will have committed suicide. My sorrow and pain in this world are greater than I can endure.

Ocey W.M. Snead

Under most circumstances, a case like this would be quickly closed. However, Dr. Simmons was immediately suspicious of Virginia and promptly called the police to join him at the scene of what he considered a crime.

Simmons noted that the state of Ocey's body revealed that she had been dead for over 24 hours. This was the only bathroom in the entire house -- surely Virginia would have found the body and called the police sooner?

Virginia insisted that she knew Ocey was suicidal, and the young woman had asked to be left alone on the second floor, so Virginia had respected her wishes. It was also noted that Ocey had been depressed and suicidal since her husband, Fletcher, left. Virginia went so far as to claim that Fletcher was dead and buried next to his daughter in Mount Hope Cemetery, which could very easily be disproved. She insisted that Ocey had "suicide mania" and was slowly "grieving herself to death." However, the ten life insurance policies taken out on Ocey's life, adding up to $32,000 -- over $1 million today -- were enough to convince the police they were right to suspect foul play.

Virginia Wardlaw was arrested the following day since she was the only one in the house when Ocey died.

The insurance companies were slow to pay the $32,000 on Ocey's life, arguing that the body found in the bathtub was not that of Oceana Snead. However, the body was positively identified by two individuals -- the doctor who had helped deliver Mary Alberta and an older woman who had taught Ocey while she was at Soule College.

A chemical expert named Dr. William H. Hicks examined Ocey's stomach and found evidence of poison. Another doctor named Maitland also examined her brain and found no evidence of a concussion. The official cause of death was drowning, with starvation as a contributing factor, though she was also diagnosed posthumously with neurasthenia -- fatigue and irritability -- from both hypnosis and starvation.

Ocey Snead was buried on December 7, 1909, in Mount Hope Cemetery next to her father, who was now suspected of being poisoned by his wife for his insurance policy, her brother, Hugh, who many now believed was pushed down the stairs by his mother, and her daughter. Little David would join them the following year.

Caroline Wardlaw Martin did not attend her daughter's funeral, although her aunt and mother-in-law, Mary, were there.

As for Ocey, although she was finally free of the three sisters and their torture, her story was far from over.

One the day of Ocey's funeral, Mayor Cardwell of East Orange called for Caroline's arrest. She was finally found on December 15, hiding at Hotel Bayard, a cheap hotel in New York, with more than 50 damning notes and papers, including multiple insurance policies, letters Ocey had written to Fletcher that were never sent, letters from Fletcher to Ocey that had been intercepted, and three suicide notes that looked strangely similar to Ocey's own note. According to reports, when the police arrived at Caroline's room, she collapsed, and it took some time before she could start making her way to the police station.

The following day, Mary was arrested, and Fletcher was found.

All three women were indicted on December 22, 1909, with three different charges:

1. Caroline and Mary threw Ocey into the tub of water, choked, suffocated, and drowned her.

2. Caroline and Mary paid Virginia to kill Ocey.

3. All three sisters aided Ocey in suicide.

This final charge ensured that the sisters would be held responsible one way or another – if not for murder, then for assisting suicide.

It didn't take long for the story of the "Bathtub Murder" to make the front page of newspapers nationwide. Rumors spread that the bones of a baby had been found in the family stove in Brooklyn. Some newspapers reported that as many as 50 forged suicide notes had been found in Caroline's possession. The public was obsessed with the suicide note written in black ink, yet the police never found paper or pens inside the East Orange house. The audacity of the crime and the ghoulishness that a mother could do this to her own child captivated audiences.

Then, in May 1910, the trial began.

The prosecution considered this a "devilishly planned murder" and stated that the three sisters were "insurance mad." They believed Caroline was the instigator, and Mary and Virginia followed along. The prosecutors - and much of the public- thought that Caroline didn't just kill Ocey for her insurance money but her husband, son, and even her nephew John, too. It was revealed that the three sisters had dowsed John's clothes in lamp oil before setting him on fire.

Much of their evidence was circumstantial – suspicions of previous murders, the multiple life insurance policies taken out on Ocey, and the family's treatment of Ocey before her death.

Everything hinged on the suicide note pinned to Ocey's clothes. The state believed it was a forgery. According to reports, the note's writing was strong and firm despite Ocey being weak and emaciated. While the three sisters only ever wrote one letter while imprisoned, the prosecution could compare the writing from Ocey's letters to Fletcher, which did not match. William J. Kinsley, a handwriting expert, was called in to testify. He claimed that two people had written the suicide note – the message itself and the signature were written by two different people, and neither matched Ocey's letters to her husband.

The prosecution called 15 witnesses to the stand, including detectives, neighbors, Dr. Teeter, who had seen Ocey just a few days before her death, the deputy county physician, Dr. Herbert, and Kinsley, the handwriting expert.

The defense tried to paint Ocey as a "dope fiend" addicted to morphine. According to Caroline's defense, Ocey had been in extreme pain on Sunday, November 28. To help, Caroline had given her morphine, the poison that would appear in her autopsy, but she accidentally gave Ocey too much. In the hopes of reviving her daughter, Caroline filled the tub with cold water. Ocey died shortly after being placed in the tub, and in a panic, Caroline forged the suicide note. The defense also claimed that some of the notes found at Hotel Bayard and the house of mystery pointed toward a possible suicide pact among the family – particularly Ocey, Fletcher, Caroline, Mary, and Virginia.

But it didn't matter what the defense said. In the eyes of the judge, jury, and public, Ocey Snead had been a victim of physical, mental, and emotional abuse.

Virginia Wardlaw wouldn't live to hear the verdict from her trial. She starved herself to death while in prison and died on August 11, 1910.

Mary was released on a technicality, left New Jersey for Colorado, and eventually settled in California, where she lived with her youngest son, Albert.

Caroline pleaded guilty to manslaughter and was sentenced to seven years in prison. When she heard her sentence, reports claimed she cried, "I do not deserve it!" She was carried from the courtroom, still in her chair, screaming. She was first sent to prison before being transferred to the New Jersey State Lunatic Asylum, where she spent the rest of her days until she died in 1913.

It would seem that with Caroline locked away and dead soon after, justice for Ocey was served. And yet, throughout the trial and into Caroline's imprisonment, her family members continued to defend her and claim that she was innocent of murdering her daughter for money.

Some family members, including Caroline's younger sister, Bessie Gertrude Wardlaw, and younger brother, Albert Goodall Wardlaw, petitioned the court to consider Caroline's diagnosed insanity when sentencing her. It was revealed that Caroline had spent some time in a sanitarium in Christiansburg, and Virginia had spent years trying to get her deemed insane.

Other members of the family – particularly Albert and Fletcher Snead – continued to defend all three of the sisters even when they were accused of murdering John Wardlaw Snead, their brother, and Ocey, their wife and sister-in-law.

Shortly after Ocey's death was announced in the papers, reporters asked Fletcher if he would return to the United States. He refused "unless requested to do so by his mother and aunts." Albert declared that there was no way his mother and her sisters could do such a horrific crime, even after Caroline pleaded guilty and was sent to prison. According to contemporary newspapers, Albert claimed Virginia was "as innocent and pure a woman as ever lived." Fletcher was adamant for years that Ocey's death was not a murder. And even as evidence was revealed exposing that Caroline and her sisters also may have had a hand in murdering John Wardlaw Snead, Colonel Robert Maxwell Martin, and Hugh Martin for their insurance money, the men stood by their side. They defended their honor -- until the bitter end.

Whatever hold the sisters had over them, it seems to have continued from beyond the grave. The three sisters dressed all in black, haunted the Wardlaw family as reminders of the horrors they committed and the spell the family continued to be kept under.

The story of the Sisters in Black and Ocey Snead, the "Bathtub Murder Victim," would continue to haunt America for years as new evidence and reports came to light.

Like so many stories sensationalized by the newspapers, it's easy to focus on the peculiarities of the sister in black and their wicked ways and not the victim – a young woman named Oceana with long auburn hair, who was once shy and beautiful before being reduced to an 80-pound skeleton, her pale skin pulled tight over her bones, floating in a bathtub with her knotted hair fanning out around her in the water.

We'll never know what Ocey thought as she was placed in the bathtub – was she ready to die, hoping for relief from the torment her mother and aunts brought on?

Or did she fight back, hoping to live out her days with little David?

And what prompted a mother to murder her own daughter all for the sake of the almighty dollar?

It's a question the public asked for years following this tragedy, and we still don't know over a century later.

"L.A.'S SLAIN ANGEL"
MARION PARKER
BY AMANDA R. WOOMER

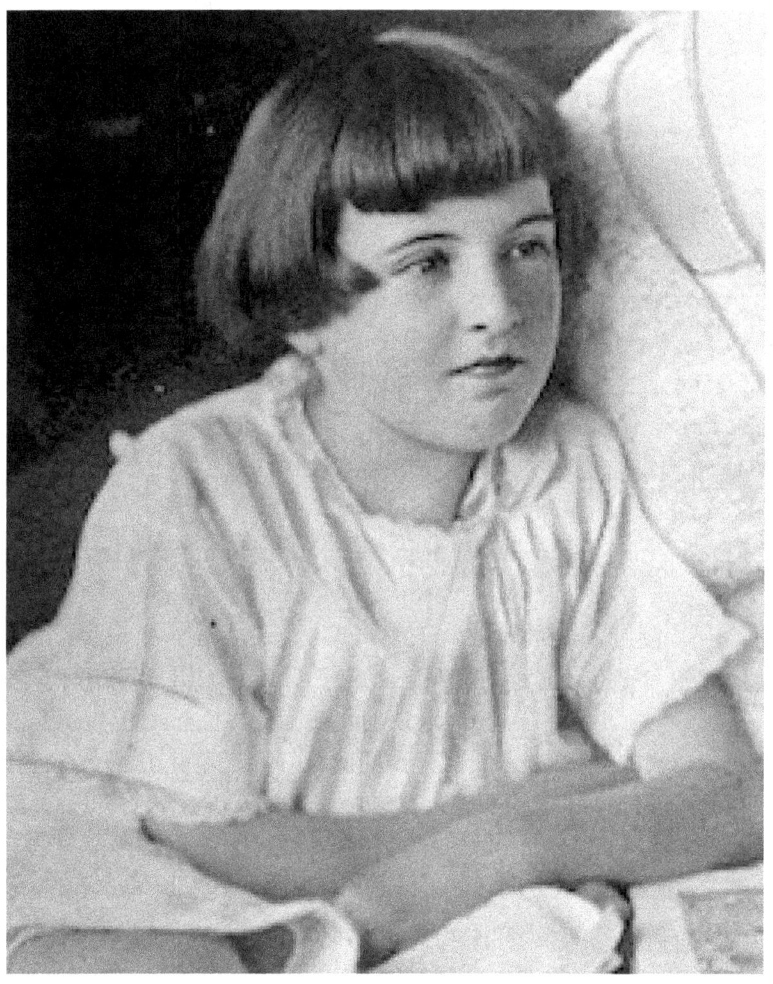

The story of Marion Parker is not for the faint at heart.

It's a story of abduction, ransom money, murder, and horror. When 12-year-old Marion was returned to her family on December 17, 1927, the ferocity of her murder made headlines across the continent. And yet, only five years later, another child was abducted for ransom –Charles Lindbergh Jr., son of the famed aviator – and Marion was overshadowed and somehow forgotten, seemingly lost to history.

Frances Marion Parker was born at 2:30 p.m. on October 11, 1915, just 10 minutes after her twin sister, Marjorie. Her parents were Perry Marion and Geraldine Parker. Perry worked at the First National Bank of Los Angeles, and the family enjoyed a comfortable life in the new up-and-coming neighborhood at 1631 South Wilton Place. The twins' older brother, Perry Willard, was almost eight years older than the twin girls. The family also had a dog named Patsy. Perry Parker described his daughter, Marion, as a tomboy focused on her family and schoolwork. But she was also a nervous child who disliked being out after dark.

Like so many murder victims, not much is known about Marion's early life – her parents weren't wealthy or famous, and so the everyday life that the family of five lived was unremarkable.

But all that changed on Thursday, December 15, 1927.

It was just ten days before Christmas, and there was no doubt a buzz of excitement among the students. Marion and Marjorie, now 12 years old, lived about a mile from Mount Vernon Junior High School. Donning a light patterned dress, tan stockings, and a pair of oxfords, Marion boarded a streetcar with her sister that would take them down Venice Boulevard toward the school. That morning several students, including Marjorie, claimed to see a mysterious man in a dark suit lurking around the school, but when they finally told authorities, it was too late.

Shortly after noon, a nicely dressed young man confidently entered the school's office. He was tall and thin, with dark wavy hair, wearing a suit and a nice pair of shoes. When the registrar, Mrs. Mary Holt, asked him if she could help him, the young man informed her that he worked at the First National Bank with Perry Parker. He told the woman that Perry had been in an automobile accident and wished to see his daughter.

To Mary Holt, this must have been a strange request – she knew that Mr. Parker had two daughters enrolled at the school – so she asked suspiciously, "Which one?"

"The younger daughter," the young man replied.

Although the girls were twins, Marion was technically younger by a few minutes, so another teacher, Miss Naomi Britton, summoned Marion to the office. While they waited for Marion to arrive, the stranger suggested that Mrs. Holt call the bank to confirm his story. She declined. Later, when questioned, she claimed she "never would have let Marion go but for the apparent sincerity and disarming manner of the man."

Marion arrived at the office, and although she did not recognize the man standing before her, she placed her hand in his, and the two walked out of the building and climbed into his blue Chrysler coupe before disappearing down the road.

As the final bell rang at school, Marjorie stood outside waiting for her sister. The minutes ticked by, and finally, Marjorie boarded the streetcar and headed home.

When she arrived, the Parkers greeted their daughter and wondered where Marion was – they knew she was nervous about traveling on the streetcar alone. Their unease turned to fear as night fell. Around 4:45 p.m., Perry called the school to see if Marion was still there, perhaps helping a teacher. When Mrs. Holt asked Parker how he was doing after the accident, he feared the worst. He quickly called the police to report his little girl as missing when a telegram arrived around 6:20 p.m. that read:

Do positively nothing till you receive special delivery letter.
-Marian (sic) Parker

It wasn't long before a second telegram arrived on the Parker's doorstep, this time stating:

Marian (sic) secure. Use good judgment. Interference with my plans
.3412dangerous.
-Marian (sic) Parker
George, Fox

The police immediately jumped into action. They got a description of Marion – four feet, six inches tall, about 100 pounds, with straight dark hair cut into a bob. The police also managed to get a description of the kidnapper from Mary Holt and Naomi Britton – white, tall, slender, about five feet, eight inches tall, 150 pounds, with dark wavy hair, and 25 to 30 years old.

These descriptions were sent out to police stations across California, and the words FIND THE GIRL were placed on all police bulletins. It was more important to rescue Marion than catch her kidnapper.

Late that night, the special delivery letter finally arrived at the Parker's home, and it was a ransom note:

P.M. Parker:

Use good judgment. You are the loser. Do this. Secure 75-$20 gold certificates-U.S. Currency–1500 dollars–at once. Keep them on your person. Go about your daily business as usual. Leave out police and detectives. Make no public notice. Keep this affair private. Make no search.

Fulfilling these terms with the transfer of the currency will ensure the return of the girl.

Failure to comply with these requests means no one will ever see the girl again except the angels in heaven.

The affair must end one way or the other within 3 days. 72 hours.

You will receive further notice, but the terms remain the same.

FATE

If you want aid against me, ask God, not man.

Included with the ransom note was a handwritten letter from Marion, revealing that she was still alive. It read:

Dear Daddy and Mother:

I wish I could come home.

I think I'll die if I have to be like this much longer.

Won't someone tell me why all this has to happen to me.

Daddy please do what the man tells your (sic) or he'll kill me if you don't.

Your loving daughter,

Marion Parker

P.S. Please Daddy. I want to come home tonight.

The kidnapper clearly ordered the Parkers to keep the police out of the affair, but by the time his warning reached the family, it was too late. Parker and the LAPD decided to continue to work together, keeping the kidnapping from the press in the hopes of hiding this fact from the assailant.

Parker had taken Thursday from work to celebrate his 40th birthday with Geraldine. The following day -- Friday, December 16 -- he returned to work, no doubt following the mysterious kidnapper's orders to "go about your daily business as usual." He also quickly gathered the $1,500 ransom -- about $25,000 today -- in the form of gold certificates and had the foresight to record each serial number so the certificates could be traced if ever used.

By the time Perry Parker returned home from work, there was still no word from "Fate," but all that changed around 8:00 p.m. when the telephone rang.

A man's voice on the other end of the phone ordered Parker to take the $1,500 and meet him at the corner of 10th Street and Gramercy Place, where he could exchange the money for his daughter.

Parker immediately jumped into his car and drove the short distance to the meeting place. As he parked his vehicle and dimmed his lights, he waited, peering into each passing car, no doubt searching for his little girl. He waited for hours, but no one ever appeared.

Sick to his stomach and wondering what had gone wrong, Parker learned that the police had followed him to the rendezvous point. Undoubtedly, the kidnapper spotted the multiple police officers and knew better than to reveal himself.

At this point, word leaked to the press, and Marion's kidnapping made the front page of the *Los Angeles Times* on Saturday, December 17, 1927.

With the public now aware of Marion's disappearance, it's said that up to 200,000 people aided the police in the search, including officers around the state, American Legion volunteers, and even local school children.

No doubt, Marion's kidnapper was starting to feel the pressure. On Saturday morning, a second special delivery letter arrived at 1631 South Wilton Place with two letters inside. The first was a furious note written by the kidnapper, threatening to kill Marion after seeing the police the night before. The second was another handwritten note from Marion:

Dear Daddy and Mother:

Daddy please don't bring anyone with you today. I'm sorry for what happened last night. We drove wright (sic) by the house and I cryed (sic) all the time last night. If you don't meet us this morning you'll never see me again.

Love to all,

Marion Parker

P.S. Please Daddy:

I want to come home this morning.

This is your last chance be sure and come by yourself. Or you won't see me again, Marion.

After the scathing letter from Marion's kidnapper, Parker confronted the police, insisting that he follow his daughter's wishes and meet the assailant alone. He knew he couldn't afford another unsuccessful ransom exchange -- his daughter's life depended on it.

Later that same day, another special delivery arrived at the house, again with two letters:

P.M. Parker,

Please recover your senses. I want your money rather than to kill your child. But so far you give me no other alternative.

Of course you want your child but you'll never get her by notifying the police and causing all this publicity. I feel however, that you started the search before you received my warning, so I am not blaming you for the bad beginning.

Remember the three day limit and make up for this lost time. Dismiss all the authorities before it is too late. I'll give you one more chance. Get that money the way I told you and be ready to settle.

I'll give you a chance to come across and you will or Marian (sic) dies.

Be sensible and use good judgment. You can't deal with a mastermind like a common crook or kidnapper.

Fox-Fate

If you want aid against me, ask God, not man.

Sadly, the second note was not from Marion, as the other two special delivery letters had included. Instead, it was another letter from the kidnapper, which did not bode well:

M. Parker:

Fox is my name. Very sly you know. Set no trap. I'll watch for them.

All the inside guys, even your neighbor Isadore B., know that when you play with fire there is cause for burns. Not W.J. Burns and his shadowers either–remember that.

Get this straight: your daughter's life hangs by a thread and I have a Gillette ready and able to handle the situation.

This is business. Do you want the girl or the 75-$100 gold certificates U.S. currency? You can't have both and there's no other *way out. Believe this, and act accordingly. Before the day's over I'll find out how you stand.*

I am doing a solo so figure on meeting the terms of Mr. Fox or else.

Fate

If you want aid against me, ask God, not man.

It is uncertain if the kidnapper had increased the ransom to $7,500 or if he made an error and accidentally replaced $20 bills with $100 bills in his latest note, but either way, it was clear that Marion was in grave danger.

The Fox - as the kidnapper now referred to himself - had warned the Parkers that they had 72 hours to get him the money. The deadline was the following day, December 18th. Time was running out, and Parker knew it.

One last letter was delivered in the early evening of Saturday, December 17, declaring the "final chance terms." According to the LAPD, it was written by an educated individual, despite their inability to number their demands properly:

FINAL CHANCE TERMS

1. Have $1500= 75-20 dollar gold certificates-U.S. currency.

2. Come alone and have no other one following or knowing the place of meeting.

4. Bring no weapons of any kind.

3. Come in the Essex Coach License number-544-995 | Stay in the car.

———— . ————

If I call, your girl will still be living. When you go to the place of meeting you will have a chance to see her. Then without a second's hesitation, you must hand over the money. (The slightest pause or misbehavior on your part at this moment will be tragic)

Seeing your daughter and transferring the currency will take only a moment. My car will then move slowly away from yours for about a block. You wait and when I stop, I will let the girl out. Then come and get her while I drive away–and I won't go slow this time. Don't attempt to follow when you get the girl.

Be sure and wait till my car pulls up ahead and stops and you see me pull the girl out before you start up. Don't act excited or think I will run away with Marian (sic).

I will do as I say–and I hope to God you will have sense enough to do exactly as I have said.

Well, it's not to worry me if you blunder again. I have certainly done my part to warn and advise you.

Fate-Fox

Around 7:30 p.m., Perry Parker received a phone call, and a familiar voice informed him of their new meeting point: the corner of West 5th Street and South Manhattan Place. He was to leave immediately with the money, park his car, and wait – the kidnapper knew his car, as noted in the final ransom letter.

Parker arrived at South Manhattan Place around 8:00 p.m. and was immediately confronted by the kidnapper as a blue Chrysler coupe pulled up next to him. The driver wore a bandana across his face to hide his identity and pointed a sawed-off shotgun at Parker.

From where he sat in his car, Parker could see Marion sitting in the seat. He called out to her, but she didn't respond even though he could see that her eyes were open. For a moment, he assumed the girl had been drugged.

Parker quickly handed the money to the stranger, and just like his final letter said, the kidnapper put his coupe into gear and slowly began to drive down the road. At 432 South Manhattan Place, he stopped, muttered, "Here's your daughter," and tossed the girl from the car before driving into the night.

Parker ran to his daughter, relief washing over his body momentarily as he fell to the ground beside her. But as he held his little girl in his arms, he immediately knew that something was horribly wrong. Marion felt much smaller than she should, her face was ghostly white, and her skin was cold to the touch.

To her father's horror, Marion Parker was dead and mutilated.

In the dim light, Parker found that he held only the torso of his precious daughter – her arms had been cut off at the elbows, and her body had been sawed in half at the waist. Her torso had been stuffed with rags, newspapers, towels, and a man's shirt. A wire was wrapped tightly around her neck and over her head to keep it upright, and her eyes had been sewn open with coarse black thread.

As Parker cradled the maimed body of his youngest child, he cried out, "My god! Look at my little girl!"

His screams alerted the neighborhood, and the police were quickly telephoned.

The autopsy on Marion Parker was performed at 9:00 p.m. by A.F. Wagner – the Parker's next-door neighbor who had watched Marion grow up over the last few years. Marion's official cause of death was "murder with exterior mutilation of its body." The autopsy brought Wagner to tears; he described it as the most horrible mutilation he had ever seen.

A theory suggested that Marion died "from fright" as her abductor was choking her and not from strangulation – her lungs, heart, and eyes did not show signs of asphyxiation. Wagner suggested she may have died from fright and exhaustion as her stomach showed signs of malnourishment. He believed that Marion didn't eat or sleep once she realized her situation. No matter how she died, it was determined that Marion had been dead for nearly 12 hours – most likely killed shortly after writing her second note to her parents.

Marion was only 12 years, two months, and six days old when she was killed.

The following morning, pieces of the grisly puzzle continued to fall into place. First, the police tracked down the Chrysler coupe to a public parking garage and held a stakeout, waiting for the owner to return.

A man was walking through Elysian Park -- now home to Dodgers Stadium -- when he found several bundles of newspapers. When he opened up the parcels, he found a pair of tiny arms severed at the elbows and two little legs. A short while later, a couple of boys found the final bundle containing Marion from her waist to her knees.

Near 432 South Manhattan Place, a woman found a suitcase. In it, there was a towel, bloody newspapers, a notebook, and black thread that matched the thread that had stitched Marion's eyelids to her brow.

With these three leads, police were able to obtain several clues -- the first was a series of fingerprints taken from the car that matched the prints on the ransom letters. If the killer had been arrested in the past, it would be easy to find a match and learn his identity. The second clue was the towel from the suitcase with a label that said "Bellevue Arms Apartments."

The police quickly headed to the apartment building only four miles away and interviewed the residents.

On Monday, December 19, the Parker family gathered around a closed casket for a private funeral service in the Little Church of the

Flowers at Forest Lawn Memorial Park in Glendale. Marion's remains would be cremated and placed inside the Great Mausoleum. Perry, Geraldine, Perry Willard, and Marjorie were finally able to say goodbye to the youngest Parker, but their nightmare was far from over.

At this point, the police had a match on the fingerprints and knew the name of Marion's kidnapper and killer: William Edward Hickman.

Hickman was only 19 years old and had grown up in Kansas City, Missouri. Friends and family that knew him growing up described him as a good boy. He loved Hollywood films, attended church, and was even elected to the student council. While living in Los Angeles the year prior, Hickman had worked at the First National Bank under the watchful eye of Perry Parker. During this time, Parker reported Hickman for cashing forged checks worth about $200. Hickman was convicted but only sentenced to probation, despite Parker's protests. He spent the next six months in Kansas City before stealing his blue Chrysler coupe on November 7 and returning to Los Angeles.

When police showed Mary Holt a photo of their suspected murderer, she cried, "That is the man who took Marion."

By the time the police identified Marion's killer, Hickman was long gone, though he took his time leaving town – almost 24 hours, in fact. Immediately after dumping Marion's body in the gutter, he stopped at a nearby diner to get something to eat, using one of his new $20 gold certificates. That Sunday morning, when the police arrived at the Bellevue Apartments, Hickman claimed to have spoken with one of them, saying, "I told them I hoped they'd catch the damned fiend who killed Marion Parker." No doubt, Hickman saw the cops literally on his doorstep as a sign to leave Los Angeles.

The greatest manhunt in the history of the Southwest was on. Radio stations aired Hickman's description and the horrific details of Marion's murder. Geraldine Parker never heard those details -- she was still being told Marion had died from an overdose of sleeping medicine to shield her from the horrors her daughter suffered.

The $50,000 reward for Marion's killer – dead or alive – nearly doubled to $100,000 after a wave of public donations. The reward - almost $1.7 million today --was the highest price ever put on a criminal's head. It was considered a fair price for the most despicable crime recorded in California's history.

Anyone who resembled Hickman was either arrested by the police or attacked by angry mobs. Both Mary Holt and Naomi Britton were called in to try to identify suspects. Some newspapers suggested Hickman had managed to elude capture for so long because he was dressing as a "modern flapper." He was interested in movies and supposedly liked to impersonate women in front of friends.

News of Marion Parker and her psychotic killer made its way as far as Alaska. A strange duality took over Los Angeles as people continued their Christmas shopping and festivities while panicking at the sight of disturbing headlines.

When the police searched apartment #315, where Hickman had stayed, they learned he had only moved in a few weeks prior under the name Donald Evans. In his apartment, they found bloody footprints in the bathroom, partly burned ransom note drafts, and newspaper clippings about the kidnapping. They also found a Christmas postcard addressed to Donald Evans that led them to believe the suitcase found on South Manhattan Place had not been Hickman's. It read:

How bout. Left 30 bucks and the suitcase. I need them both.
-Joe

Initially, police assumed Hickman would head east to Kansas City to be with his family, though they also warned Mexico to carefully monitor their borders just in case he tried to flee the country.

All was quiet for a day before Hickman was spotted on Tuesday, December 20, in Albany, Oregon, at a gas station, driving another stolen car – this time a green Hudson Super Six sedan. The gas station attendant informed the police the following day.

On Wednesday, December 21, Hickman used another $20 bill at a haberdashery -- a men's clothing shop -- in Seattle, Washington. With his ransom money, he purchased a pair of gloves and some underwear. Police were able to track this exchange thanks to Parker recording its serial number before handing it over to Hickman just four days prior.

At 6:30 a.m. on Thursday, December 22, another gas station attendant spotted Hickman in Portland, Oregon, and immediately reported it to the local police. After a quick but frantic car chase, William Edward Hickman was arrested outside of Echo, Oregon. In his car were the sawed-off shotgun and $1,400 of the $1,500 ransom.

When word reached the Parkers of Hickman's capture, Perry Parker is recorded as saying, "I'm glad, very glad." No doubt Marion Parker would see justice served.

Hickman immediately denied killing Marion Parker, instead laying the blame on a man named Andrew Kramer. The only problem was that Kramer was already serving time in jail, and the police knew that. To add even more doubt to Hickman's story, his ransom notes only ever used singular pronouns. He wrote to Parker, "I'm doing a solo," and he still had almost all of the ransom money on his person -- surely, he would have split it with any accomplice he might have had immediately.

On Christmas Day, while locked in the Pendleton Jail, Hickman tried to kill himself. This was the first attempt of many to follow.

Local bureaucracy quickly brought Hickman back to Los Angeles to face the City of Angels and its fury. While traveling by train, Hickman abandoned the story of Andrew Kramer as a possible accomplice and finally admitted to the horrors he had committed.

Hickman assured the police that this was not an act of revenge against Perry Parker after he had reported him for forgery – he simply wanted the ransom money to pay his way through Park College, a Bible college in Kansas City. He knew that Parker would have access to the $20 gold certificates. While he didn't know Marion's name, he had seen her visit Parker at the bank several times, making her the perfect target. He never realized there were two sisters - twins - and that Parker had more than one daughter.

After Hickman and Marion left school, he claimed he took her to the movies to make her feel comfortable around him.

For the next two days, Hickman kept Marion cooped up in his tiny apartment, forcing her to write notes to her parents that he would include with his diabolical letters.

On the evening of the attempted ransom exchange, Hickman claimed he brought Marion to his stolen car and drove to the rendezvous point, where she saw her father. Nervous about the police presence, Hickman drove away, and Marion became agitated. It was clear she was starting to grow restless.

On Saturday, December 17, he made her write one final note that he included in the special delivery. He tied her to a chair before leaving to mail the letter. When he returned, she began begging him to let her go – to drop her off in front of her house and drive away. He feared she would bring attention to the apartment, and so he decided her had to kill her.

With Marion still tied to the chair, he approached her from behind with a dishtowel. He wrapped the towel tight around her neck and squeezed. She struggled and squirmed for about two minutes before she slumped forward, motionless.

At this point, Hickman claimed, "She felt perfectly safe, and the tragedy was so sudden and unexpected that I'm sure she never actually suffered through the whole affair, except for a little sobbing which she couldn't keep back for her father and mother."

Turning his phonograph on, he started listening to the Broadway Nitelites singing *Bye, Bye Pretty Baby* and grabbed a large knife from the kitchen.

Dragging her still-warm body to the bathroom, Hickman removed her patterned dress, shoes, and stockings before placing her nude body in the tub. Some reports claim he hung her upside-down, while others say he laid her in the tub, her head over the drain. Whatever position he put her in, Hickman then slit her throat and drained the body of its blood.

Once this gruesome act was complete, he got to work making the body easier to transport. He disarticulated Marion's arms and legs with a kitchen knife, sawing them off at the elbows and knees. He then began to saw her torso in half at the waist. At this point, the body jerked violently – "It flew out of the tub." This horrific detail, along with the fact that neither chloroform nor any other type of anesthetic was in Marion's system at this time, leads some to believe Marion might have somehow still been alive at this point and able to feel everything. Others suggest the body's sudden reaction resulted from Hickman cutting through her spinal cord, causing a reaction similar to a chicken still being able to run around without its head.

Once Marion was cut into six separate pieces, Hickman wrapped the arms, legs, and lower torso in newspapers and placed Marion's upper torso in the old leather suitcase. He then decided to unwind a bit by going to the movies. Unsurprisingly, he couldn't enjoy it because he "felt kind of punk."

While at the movies, Hickman came to an unsettling realization -- Perry Parker would want to see proof of life before exchanging the ransom for his daughter. While out, Hickman stopped at a local store and bought rouge and face powder before returning to his apartment and getting to work once again.

Pulling what was left of little Marion from the suitcase, he washed the blood from her naked torso and combed her hair. He wrapped wire around her throat so tight it cut into her skin and wound it over her head to help prop her head up. Using the makeup he had purchased, he applied it to her pale face and then sewed her eyes open. Lastly, he pulled Marion's familiar light-colored dress on "as a little girl would dress a doll."

The crimes that Hickman admitted to were horrific, even for the seasoned police officers of the LAPD. When Hickman arrived in Los Angeles on December 27, it was said that over 4,000 enraged residents were there to see the madman that had killed an innocent girl. The police force quickly and efficiently transported Hickman from the train station to the Hall of Justice. By 10:15 a.m., he was booked, locked in a cell on the twelfth floor, and had confessed in front of district attorney Asa D. Keyes, who was so sickened by the brutal retelling he "had to seek air." Keyes would push for a quick trial and settle for nothing less than the death penalty.

As word spread that Hickman had arrived, crowds began gathering outside the jail, and traffic nearly reached a standstill. Hickman's cell was known as the "jewelry tank" since it housed prisoners who wore irons and manacles. He was separated from his fellow inmates to preserve his life long enough to stand trial. He did not have to wait long.

A jury of eight men and four women was selected, and the "trial of the century" began on January 25, 1928. People waited in line for hours, hoping to get a seat in the courtroom. Those who were lucky enough to get a seat were searched for weapons. Crowds stood outside, waiting to hear any news that might leak out. Edgar Rice Burroughs (the author of *Tarzan*) reported on the Hickman story for the *Los Angeles Examiner*, and opinion pieces in papers suggested Hickman, "the beast in human form," should have portions of his flesh removed by the executioner so his death could be as long and painful as possible.

Despite the blatant hatred the public had for William Edward Hickman, his defense entered a plea of "not guilty by reason of insanity" – the first of its kind in the state of California. According to Hickman's defense, a deity called "Providence" had ordered Hickman to kidnap Marion and murder her. However, prison guards and psychologists contradicted the defense's claims of insanity. Hickman was well-spoken and coherent. He kept his story straight and even went so far as to ask others how he could "act crazy."

Dr. Cecil Reynolds, a noted psychiatrist, declared Hickman sane. He said, "I consider Hickman a cold-blooded monster in full possession of his facilities, which are above the average of the human being of the same age and station."

Multiple women's organizations called for capital punishment. Their petition received the endorsement of 40,000 club women in Southern California alone.

Death threats were sent to Hickman, as well as the judge and jury, if he was acquitted.

Shortly after Perry Parker testified on February 8, 1928, the jury deliberated for less than 45 minutes before returning with the guilty verdict. To the relief of the Parker family and the public, Hickman was sentenced to death by hanging.

On October 19, 1928, William Hickman walked up the 13 steps to the gallows at San Quentin Prison. At 10:10 a.m., he fainted just as the black bag was placed over his head. The trapdoor opened, and as he fell, he hit his head on the platform, keeping his neck from breaking. Instead of a quick death, he twitched and jerked violently as he was strangled for several minutes -- just as Marion had.

At last, justice had been served.

In the following years, Marion and her tragic death became the subject of several murder folk ballads, including two in 1928 alone by Vernon Dalhart and Blind Andy. But soon, Marion would be forgotten, her grisly murder overshadowed by so many others that plagued Los Angeles.

The last member of the Parker family – Marjorie – died in 1987, and around this time, a ghost story connected to the sad tale of Marion appeared.

Starting in the 1990s, the new owners of 1631 South Wilton Place started experiencing unexplained phenomena. They reported hearing the sound of footsteps in the otherwise empty house and would also see objects moving on their own. The family pets would react to something that no one else could see. Lights would sometimes turn on and off on their own, and doors would open and close without assistance.

Although ghostly activity can be unnerving, the owners insisted that whatever was there was a friendly, child-like spirit. Several years later, a psychic medium confirmed that the ghost was Marion.

It seems like a fitting ending to the story of Marion Parker. After all, she just wanted to go home.

"YOUR UNFORTUNATE WIFE"
MINNIE PETERS
BY TROY TAYLOR

Although forgotten today, the death of Minnie Peters in Cleveland in 1906 caused a sensation like few others in the city's history. It remains Cleveland's most infamous "locked room mystery," and the horrific event led to one woman dead, one man arrested, and numerous family members and friends under police suspicion and the scrutiny of sensational newspaper stories.

It's also a tragic death that remains unsolved well over a century after it happened.

The "Minnie Peters Strange Death" story began exactly at 6:00 p.m. on Friday, November 16, 1906. At that moment, Albert Peters, a fortyish jack-of-all-trades with a large black mustache, returned home to find that the door to his apartment on the second floor of 3805 Payne Avenue was locked. He knocked, but there was no reply from his wife, Minnie. Without a key, he went downstairs to the grocery store on the first floor of the building. The building's owner, Henry Soeders, operated the store.

When Albert walked in, he found Henry and some of his neighbors. "Something is wrong, and I can't get in," Albert said.

Accompanied by Henry Soeders and next-door neighbor Michael McNierney, Albert led the way to the darkened three-room apartment upstairs. He bent down, peered through the keyhole, and spied the key in the lock, inserted from the other side.

After discussing a few options, they decided to pry open the apartment's pantry window, which opened onto the public hallway. The three men forced the window open, and Albert crawled through. The two men in the hall could hear his footsteps as he walked to the door and opened it for them.

They entered the front parlor, and Henry Soeders lit a candle so they could see. The lights were out, and the apartment was filled with shadows.

In the flickering light of the candle, though, the men were startled by a fearsome sight - Minnie Peters, lying motionless on the floor.

She was in a horrible state. Lying on her left side with her hair partially concealing her face, the 45-year-old Minnie lay unmoving in a pool of congealed blood. Blood was spattered on everything in the room - the floor, the walls, the rug, pictures on the walls, and a mirror that, oddly, had been placed against a rocking chair close to the corpse.

Even with her head caked with gore and her knot of long, dark hair, it was obvious that Minnie's head and been bashed in with savage ferocity. Her skirts were pulled up to her waist, exposing her underwear and stockings, and under her left side was found a heavy, blood-covered machinist's hammer.

Sinking to his knees next to his wife's body and then pitching forward to fling himself on top of her body, Albert Peters wailed, "My God! My God! Didn't I tell you long ago not to kill yourself?"

What? How could such a brutal attack be a suicide?

As Albert began to lapse into a stream of sobs and German phrases, Henry Soeders sensibly suggested they call the police.

When Cleveland police detectives Lieutenant Frank Smith, Captain Schmunk, and Sergeant James Doran arrived at the apartment, they found the scene almost the same as when Albert and the other two men had earlier entered the room.

Minnie had definitely been dead for some time, they realized, and they also noted two puzzling details - all of the furniture in the room had been pushed back against the walls, and there was a mirror propped up against a rocking chair near the body. Next to it was a small saucer filled with varnish.

With nothing more to go on, they did the expected thing and took Albert into custody for questioning. Seven hours later, after a vigorous interrogation during which he maintained his complete innocence, he was booked as a "suspicious person." He was assured there would be more inquiries and questioning in his future.

Albert's story was plausible, allowing for a few minor inconsistencies caused by his initial reluctance to be open and honest about the intimate details of his marriage to a woman who could be described as "troubled" at best.

Married for 15 years, Albert and Minnie had come to America in 1892, leaving behind two children from Minnie's previous marriage in a German orphanage. In Germany and in America, their marriage was not a happy one. It was continually upset by Minnie's ongoing physical and mental problems, causing them to move frequently in hopes of settling her health. They lived in dozens of places before settling in Cleveland in April 1906. Even then, over seven months, they had lived in six different apartments before moving into the one on Payne Avenue.

Where they lived didn't seem to matter much, though. Minnie was a desperately unhappy woman wherever she event, which had caused an estrangement from most of her relatives. She seemed determined to make her long-suffering husband, Albert, as miserable as she was. He characterized their life together: "My whole life was bound up in that woman, and I did not consider any sacrifice too great for her. When she began to experience these strange spells, thenceforward I suffered as much as she did."

According to Albert and in statements from friends and relatives, Minnie's sufferings had become especially morbid and ominous during the few months preceding her death. Depressed and bedridden and often acting in a demented manner, she became convinced that some unknown enemy was pursuing her. This led to constant talk about suicide.

Once, on a train coming east from California, she had begged Albert for a knife. She wanted to slash her wrists before some mysterious man could throw her from the train.

Shortly after that, Minnie tried to slash her throat with Albert's razor and then tried to drink carbolic acid - or so Albert said.

On Sunday, November 11, just five days before her death, Minnie had proposed a suicide pact to her husband. She allegedly told him, "I don't care for my life. I have nothing to live for but you, and if we could go together, I'd be happy." Albert refused but said he heard her praying later that night that God would take them both in their sleep.

Two days later, Minnie insisted they make new wills, each leaving everything to the other in case of death.

Then, on Thursday, November 15, she wrote a note to Albert that said, "This is my last day. They are going to take me to Newburgh (insane asylum)." Like all of Minnie's letters to her husband, it was signed:

Your Unfortunate Wife

When he left her on Friday morning to go to work, around 6:00 a.m., she had walked with him to the stairs. "This is my last day," she said to him again. "Kiss me goodbye. Goodbye, Papa."

No food was found in her stomach during the autopsy that followed her death. Albert told detectives that she had not eaten in at least three days.

That was enough for Cleveland's police chief, Fred Kohler. After hearing that several witnesses interviewed by the police spoke about the great care Albert took of his difficult wife, he ordered the man's release from jail on Sunday, November 17. Kohler then issued a statement declaring that Minnie had killed herself, "beating her skull into fragments with her husband's machinist's hammer."

Many of the officers under Kohler's command were skeptical, as was Cleveland's mayor, Tom Johnson. But Kohler defended his belief, telling the mayor, "The woman was insane. She had repeatedly threatened to take her own life. She told her husband when he left that morning that he would never see her alive again."

When the still-dubious Johnson asked how the frail woman could have lifted the hammer enough times to bash herself in the head so many times that her skull was shattered, Kohler had an answer, too. "The frenzy of insanity," he replied. "It gives great strength. I have seen people who have nearly cut their own arms off in committing suicide who afterwards cut their throats."

Kohler's decision to release Albert - along with his comments about the case - quickly drew the scorn of the public and the press. Jeering at his claim that Minnie committed suicide, the *Cleveland News* suggested Kohler was "working apparently on the Cleveland police theory that every murder case is a suicide unless the murderer surrenders himself."

Dr. Louis Siegelstein, who had just completed Minnie's autopsy, was even more blunt: "Anyone who says this murder is a suicide is ridiculous. Any one of the six wounds was a fatal one. It is out of all possibility of belief that a human being could have inflicted those injuries on himself. It could not have been done by man, woman, or beast. And that is the opinion of two other doctors who also examined the body."

One of those doctors, Assistant County Coroner J.T. Kepke, supported the statement. He asserted, "There is not a particle of doubt that the woman was brutally murdered." Dr. C.L. Jaster of the Newburgh Asylum - who knew a thing or two about insanity - also chimed in, saying that it was a "practical impossibility" for even a maniac to inflict such injuries on herself."

The public and the press took sides, most supporting the coroner. One headline screamed, "How Could A Corpse Take Its Own Life?" and expounded on the evidence from the autopsy that made a suicide verdict almost unthinkable.

Using the round end of the machinist's hammer, Minnie was hit 12 times in the skull. These were severe blows; even half would have caused unconsciousness or death. Two of the blows had been forceful enough to drive broken pieces of her skull into her brain. How was she supposed to have continued hitting herself after that?

In addition, the chaos in the parlor, the blood spatter all over the room, and the condition of her clothing all pointed to an attack by a homicidal assailant. And, as all who knew Minnie testified, she was too weak to have wielded the heavy hammer. "To assert otherwise," Dr. Siegelstein concluded, "is to violate good sense."

Publicly shamed in the papers, Chief Kohler refused to back down. Denying that the hammer blows had killed Minnie, he insisted that she choked on her own blood instead. Noting that all the windows and the only door to the apartment were locked from the inside and that no one said anyone had entered it on the day of the murder, Kohler scoffed at the idea of some unknown intruder. Since Albert's alibi checked out - Dr. Corlett swore he had been at his house on Euclid Avenue all day - Minnie's death could only be a suicide.

She had been depressed for a long time and had told her husband it was her "last day." The murder scene, as far as Kohler was concerned, proved that she had carried out her self-destruction with admirable precision. In fact, Kohler even spelled out how she'd done it, basing it on what he called "other housewife suicides." He told the newspaper:

Police records show similar incidents. The woman prepared for death - cleaned her house from parlor to kitchen - changed her clothing from the skin out - burned her papers - placed the mirror at the chair - then took a machinist's hammer and pounded herself - the blows increasing in force as her frenzy advanced.

She placed the looking glass on the rocking chair in such an angle that no one could see her reflection therein without standing up. This is a common practice for would-be suicides to stand before a mirror, the looking glasses frequently being shattered by the body striking them in the fall.

It is not the function of Coroner Siegelstein to say how this woman came by her wounds. If I should declare that the woman was murdered, I would be hotted out of office by the men under me.

Based on what the men under him were saying? Probably not.

Dr. Siegelstein immediately fired back a reply in the next day's paper. When asked why he was sticking to this murder theory in light of the police chief's statements, the coroner replied: "I have only begun to stick. In the annals of surgical history, there is no case of a person receiving wounds similar to those Mrs. Peters received and retaining consciousness long enough to strike a second blow."

So, what really happened? The story isn't over yet.

Minnie's funeral was held on Monday afternoon at the Flynn and Froelk Mortuary. It was attended by what the press called "morbid persons, mostly women." News articles included the sensational rumor that a mysterious woman was seen "gloating" over Minnie's open casket.

Reporters also couldn't help but add that when her casket was lowered into the ground at Monroe Street Cemetery, Albert was heard muttering that it wouldn't be long before he was with her.

Anyone who believed the coroner's inquest would settle the dispute between Dr. Siegelstein and Chief Kohler about Minnie's death was very disappointed. The inquest started on Monday, November 19, and the jury called several dozen witnesses - most of whom gave evidence that supported *both* theories about the cause of death.

Friends and family of Albert Peters testified about Minnie's persistent mood swings, depression, irrational fears about a phantom stalker, and frequent threats of suicide. Their recollections of the mentally disturbed woman were amplified by a note - or rather the faint impression of a note on the top sheet of a paper tablet -found by Chief Kohler himself while searching the Peters apartment two days after the murder. Verified as her handwriting and magnified to be legible, it was translated from German by Henry Soeders' daughter, Annie. Minnie last missive seemed to be the final cry of a woman at the end of her psychological rope:

Schmidt, Girgin Soeders said nothing. To this I can swear. This was all that was wanted to set these people upon me. What is worse, you do not care for me. Dear friends, forgive me. If you can come as soon as possible.

Your Unfortunate Wife.

The note didn't make a lot of sense, and it took some time to puzzle it out. "Schmidt" was Max Schmidt, a family friend and man the police initially suspected might be Minnie's lover. But after a long "chat" with him, Kohler's men concluded that his interest in Minnie had been genuinely platonic. Minnie's fears about people being "set upon" her turned out to be the unfounded delusion that landlord Henry Soeders was about to evict them. But the main part of the note clearly demonstrated Minnie's fears of impending doom. Her anxiety seemed to indicate that her suicide was inevitable - and was happening soon.

Chief Kohler's insistence that no intruder could have entered the Peters' apartment seemed to be supported by Annie Soeders' testimony that she had been working in the building all day and hadn't seen anyone else.

With the key left inside that locked door, it seemed impossible that anyone could have entered the apartment during the critical 12 hours between when Albert left for work and when he returned that evening.

But Dr. Siegelstein wouldn't let Kohler run roughshod over the inquest. Soon, a small parade of surprise witnesses arrived to challenge the chief's suicide theory.

In the first place, there was no proof that the Peters apartment had been locked from the inside when Albert and the other men arrived at the door on Friday evening. The other men had merely accepted Henry's claim that the door was locked - they didn't try it themselves. After Albert crawled through the pantry window and came around to let them inside, they neither saw nor heard him actually unlock the door.

Henry Soeders reluctantly admitted on the stand: "I do not know who killed this woman, but even if what I am about to say would hang Albert Peters, then I must say it - it is the gospel truth that Peters never unlocked that door. He swung it right open. There was no turning of the key and no sliding of a bolt."

The greatest challenge to the suicide theory came from Conrad Voth, a journalist for a German Baptist periodical, whose office was directly across the street from the grocery store and apartment building.

He had contacted the police on November 18 to claim that he had seen a mysterious older man at the Peters apartment around 12:30

p.m. on the Friday Minnie died. Appearing for a few seconds at the second window from the apartment's southeast corner, the man looked down at the street and then withdrew.

But after Chief Kohler heard about the witness, he dismissed Voth's sighting, laughingly calling the mysterious man a "phantom." But Dr. Siegelstein took it seriously and made Voth his star witness at the inquest.

Repeating his claim, Voth described the man he had seen as about five feet, eight inches tall, between 50 and 60 years old, well-dressed in a black cloak, wearing no hat, and wearing a well-trimmed beard. He said he would certainly recognize the man if he ever saw him again.

Kohler's men did what they could to disparage Voth's statements, claiming that he had failed to identify other figures at the same window and that his eyesight was poor. But Voth stubbornly stuck to his story and succeeded in embarrassing the police on the stand by correctly reading distant address numbers through the window of the building where the inquest was held. Voth's solemn and precise testimony made a lasting impression, even if he did conclude it with a comment about the dead woman's private life: "I would not be surprised to learn any time that a man had been found, a man whom Mrs. Peters had known, and known intimately, though without the knowledge of her husband."

Was this just speculation - or had Voth seen other things while looking out his office window toward the Peters' apartment building?

Jake Mintz, Cleveland's most famous private detective at the time, echoed his comments the following day in the newspapers. He theorized that Minnie had been murdered by a "moral degenerate," an unknown man who had "loved her better than her husband." Dismissing Albert as a stooge, he said it was useless to question the man further: "Do not ask Peters who he suspects, for he is a man who would never suspect anyone of anything."

More support for the unknown intruder theory - perhaps Voth's bearded stranger - came on Thursday with the dramatic testimony of Isadore Rosenthal, a boy who lived in the neighborhood. He told the jury that he had been standing in the Grenloch and Gensert shoe store - next door to the Soeders grocery store and just below the Peters apartment - when he heard a sound "like a body falling" overhead. He mentioned the noise to the store proprietor at the time, but they were too busy to pay much attention.

The inquest finally ended on November 22, with the question of the cause of Minnie's death still undetermined. But Dr. Siegelstein and Chief Kohler continued their public feud, each determined to have the last word.

Even before all the testimony had come in, Kohler had already declared, "This incident is closed." And on Friday, after the inquest ended, he stated angrily, "The coroner jumped to conclusions, which he has since come to realize were wrong, and now he is exerting every effort to vindicate himself in his prejudged verdict. I'm just vexed. It's ridiculous, preposterous, asinine. He snaps his fingers at a trained police force, trained for just such action as the solving of death mysteries, and tells us to paddle our own canoe, that he'll paddle his!"

But County Coroner Siegelstein did have the last word, which came with his official inquest verdict on December 1. He wrote:

Minnie Peters came to her death from hemorrhage of the brain and a fractured skull, which were caused by said Minnie Peters having been struck a number of blows over the head with a blunt instrument by an unknown person.

And that ended the Minnie Peters mystery - well, sort of. She hadn't committed suicide, according to the coroner, but no one was any closer to finding out who killed her. And given the attitude of the police chief - and the very public feud he was part of - no one would be looking for her killer either.

Albert eventually agreed that Minnie could not have killed herself, saying, "She would have left a note clearing me. She told me many times that she would be murdered, but always promised me faithfully that she would not harm herself."

His story certainly changed.

Albert was fired from his work for Dr. Corlett because of the bad publicity about the murder but soon found another job and new bloodstains-free lodgings. What became of him after that is unknown.

Chief Kohler closed the investigation into Minnie's murder, believing he had been right all along. And before he dismisses the chief completely, there is something to consider - he may have been right about Minnie killing herself.

Six months later, Chief Kohler claimed to have the last laugh in the Peters case when Frank E. Woodworth of Painesville, Ohio - perhaps inspired by the news stories - tried to kill himself with a heavy hammer. Despite being a large and muscular man, Woodworth failed in his attempt. He didn't fracture his skull, and he didn't even lose consciousness. When baited by newsmen as to why the strong Woodworth failed where Minnie had allegedly succeeded, Kohler replied, "Woodworth didn't have Mrs. Peters' nerve."

But there were other cases - almost identical to Minnie's - that did bolster Kohler's theory:

Four years earlier, in 1902, Henry L. Dauernheim, a 50-year-old paper merchant from St. Louis, had killed himself by beating in his skull with a heavy sledgehammer.

Just 19 months after Minnie's death, Rachel Goldfadoon of Cleveland tried to kill herself with a hatchet. She didn't succeed, but she did inflict seven nasty wounds to her head without passing out.

In March 1911, businessman William Staum of Syracuse, New York, beat himself to death with a hammer under circumstances that were eerily close to those of Minnie's case. Found lying in a pool of blood, Staum had locked his door and had hit himself ten times with a heavy hammer, shattering his skull and penetrating his brain several times. The official coroner's verdict? Suicide.

So, who was right? The police chief or the coroner? Was Minnie murdered, or did she kill herself? If it was a suicide, how did she manage to hit herself so many times, damaging her brain and shattering her skull, and still manage to keep going? And if she was murdered, who killed her - her husband or the mysterious bearded man?

We'll likely never know, and the story of Minnie Peters will continue to be Cleveland's most baffling unsolved, locked room mystery.

"QUEEN OF THE COMSTOCK"
JULIA BULETTE
BY AMANDA R. WOOMER

The history of sex work is shrouded in mystery, much less the unique stories of individual sex workers. The little we know is written by men – either those trying to control women or those soliciting them.

Often, prostitutes are nameless blips in history, intentionally forgotten because of the stigma surrounding their profession. However, several women – soiled doves, fallen women, and good-time girls, as they were often called – have managed to make their mark on a community and find notoriety, fame, and affection in death.

And that was something they may not have had in life.

Much of Julia Bulette's life is intricately mixed with folklore, making it difficult to determine the details of her life aside from those surrounding her gruesome death. Some stories claim that she was born in England - possibly London or Liverpool - in 1832 before her parents immigrated to New Orleans when she was two years old. Another story suggests that Julia was a "quadroon" - one-quarter African American - with her father, a Frenchman, marrying a well-respected black woman after moving to Mississippi.

It's believed that by the time she was 16 years old, Julia had a successful business set up in New Orleans, working as a highly elite prostitute. Her being well-read and well-spoken certainly helped set her apart from some of her competition. One fact that we do know about Julia is that she never worked out of a brothel – she was always an independent contractor.

During the San Francisco gold rush (1848-1855), she made her way west to strike it rich among the miners. However, when she arrived in California, she found the sex market was oversaturated with far too many fellow sex workers, and she couldn't charge nearly as much as she was making in New Orleans. Gradually over time, Julia migrated to Sacramento and then Carson City. While in Carson

City, she met a man named Thomas Peasley -- whom some considered the love of her life -- and he convinced her to move to Virginia City with him, where he would establish the first fire department.

Now 31 years old, beautiful, tall, and slim, with dark eyes and hair, Julia instantly won over the hearts of the men in Virginia City. Legends claim that Julia was the first woman to arrive in town when the Comstock Lode – the largest discovery of silver in the country – was discovered in 1859, making her *extremely* popular. However, this is a tall tale since Julia didn't arrive until 1863. By then, the town was established with gentlewomen of society, teachers, and a number of fellow prostitutes. But that didn't make Julia any less popular among the community of Virginia City, and she made new friends and patrons quickly and easily.

Virginia City was a rough, wild west mining town. Brawls and duels were part of everyday life. Various types of brothels existed, ranging from high-end parlor houses with educated, well-spoken, disease-free working girls - with services costing up to $10 per client - to brothels that forced Chinese immigrants into sex slavery, charging just a few cents.

The 1860 census shows 2,390 men living in the mining town alongside just 118 women. In 1860, Virginia City was comprised of "half a dozen stone houses built last fall (1859), some twenty-five wooden houses, and several hundred tents." But by the time Julia arrived just a few years later, schools, hotels, and even an opera house had been built.

Julia settled into a small rented two-room crib - known as Crib 1 - at 4 North D Street, part of Virginia City's "Sporting Row" - the red-light district before there was an official "red-light district." As an independent worker, she competed with parlor houses, bawdy houses, and streetwalkers.

Local legends have grown around her time as a sex worker in Virginia City. Stories claim that she helped nurse the sick during flu epidemics when the women of society wouldn't get their hands dirty. She served soup to the homeless. She and the other prostitutes in town would throw balls to raise money for widows and orphans. Julia also supposedly led a team of prostitutes who nursed community members back to health after the drinking water was contaminated with lead.

While these stories might not be based on fact, it was well-known that Julia Bulette was extremely charitable, and one of the beneficiaries of her charity was the local fire department, run by Tom Peasley. Julia would donate her money to support Virginia Engine Company No. 1, as well as her time. During emergencies, she would be found working the brakes of the water pumps, helping the firefighters put out the flames. Peasley claimed, "She can man a brake as good as she can break a man." Eventually, Peasley, now the fire chief of Company No. 1, would make Julia an honorary company member. She was gifted a feminine uniform complete with a fire shield, shirt, belt, and helmet with the number one embossed on it. She was the only woman to be an honorary member, and today, the only known photo of her shows her in her uniform.

For several years, Julia found success. While the wholesome women in town wouldn't have much to do with her, her kindness and generosity won over the rest of the community. Those that solicited her for her business expressed that she was always compassionate and warm. She was known to throw lavish parties for her friends and patrons. Her clothing was fashionable yet conservative – she fancied dark colors though she did have an impressive collection of lingerie. While she never made a fortune like the madams running the brothels, she did manage to build up an assortment of furs, silks, and jewels, which were sometimes given to her as payment by her customers.

Her house wasn't luxurious in any way – it was a two-room crib that sufficed for what she needed it for. The parlor had a stove to keep it warm in the winter and seating for 12 guests. It had ornate furniture and lace curtains. Her bedroom was inhabited chiefly by a large bed where she conducted business transactions. There was no kitchen and no place to sit and eat. Instead, she would join her neighbor, friend, and fellow prostitute, Gertrude Holmes, next door for every meal.

In 1866, Julia's comfortable life seemed at an end when Tom Peasley was shot and killed in Carson City. Her best friend, likely lover, and original ally in Virginia City was gone, and things would only worsen for Julia.

She was now 34 years old, and as she was getting older, she knew she couldn't continue to charge the amount of money she wanted for her services. She started drinking heavily and taking laudanum - a mixture of opium and alcohol. Julia began to see a doctor twice a week for an undisclosed illness. Her doctor bills started piling up, as well as her alcohol bills. She was grieving the loss of Peasley and extremely depressed, not to mention a recent ordinance that banned her from sitting in the local opera house, adding to her ostracization and loneliness.

On the evening of January 19, 1867, Julia ate dinner with Gertrude Holmes. Around 11:00 p.m., she excused herself, telling her friend she was meeting someone at midnight.

No one knows whom Julia Bulette met in her crib that night, but it didn't take long for others to discover that whomever her late-night customer was, he had certainly not been a friend.

Around 11:00 a.m. on January 20, the handyman hired to build Julia's fires each day arrived. He noticed Julia was still in bed with the blankets pulled over her head. Assuming she was still asleep after a night of work, he quickly finished his task and left. Shortly after, the truth was discovered.

Conflicting reports claim that Julia's maid - also named Julia - was the first to find her. Others suggest that Gertrude Holmes brought a meal over after Julia missed breakfast. A third report says that another neighbor that lived on D Street, Mary Jane Minieri, made the gruesome discovery. Whomever it was, they found the parlor in perfect order. However, in the bedroom, once the blanket was pulled away from Julia, a brutal crime scene was revealed.

Julia was dead in her bed, lying on her left side with a large pillow hiding her face. Her nightgown was in disarray, revealing that there had likely been a struggle between the assailant and his victim. The bolster beneath her was covered with blood, seemingly caused by a heavy blow to her right temple. Investigators quickly realized she had been struck with a piece of wood – there were two holes in her right temple made by a stick and pieces of bark still clung to her hair – though the weapon would never be found. Bruises around her throat showed that she had been strangled, and her nightgown had been ripped open to reveal her breasts.

Alf Doten, a reporter for the *Territorial Enterprise* and *Gold Hill Daily News*, known for his in-depth diaries that captured life in the West, wrote after visiting the crime scene, "Worst murder ever in this city – horrible."

Julia was certainly not the first prostitute to be murdered in Virginia City in the nineteenth century. It was an unfortunate common occurrence. But Julia was such an integral part of the town that her death shook the community to its core. A beloved citizen had been murdered in her own bed. At the time, it was considered the worst crime committed in Virginia City's eight-year history.

As the authorities tried to imagine who would kill a respected community member, a motive was quickly revealed – all of Julia's silks, furs, jewelry, and valuables were missing.

Dr. Bronson performed the autopsy with the help of Dr. Gaston and Dr. Green. According to their findings, Julia's official cause of death was strangulation – her brain and the blood vessels in her head were swollen. Despite the heavy blows to her temple, there were no fractures in her skull or any other evidence of violence below the neck.

Julia's body was taken to No. 1's engine house on the morning of January 21 and was kept there until her funeral that afternoon.

That Monday was cold, and sleet poured down on the town as it mourned the loss of their cherished courtesan with a heart of gold. Saloons, businesses, and even the mine shut down as the city was draped in black wreaths and streamers -- a sight not seen since the assassination of President Abraham Lincoln two years prior.

The firefighters of the Virginia Engine Company No. 1 led the procession as a horse-drawn carriage transported Julia's body through the town to her final resting place. A parade of 16 carriages carried friends, fellow prostitutes, and mourners as the Nevada militia band played *The Girl I Left Behind.*

Newspapers printed glowing eulogies. The *Territorial Enterprise* remembered her as "being of a very kind-heart, liberal, benevolent, and charitable disposition, few of her class had more true friends." The *Virginia Daily Union* wrote, "...her purse ever being open to the demands of charity." Even today, a plaque near her former home reads *Angel of miners. Friend of firemen. Administrator to the needy.*

Although she was an active and giving community member, her vocation was still the center of attention and brought judgment even in death. It was noted at her funeral that Reverend Martin preached where "the gospel seed is seldom permitted to be sown," and the *Gold*

Hill Daily News wrote, "Let her faults be buried with her and her virtues live." Some couldn't help but cast judgment on her choice of profession. She was not permitted to be buried in the newly established Silver Terrace Cemeteries. Instead, she was placed in Flowery Hill Cemetery, the town's original cemetery that was no longer in use. Today, no one knows where Julia Bulette was laid to rest – the grave marked as a tourist attraction is likely fake.

After the funeral, the police began tracking Julia's killer but wouldn't make any headway for months, and when the killer was finally found, it was thanks to two women.

In May 1867, another independent prostitute named Martha Camp awoke in the middle of the night to find a man with a weapon standing over her. She immediately screamed. Luckily for Martha, her outburst frightened the would-be assailant, and he fled. Police were able to track the man down as he attempted to leave town.

It seemed Virginia City had found its possible suspect.

The *Virginia Daily Trespass* wrote of this brush with death:

It is not at all improbable that the same man who so foully murdered Bulette attempted to murder and rob Camp last night.

At this same time, in Gold Hill - just five miles south of Virginia City - a woman named Mrs. Cazentre came forward with another clue in the mystery of Julia Bulette's murder. After overhearing a pair of men discussing the belongings stolen from Julia Bulette's crib, Mrs. Cazentre realized she had unintentionally purchased a bit of silk that may have belonged to the murdered woman. She informed the authorities that she had purchased it from a drifter who assured her he was selling it on behalf of an impoverished widow whose husband had died in a nearby mine. When examined by the local dry goods merchant, Mr. Rosener, he confirmed that he had sold it to Julia Bulette.

During this era, drifters could be jailed for vagrancy, so when Mrs. Cazentre told Judge Jesse S. Pitzer that the silk had come from a drifter, he quickly brought her to the jail to see if she could identify the man who had sold her Julia Bulette's silk.

She could. And his name was John Millain, a Frenchman and a criminal who had fled his homeland after the Crimean War.

Although he spoke very little English, Millain ran a business in Virginia City washing clothes, which is how he crossed paths with Julia. According to reports, the large, heavy-built 37-year-old man was hired to wash her clothes and, in so doing, became familiar with the layout of her house and what she owned that might have been of value.

Shortly after Mrs. Cazentre identified John Millain as the man who had sold her Julia's stolen silk, the authorities discovered a trunk in his home filled with the rest of the prostitute's missing valuables. Inside was one pair of large coral ear drops, one jet set, a cross, a breastpin and ear drops, a long gold chain with miniature charms of scissors, a thimble, and a needle case - all made of gold - one set of enameled sleeve buttons, a silver brick with the name "Julia" engraved on it, a heavy gold ring, a pair of red silk stockings, a sable cape, a muff and wristlets, a black silk dress, a scarlet silk dress, a purple silk dress, a silk breakfast cape trimmed with white down, an opera hood of white silk and purple velvet trimmed with swan's down, a silver cup with "J.C.B." on it, a gold watch, handkerchiefs with Julia's name on them, silk cords, and lace trimmings.

At this time, there was no question in anyone's mind that the Frenchman, John Millain, was guilty of Julia Bulette's murder. The papers quickly credited the two women responsible for finding him: Mrs. Cazentre and Martha Camp.

Judge Richard Rising was assigned the case, and he wanted to avoid any vigilante justice in the form of lynching, so the trial was quickly set for June 26, 1867. The trial lasted only eight hours without a single witness for the defense. John Millain - with what little English he could muster - claimed he had not murdered Julia Bulette. He was drunk that night, he claimed and had acted as the lookout as two other men entered the crib and killed her. He was simply holding onto the trunk full of the dead woman's belongings. The prosecution quickly pointed out that Millain profited from Julia's death by selling her valuable clothes and jewels.

All the evidence against Millain was circumstantial. Still, the jury deliberated for a short time before swiftly declaring him guilty, partly due to the fact that he was uneducated and poorly dressed and also because he was a foreigner.

When the verdict was read out loud, it was said that the bell of the Virginia Fire Engine Company No. 1 rang in celebration.

On July 5, 1867, John Millain stood again before Judge Rising. Calmly, with his arms folded and his eyes cast down, he listened as he was sentenced to hang on the gallows for the murder of Julia Bulette.

Justice was finally served in the eyes of Virginia City on April 24, 1868.

John Millain boarded a carriage, surrounded by the National Guard and armed deputies, as he was transported to the gallows approximately one mile outside of town. It's said that between 3,000 and 4,000 people descended on Virginia City to witness the hanging, including Mark Twain, who was in town at the time. Men, women, and children of all social classes and ethnicities – Chinese immigrants, Indigenous populations, mothers carrying their little ones, people from the city, and country folk – lined the streets, making it nearly impossible for the wagon carrying Millain to pass. The *Janesville Gazette* reported:

Only by scolding, pushing, and threatening with a bayonet was there enough room to proceed.

As John Millain arrived at the gallows, he spoke in French for a few minutes, allegedly cursing his lawyer, the Virginia City police, and the prostitutes that testified against him. He maintained his innocence as he shook the sheriff's hand and kissed the chaplain.

Before a bloodthirsty audience hellbent on justice for their beloved Julia, Millain removed his slippers and opened his collar as the noose was placed around his neck. A black bag was placed over his head, and the moment the trapdoor sprung beneath his feet, his neck snapped, killing him instantly.

Mark Twain, one of the thousands that had shown up for the execution, was back in town to give a lecture at the opera house on April 27 and 28. He had written for the *Territorial Enterprise* from 1861 to 1864. Twain described the hanging for the *Chicago Republican* newspaper:

I believe that if ever it would be possible to see a man hanged, and derive satisfaction from the spectacle, this was the time. For John Melanie (sic) was no common murderer... he was a heartless assassin.

Around this time, the stolen belongings were returned to Julia's friends and auctioned off to try to pay off her debts. Her estate amounted to $875.43, not nearly enough to pay back what she owed the debt collectors.

Julia died alone, depressed, ill, and in debt. And as the decades passed, she was all but forgotten. All that was remembered seemed to be the heinousness of her death. But all that changed in the mid-twentieth century when Virginia City saw a need for Julia and gave her a new life.

As the mines along the Comstock Lode began to shut down, Virginia City needed to find a new way to boost the economy. Tourism was the name of the game, and what better way to lure in tourists than to create a wild west town ruled by the Queen of the Comstock?

Julia Bulette quickly became a folk heroine, presented as a prostitute with a kind and giving spirit - which was true - and specifically as a madam that made her fortune and rode around town in gilded carriages - which was not true. Her picture hangs in several bars in town today, the Virginia and Truckee Railroad named its club coach after her, and the town has erected a makeshift grave where people visit the larger-than-life courtesan, Julia Bulette, whose personality could "pack a punch."

Sadly, the real Julia has been lost to history, and the little we know about her is told through the eyes of men, and even then, her presence is scarce.

There's no mention of her in Mark Twain's book *Roughing It*, though he lived in Virginia City at the same time as Julia, and when he did write about her for the *Chicago Republican*, he referred to her as only a "woman of the town." We have vague details of her life, mostly surrounding her untimely death.

The truth behind Julia Bulette's life and death may never be fully revealed. While it can be said that she is another example of how sex workers are lost to the annals of history, she is one of the lucky ones, for at the very least, we know her name. And not only has she become a beloved figure in death, but she was deeply cherished in life, a feat not accomplished by many sex workers.

This simple truth is evidence that despite all the tall tales surrounding Julia Bulette, we know one thing for sure: she truly was a prostitute with a heart of gold.

"I HAVE KILLED MY DAUGHTER" MAGGIE SHEFFIELD

BY TROY TAYLOR

On a hot summer day in 1893, a little girl named Maggie Sheffield was murdered against a backdrop of music and laughter at Rocky Point Amusement Park in Warwick, Rhode Island.

As if this was not bad enough, Maggie's killer was someone she knew, loved, and trusted - her own father, Frank Sheffield.

In the days that followed this brutal crime, people in the community seemed to be more concerned about Frank than they were about his young and innocent victim. Rumored to be insane or addicted to narcotics, he pleaded insanity at his trial.

The more his story was sensationalized in the newspapers of the day, the more that little Maggie was forgotten, becoming a footnote in the story about her gruesome death.

And perhaps this is the reason why Maggie Sheffield's spirits refused to rest and why she remained behind at the seaside amusement park until it closed a century after her death.

Frank Sheffield was born in Woodstock, Connecticut, on August 9, 1850, the son of a Methodist minister, John Franklin Sheffield, and his wife, Charlotte.

While Frank was young, the family moved often, following the call of God wherever he saw fit to move the minister and his family. When Frank was 10, the family moved to Rhode Island and remained there for many years to come. Charlotte died in 1875, and John later remarried a woman named Mary Segur.

Frank and his siblings, Mary and Charles, had grown up listening intently to their father's sermons. Like other Methodists of the time, John Sheffield did not believe one could be saved by good deeds alone. It was also necessary to have the strongest faith in the Lord. Redemption would come, and all who believed in God would go on to heaven, even if they had not always avoided committing wicked deeds during their life on earth. Faith was everything, and any man could be saved.

Frank considered going into the ministry himself and even began his studies for a time, but he changed his mind before becoming ordained. He never said why but never spoke of becoming a minister again. Instead, he entered the education field, as did his sister and brother. In the mid-1870s, he became the principal of the East Greenwich School.

On December 15, 1876, he married Mary Ann Hill of Mystic, Connecticut. Her father, Mason Hill, was a well-known and respected master shipbuilder, and while he had a life of prestige and wealth, he'd also known great tragedy. His first wife, Mary Ann, had drowned at the age of 28 when a boat she was traveling in overturned on the Mystic River on July 4, 1853. He remarried Margaret Wheeler, and the couple had many children together, including Frank's new wife, who had been named after her father's beloved first wife.

After Frank and Mary Ann were married, they moved into a house next door to her parents on Greenmanville Avenue in Mystic. Their first child, a son, was born on January 11, 1880. He was named Mason after Mary Ann's father.

Later that year, the family moved to Pawcatuck, Connecticut, where they rented one floor of a three-family home on Liberty Street. Frank had just taken over the principal position at the newly built Palmer Street School in town.

While working there, Frank was injured in a freak accident that resulted in an injury that would plague him for years. As he was in the process of ringing the large school bell one day, the bell somehow swung in a way that struck Frank solidly in the head. He was knocked down, and while he turned down medical care for the blow, those who knew him said that the accident caused him severe headaches for the rest of his life.

While living in Pawcatuck, Mary Ann gave birth to the couple's second child, a little girl named Maggie, on January 31, 1888.

Tragically, Maggie's birth ended the life of her mother. Just one week later, Mary Ann died at the age of 33 after suffering from peritonitis - a condition caused by a hemorrhage of the membranes lining the pelvic wall. Her abdomen became so inflamed that it caused her lungs to swell. Already in intense pain, she struggled to breathe, which at first was difficult, then impossible.

Frank lost his wife, and Maggie lost the mother she would never know. Mary Ann was buried at the Elm Grove Cemetery, just down the road from her parent's home.

Frank was devastated and, in despair, decided that he could not care for two small children alone. Mary Ann's parents took in Mason, and Maggie went to live with Frank's parents in Danielsville, Connecticut.

Frank remained alone in the house he'd once shared with his family.

A year after Mary Ann's death, Frank resigned from the Palmer Street School and became principal of the Liberty Street School, which was closer to his house. While he was there, though, he contracted a bacterial infection that caused him to lose his job in 1890. By that time, he had already remarried.

Frank had married Nancy Armeda, the 37-year-old daughter of his former landlord, on November 27, 1889. Nancy was a professional dressmaker and knew well the mournful feeling of loss that her new husband carried. She had already lost her mother, four sisters, and, less than a year earlier, her father, too.

But she would not be prepared to deal with everything that being married to Frank would entail.

Frank moved into a home that Nancy owned and secured a new job as a clerk in the New York, Providence's freight department, and Boston Railroad's depot in Westerly, Rhode Island. But the job would not last long. Frank's poor health continued to plague him, and he was soon let go by the railroad.

On October 14, 1890, Nancy gave birth to the couple's first child, a girl named Sarah. Frank had started working as a rent collector, but his heart wasn't in it, and he was having trouble getting over his tainted past.

Everyone who knew him could tell something was wrong.

All the faith his father had instilled in him was gone. He wanted nothing to do with religion and refused to even speak about it - unless he was arguing with someone about it and believed he could somehow do something to fray their beliefs.

His behavior shocked and hurt his father, and later, after the murder, his father would say that his son would not have done that on his own - A demon had obviously possessed Frank.

No one will ever know what was truly going through Frank's mind in the years that followed Mary Ann's untimely death. Perhaps he had been driven mad, or perhaps he needed someone to blame for taking his wife away. He may have blamed God, but he may have also blamed the little girl whose birth had killed Mary Ann. Frank may have wrestled with the idea amid all the other confusion in his mind.

Nancy may or may not have realized - or accepted - that something was terribly wrong with the man she had married. Regardless, she gave birth to the couple's second child, a son named Amos, who was named for Nancy's father, on August 2, 1892.

However, that little boy would never really get to know his father. He would be just celebrating his first birthday when his father committed an unspeakable act that would cause him to be locked away for the rest of his life.

On Sunday morning, August 27, 1893, Frank rose early from his bed. After getting dressed, he told Nancy he needed a few things and would walk down to Richmond Brother's Grocery, a short distance from their home. Nancy thought his errand could wait until later. She had already started making breakfast.

"Breakfast will be ready soon," she protested.

But Frank ignored her and walked out the door. No one knows where he went and what he did immediately after that, but he didn't come back home. His breakfast grew cold on the table.

Later that morning, he showed up at the train depot on Railroad Avenue, where he had worked several months earlier. He went to the ticket booth and handed over far for transportation to Providence.

A man standing nearby recognized him. "Where are you off to?" the man asked.

"I'm going to Attleboro to get my child," Frank replied.

Even though his wife was waiting for him at home with no idea where he was, Frank left town on the 8:18 a.m. train for the city.

When he hadn't returned home after several hours, Nancy became worried and started looking for him. She had good reason to be concerned. Frank had been seeing a doctor and privately informed Nancy that her husband was not well and that she should make sure he didn't wander off alone. The doctor had no idea what might happen.

Concern turned to worry, and Nancy enlisted the help of Frank's friend, Dennison Hinckley. He was an undertaker and part owner of Hinckley and Russell, a furniture store and undertaking parlor in nearby Westerly. The two men had been good friends for a long time.

Nancy also sent telegrams to Frank's family, including his sister in Attleboro, to see if they had seen him or heard from him. Unfortunately, Frank's sister Mary wouldn't see the message until the following day.

Mary and her husband, Methodist minister George Brightman, had been entertaining guests at their home for the past ten days. Her father and stepmother had come to stay with them for a short time, and since Maggie lived with them, she was there, too.

At noon, the front doorbell rang at the Brightman home. Mary was surprised to see her brother Frank standing on her doorstep. She was further surprised when Frank told her he was there to see Maggie and take her away with him.

Alarmed by Frank's disheveled appearance - and aware of his recent mental issues - Mary urged Frank to come in, lie down, and rest for a bit. He would feel much better after a nap, she assured him.

But Frank was only impatient with the delay in taking custody of his daughter and declined the offer. He was too eager - too desperate, really - to take his daughter and be on his way.

George Brightman returned from morning church services just in time to find his agitated brother-in-law in the foyer of his home, adamant about collecting his child and leaving. The strange way that he was behaving immediately set George on edge. By this time, Maggie, hearing the commotion, joined her father, aunt, and uncle in the foyer. George didn't like the way that Frank was looking at the little girl.

There was something wrong about it.

Even Maggie could see that things weren't quite right with her father. "Why are you looking at me like that?" she asked him.

George tried to reason with Frank. He also attempted to convince him to get some rest and then go home. Eventually, Frank agreed, and with a sigh, he settled himself on a couch in the parlor and slept for several hours.

George immediately sent a telegram to Nancy to let her know that Frank was there - but just like the telegram that Nancy had sent to the Brightmans, it was delayed until the next afternoon.

When Frank woke up later that afternoon, he seemed calmer and more like his old self. He joined the family at the supper table and enjoyed a large meal. He was persuaded to stay the night at the Brightman home since everyone assumed that Nancy knew where he was because of the telegram that had been sent to her.

The next morning, Mary finally received the telegram from Nancy, asking if she knew where Frank was. She was now worried and confused. She took her father and stepmother aside and shared the message with them. They didn't understand why Nancy had sent the telegram when they'd already informed her of the situation. They had no idea that it had been sent the previous day and that, on Monday, Nancy still considered her husband missing.

Worse, while the three spoke privately, Frank had quietly taken his daughter and walked away from the house.

George had been conducting a funeral service when Frank left, and when he returned home, Mary quickly told him that Frank had slipped out of the house and had taken Maggie with him. They quickly contacted other family members, and a search was started.

After speaking to several people in town, it was discovered that Frank and Maggie had left Attleboro on a trolley bound for Pawtucket. The police there were notified to be on the lookout for him, and Nancy was also contacted so she would be aware of what was happening.

By noon, Frank and Maggie had arrived in Providence, where he purchased tickets for the 1:00 p.m. departure of the *Bay Queen* steamship. Once on board, Frank decided he was hungry and asked the purser if he and his daughter could get off the boat at Silver Spring -- one of the many resort towns located along Narragansett Bay -- for dinner. The purser explained that the ship didn't stop at Silver Spring - only at Rocky Point Park and Crescent Park.

Frank grumbled and stomped away, pulling his daughter by the hand. Other passengers would remember Frank because of his scruffy appearance, strange vacant stares, unusual body movements - and the look of fear on Maggie's face.

Frank took Maggie off the boat at Rocky Point, paid the 10-cent fare, and went straight to the park's Shore Dinner Hall. At a table, Frank ravenously devoured clam cakes, chowder, lobster, and fish.

Maggie ate very little but talked a lot and often smiled, perhaps hoping to please her father and make him happy with her. She was also excited to be at the amusement park. Maggie rarely saw her father, and he never seemed to like her very much. But now that he was taking her on a special outing - just the two of them - well, that must mean that he loves her very much.

Maggie couldn't have been happier at that moment.

Even if Maggie didn't see it, the waiters in the dining hall noticed Frank's bizarre behavior and later testified that, as Maggie continued to talk and laugh, it was obvious that Frank was trying hard to pay attention to her, but his gaze continued to be pulled to his plate of half-eaten food. He looked at the hall wildly and then stopped sometimes to stare at nothing.

When Frank finished his plate of food, he ordered another and finished it, too.

After that, he took Maggie by the hand, and they started up the hill that led toward the theater and the high cliffs that loomed above one edge of the park.

It was now 3:30 p.m.

The happy little girl walking next to her father would be dead in less than an hour.

Before and after that terrible day in August 1893, Rocky Point Amusement Park was one of the premier attractions on the Atlantic seaboard. It was known as a place for exciting rides, amazing attractions, and, of course, the best seafood dinners that money could buy.

The area had been developed from a picturesque estate, a portion of which had been used for picnics and sailing excursions as far back as the 1840s. In time, more attractions were slowly added, like the sea swing. This large apparatus built several feet out into the water, spun around in a circle to the delight of those in the suspended swings. A roller coaster followed a few years later.

The owners of other excursions began landing at the park, but many of them made the short walk from the park to Horn Spring, a short distance away. Horn Spring was a haven for gambling and liquor, and its shore dinners - a common term for seafood at the time - were managed by an expert cook named Smith Shaw, who drew many customers. They came for his food but also the roulette wheels, card games, dance hall, and free-flowing booze.

The owners of what came to be known as Rocky Point built a large fence to keep patrons from other parks off their property. They also erected a fence across the end of their wharf, so entrance was permitted only to those who were there to visit Rocky Point.

Rocky Point next built the large Shore Dinner Hall. One of the park's owners was a former sea captain named William Winslow, and his wife began cooking all the food. In 1859, "Mother Winslow's" menu included baked clams, sweet corn, baked fish, fish chowder, and brown bread - all for 40 cents. That seems cheap, but it's the equivalent of about $15 today.

The park continued to grow, hiring so many staff members that a dormitory called Rock Cottage had to be built on the grounds. There was also Forest Circle, a theater that later became a gambling hall, providing some of the best musical acts, comedy programs, and minstrel shows.

A carousel, bowling alley, and other simple amusements were added to the park, but when Byron Sprague purchased the park in 1865, he made many changes. He constructed a 10-story octagonal observatory that allowed visitors to climb the spiral stairs and enjoy a breathtaking view that stretched for miles. He also built a hotel, a massive three-story structure with 300 rooms, its own boathouse, and a livery stable.

Located next to the hotel was the Mansion House, Sprague's own summer retreat. The top floor was his home and office, while the ground floor offered a café, which served everything from sandwiches to full meals. The mansion faced the bay and provided an incredible view of Newport.

The American Steamboat Company later purchased the park, and more changes followed. By the 1870s, Rocky Point had grown to include many new amusements, like a shooting gallery, trained animals, circus performers, musicians, dancers, and dancers zoo animals, and a cage filled with monkeys.

As more and more people came to the park, the company struggled to keep up with the transportation demands. They built more docks and put more boats into service. Trains carried passengers to the park, dropping them off at the Canal Street depot so they could walk to a steamboat wharf and take a boat to their destination.

Despite the new thrilling amusements that had been added to the park, one of the biggest draws was still the Shore Dinner Hall. Rhode Island had become famous for its clam bakes, and many believed no place did it better than Rocky Point.

Bushels of clams were dug from the sand along the seashore, while large pits were filled with wood and lined with rocks. The wood was set on fire and allowed to burn out. Then, the ashes would be raked out while the rocks were still hot. A piece of wet canvas was laid over the rocks, and lobsters were placed on top of it. Seaweed soaked in saltwater was placed over the lobsters and each layer that followed to keep the steam inside the pit. Ears of fresh sweet corn were added next, then potatoes, then the clams. Another large canvas soaked in saltwater was placed on top, and the meal was allowed to cook for several hours.

The clam bake was eaten in the reverse order of how it was built. Once the clams were opened by the heat, they were enjoyed first, giving the corn, potatoes, and lobster more time over the heat. Drawn butter was always on hand, and watermelon usually provided the ending to the feast.

At Rocky Point, it was not uncommon to see a lingering plume of white smoke hanging above the park from the clam bakes. The clouds carried with them the decision scent of steaming seafood on the breeze.

The Rocky Point Hotel continued to offer fine accommodations for guests to the park until March 16, 1883, when a fire broke out and burned it to the ground. Before the blaze could be extinguished, the fire claimed the Shore Dinner Hall, the boathouse, and many other structures. Everything else was rebuilt, but the hotel was not.

In 1888, Rocky Point changed hands again. A former New York theatrical agent named Randall Harrington invested much time and money into updating and freshening the park. He added a large outdoor refreshment garden, a baseball field, and a grandstand that could seat up to 10,000 people.

Other popular attractions were the camera obscura, an optical device that projected images on a screen, and a giant waterslide called the Big Toboggan. After the idea debuted at the 1893 Columbian Exposition in Chicago, the park also added a Ferris Wheel, named after creator George Ferris, who had unveiled the first one at the World's Fair. The much smaller wheel at Rocky Point had 16 cars that each held two passengers, who got an unforgettable view of the bay from the top of the ride.

There was barely enough time in one day for families to take in all there was to offer at the park in 1893. Many took home a souvenir portrait from the photography studio, where they could choose an artificial backdrop from one of the entertaining selections offered.

Rocky Point opened each year during the first week of July and stayed open until after Labor Day. Guests were welcome from 8:00

in the morning until 6:00 in the evening. Alcohol wasn't allowed on the grounds; on Sundays, the park was closed except for baseball.

On August 4, 1892, the park would earn a place in America's infamous history when the police department from Fall River, Massachusetts, decided to schedule a vacation day for its officers to visit the park.

While they were there, the father and stepmother of a young woman named Lizzie Borden were brutally murdered back home in Fall River.

Just over a year later, though, the park itself would be the scene of another murder - when little Maggie Sheffield was beaten to death.

It's easy to understand why Maggie Sheffield was so excited to be visiting Rocky Point with her father.

There was so much to see for a child -sights, sounds, music, and laughter. The carousel, the flying swings, the roller coaster, and the train ride, all of them whirling, twirling, steaming, jangling, and ringing with frantic melodies. The little girl didn't know where to look next. There was so much to see - it was overwhelming.

But as her father led her along by the hand, Maggie realized with dismay that they were not stopping. They walked past the gaiety and the cheerful noise and the loud music and walked down to the shore of the Atlantic Ocean. The delightful cacophony of the park faded a little for Maggie, and she looked back over her shoulder in disappointment, wondering if she'd ever get to see the rides, animals, and attractions up close.

She wouldn't.

While the sounds of Rocky Point faded for Maggie, everything got louder inside Frank's head. It was all swirling together in amplified chaos. He had to make it stop. He bent down and picked up a large rock lying on the sand. He then turned to look at his five-year-old daughter.

The next sound he heard was a scream.

Two young couples, sitting a short distance away, had been enjoying the warm summer day when startled by the sound of the cry. One of the boys, Arthur Skirron, quickly got up and rushed over to see where the sound had come from. He was nearly halfway over the knoll where the beach was when a man came toward him. He was dirty, his clothing was rumpled, and he had a mad look in his eyes. He glanced at Arthur and kept walking without uttering a word.

Arthur kept going and climbed to the top of the slope that led to the beach. He looked down and went numb from the horror of what he saw.

A little girl was lying on the sand. There was a pool of blood surrounding her head. Neatly clad in a pretty dress and shoes, her head had been crushed, and blood covered her face.

Arthur suddenly realized the girl was still alive - and he ran for help.

He sprinted across the sand and then took the path toward the park's main office. The manager, Randall Harrington, was outside, and Arthur blurted out that a little girl had been badly injured and needed help. A house painter, Robert Quinn, was nearby and heard what Arthur said. He joined the other two men as they ran back toward the beach.

The girl - whom they'd soon know was Maggie Sheffield - was unconscious but still breathing.

With no time to waste, Harrington and Quinn gently picked up the small limp body of the child and carried it to the closest building, the park's theater. They summoned a doctor for help, but it took him nearly 20 minutes to arrive. By the time he ran through the door, Maggie had died.

Meanwhile, her murderous father had walked out of Rocky Point Park and headed toward the nearby Warwick Club, a private association for local businessmen. In the parking lot outside the club, he walked up to Newell Belcher, a hardware dealer from Providence, and another man, Daniel Remington.

"I wanted to be turned over to an officer," Frank loudly announced. "I have killed my child."

The two men were stunned and likely unsure of what the strange man had just said.

But Frank kept talking. "Why I did it, I don't know. I did not know that I had done anything until I had killed her. I did not know I had struck her until I saw the blood."

At that point, Frank began to shake and tremble. His knees gave out, and he collapsed in the parking lot. Belcher and Remington at first assumed he was insane, spouting words about his delusions, but when Frank asked again to be turned over to the police, they decided to comply with his wishes. It was, they thought, better to be safe than sorry.

They walked him back onto the grounds of Rocky Point and handed him over to Randall Harrington, who was not only the manager but also a police constable. They repeated what Frank had told them, and Harrington, having just left the bloody crime scene and witnessed the painful death that followed it, placed Frank under arrest. Harrington arranged for Frank to be taken to the county jail and put him in the lockup cell on the park grounds until officers arrived.

News of the murder quickly spread throughout the busy amusement park. Visitors lost interest in the popcorn, cymbal-playing monkeys, and trapeze artists and wanted news of the tragedy to satisfy their morbid curiosities. It seemed to be the general consensus that whoever had murdered the little girl should be hanged - right there in the park, if necessary.

While awaiting the arrival of more police officers, Harrington returned to the bloody scene on the beach. As he looked things over, he picked up a large rock that he assumed could be the murder weapon. It was nearly 10 inches long and two inches wide on one end. The other end was tapered to a point with square edges. The thicker section was smeared with Maggie's blood, and strands of the girl's hair stuck to it.

Sitting in the cell back at Harrington's office, Frank shifted and squirmed on the bench inside. He kept nodding his head back and forth and mumbling to himself. He kept asking in a low voice why he had committed the terrible act that caused the death of his daughter. Each time he asked, he paused as if waiting for someone to speak up and explain his violent behavior. No answers were offered - not by those who sat watching him and not by the voices inside of his head. Soon, he started asking to simply be shot.

Around 7:00 p.m., two police officers, Sanford Kinnecom and Frank Holden, arrived to take Frank to the East Greenwich County Jail. Frank told the officers that he had a history of insanity and killed his daughter under the influence of something he couldn't control.

This was his first effort to rid himself of responsibility for his crime - it wouldn't be the last.

"I could not have struck her if I knew I was hurting her," he tried to tell them.

The officers weren't sure how to reply to that. They didn't understand what had happened, but when they learned the details from Harrington, they asked Frank why he had brought Maggie to Rocky Point that day.

He didn't know, Frank told them. He claimed to have no recollection of when he got there or even how he got there. I recalled going to Attleboro to bring her home, but the time between leaving his sister's house and striking Maggie on the head was allegedly missing from his memory. The sight of his daughter's blood finally snapped him back to reality.

After Frank was taken away, the authorities sent telegrams to Frank's family, informing them of the day's horrible events.

Frank was in jail, they said, and their little Maggie was dead.

George Brightman had been in a meeting at the church when a newspaper reporter arrived to speak to him. That was how George learned of the tragedy. He hurried home and arrived just in time to receive the telegram that was supposed to have been delivered two hours earlier. He had to deliver the news to the rest of the family, and now someone had to go and claim Maggie's body. She had been taken to the undertaking rooms of Thomas Monahan in Providence.

He arrived there sometime around midnight and had to wait until medical examiner Moses Fifield was finished with the autopsy. He said that Maggie's skull had been so badly fractured that her brain had protruded through the top of her head.

The authorities called Frank's former in-laws early the following day for an interview. Mason and Margaret Hill told them that they had recently received three postcards from Frank, informing them he was in Attleboro and in good health. After they heard he had gone missing and had taken Maggie with him, they became very concerned.

The Hills had long believed there was something very wrong with Frank since he had aimlessly wandered away from home and showed up at their door. They believed his problems had started because he'd overworked himself at the railroad freight depot in Westerly - or perhaps when the school bell had hit him. They only saw him occasionally but believed that he loved Maggie very much, favored her even, and never suspected he might do anything to hurt her, despite his mental issues.

Mason Hill added with a tear in his eye. "Maggie," he confessed, "was the sweetest little thing you ever saw."

Later that morning, an official arrest warrant was sworn out for Frank, and Deputy Sheriff Michael Lynch took it to the jail. He was accompanied by court clerk Thomas Tilley and Frank's friend, the undertaker Dennison Hinckley. The men walked down the corridor and found Frank reclined on his cot, his head on a pillow, staring at the ceiling. Deputy Lynch wished him a good morning and asked him to get to his feet. Frank stood up, walked out of the unlocked cell door, and followed them into another room.

Frank was seated in a chair and listened to the warrant being read aloud to him, charging him with willfully, maliciously, and feloniously assaulting and killing his daughter. Once the warrant was read, Thomas Tilley asked him how he wanted to plea to the charge - guilty or not guilty?

Frank didn't say anything for a moment, and then he let out a groan of agony. "I killed my little girl," he said.

Dennison Hinckley awkwardly tried to comfort him. Frank just stared at him as if looking at a complete stranger. Slowly, he seemed to realize who he was.

"Did you sleep last night?" Dennison asked him.

"I don't know," Frank replied. Guards at the jail had noticed just before midnight that Frank's short intervals of sleep were interrupted by something that seemed to cause him pain.

And then he became agitated. "I must go to Mystic today and see my boy," he announced.

Dennison and the others in the room knew Frank was not going to Mystic or anywhere else. As for Dennison himself, he needed to return to Westerly so that he could prepare the body of his friend's daughter for burial.

When Frank was returned to his cell, he was given a telegram from Nancy, promising to come to the jail and see him later that day. Before she arrived, Reverend Smith Goodenow of the First Congregational Church, which Nancy attended, arrived to visit Frank. The two men spoke of happier things for a bit, but eventually, the conversation turned to the events at Rocky Point.

"I can remember being with Maggie among the rocks at Rocky Point," Frank told the minister. "The last thing I recall is Maggie asking me for my handkerchief so that she could tie it into the form of a doll."

He said he remembered nothing after that. His next real memory was the look in Maggie's eyes as she stared up at him with blood gushing from her head.

Frank wept as he spoke. "I don't remember picking up the stone or striking her with it." Then he added something that likely seemed strange to the reverend at first, "They charged me with murdering two girls, but I can't remember killing but one and that was my little Maggie."

Frank had been confused by the arrest warrant. In it, Maggie had also been referred to as "Eliza Roe," an alias like "Jane Doe." The police had used it to reference Maggie before they learned her identity. This had been explained to him by Deputy Lynch, but he'd forgotten it, and now he had come to believe that "Eliza Roe" was another child who had been killed.

Frank then informed the minister that he was expecting a visit from his wife and was very concerned for Nancy's safety. He requested that the guards not let him out of his cell while Nancy was there. He explained that he feared he might go violently insane again and, this time, harm his wife.

"I have terrible pains in my head," he told the minister and said he knew he was in a bad situation.

On Wednesday afternoon, Maggie's body was laid out in her father's home while her Uncle George preached a funeral service with the assistance of Reverend Goodenow. It was a simple ceremony - one hymn, a prayer, and some brief remarks. Her body was then taken to Elm Grove Cemetery and placed in the earth next to her mother.

On September 5, 1893, a preliminary hearing was held at the Kent County Courthouse. Frank was brought into the courtroom wearing a somber black suit. He joined his attorney, Nathan Lewis, at the defendant's table.

Lewis was a Civil War veteran, former politician, and circuit judge who was well-respected and staunch in his belief that Frank was insane at the time of the murder. He confidently entered his client's plea of not guilty. He believed that Frank fit the description of the law that stated that a person without the capacity to tell right from wrong at the time of the crime could not be held responsible.

While Lewis addressed the court, Frank sat silently in his chair, alternating between looking incredibly bored and covering his face with his hands.

When Lewis was finished, the prosecuting attorney - who was also the coroner - began to speak. Albert Greene was also a Civil War veteran, a graduate of Brown University, and the Michigan School of Law. He had served as the president of the Warwick Town Council for three years and was also widely respected. Greene was convinced of Frank's guilt and intended to make him pay for what he'd done to his daughter.

Standing before the judge's bench, Greene held up a brown paper bag and carefully removed a little girl's dress and shoes. Both were darkly stained with blood.

He called Officer Kinnecom to the stand and asked the policeman if he could identify the two articles of clothing. The officer nodded and stated they had been worn by Maggie Sheffield at the time of her murder. When he heard this, Frank removed his hands from his face and looked at the witness. He then tore his gaze away and stared down at the top of the table.

No defense was offered during the preliminary hearing, but Judge Warner felt enough proof had been offered to hold Frank over for trial. As Frank was being led out of the courtroom, his calmness disappeared, and he let out a wild yell and became aggressive and angry. Several officers were forced to restrain him. Frank flung them back against the wall, and they all fell in a heap on the floor.

Nathan Lewis was more determined than ever to prove his client was insane.

The following day, Lewis went to see Judge Pardon Tillinghast and asked him to order a psychological examination of his client. But Lewis was told that the judge would only be allowed to do this if he was given jurisdiction over the trial. Lewis prepared the petition and went to see if Deputy Sheriff Amasa Sprague would sign it.

Meanwhile, expecting Lewis to return with a signed petition, Tillinghast contacted a doctor and asked him to go to the jail and perform a complete examination of Frank.

But there was a problem. When Lewis brought the paperwork to Deputy Sprague, he balked at giving an immediate signature. He wanted to consult with the attorney general first because Sprague had his own opinions about whether Frank should be examined. Lewis was forced to wait several days, and then Sprague contacted him to say he had decided not to sign the document.

Lewis tried to change his mind, but Sprague refused again. The defense attorney then visited the Office of the Rhode Island Agent of Charities and Corrections to appeal for help. When he arrived, he was told that the officer he needed to speak with had left on a trip to Chicago to see the World's Fair. Nothing could be done until he returned.

More time passed, but when the man returned to the office, Lewis immediately went to see him. He told Lewis there was nothing he could do. A proper psychological exam would require Frank to be transferred, and if Deputy Sprague wouldn't allow this, their hands were tied.

But Lewis explained that he was not asking for Frank to be moved - he just wanted him to be examined so that a determination could be made regarding his sanity or lack of it. If Frank did turn out to be insane, it would still have to be proven before the judge would order him to be moved to a hospital.

But the officer stubbornly refused to help. He informed Lewis that he didn't think Frank would be tried if he was moved to a hospital and, therefore, it was best that he remain in jail.

Public opinion had already turned against Frank because of his daughter's murder, and now it seemed to Lewis that the authorities were biased against him, too. It was obvious that the officer and the sheriff's deputies wanted to make sure that Frank paid for his crime - whether he was in his right mind or not.

Lewis angrily asked the man why he would want to try an insane man who was not legally responsible for his acts.

Perhaps, the officer suggested, it was not as simple as that. "He might have brought it on himself," the man shrugged.

After all, there had been rumors going around town that Frank had been a regular user of cocaine for at least the past five years, while others claimed it was opium that he was using.

This was when our story takes yet another turn.

In 1893, cocaine was sold over the counter in pharmacies nationwide, both in pure form and as an ingredient in medicine given to babies, children, and adults. In 1886, it had even become the main ingredient in a new soft drink called "Coca-Cola." It was almost revered for its restorative power and was widely endorsed by eminent physicians and psychiatrists, which were referred to as alienists at the time. Sigmund Freud used cocaine, recommended it to patients, and believed it was a reliable cure for opium addiction.

If Frank Sheffield was using cocaine, this was likely what he used it for - to cure his need for opium. His symptoms didn't fit with cocaine, which usually brings high energy, extreme talkativeness, and a lack of hunger. Frank was often hungry, especially on that final day, asking to leave the boat for food and eating a large meal at Rocky Point. Cocaine can erase the appetite, and heavy users might go without eating for a day or more.

Opium was a different kind of beast. Like cocaine, the dark brown, gummy substance was sold right over the pharmacy counter and, more commonly, was an ingredient in dozens of medications, from cough syrup for children to pain relievers for adults. One of the most popular was laudanum, found in almost every household's medicine cabinet. It could also be injected or smoked.

Unfortunately, many of Franks' behaviors fit those associated with opium. It causes headaches and ringing in the ears. Even though Frank attributed those symptoms to being hit by the school bell, it also might have been a side effect of opium use. It could also cause objects and faces to appear faded and distorted, explaining Frank's habit of staring strangely at things around him. Sounds and words may not be heard clearly, explaining Frank's response when people spoke to him. Opium can also cause a user to be restless and wander aimlessly, which Frank was prone to do, leaving home for hours at a time. It could also cause severe memory loss.

However, Frank didn't fit all the signs of opium use. He didn't obtain the calm, serene feeling most users spoke of or the lack of worry that most achieved. Typically, it would be out of character for someone who was a heavy opium user to suddenly kill someone.

Perhaps Frank was using opium and cocaine, too, using one of them to cease his reliance on the other. Or maybe those were just rumors made up to explain his strange behavior. He may not have used drugs at all.

It's also possible - even more likely - that Frank was just out of his mind.

Frank's trial for the murder of his daughter began on October 9, 1893. He arrived in the courtroom wearing a neat black suit. His usually close-cut beard had grown several inches since he'd been arrested - but it did nothing to hide the look of utter despair on his face.

He was seated between Nathan Lewis and his brother-in-law, George Brightman, at the defense table. The courtroom was packed with witnesses and the curious, and as more people pushed through the doors, the seats were filled, and it became standing room only.

When Frank's wife, Nancy, entered the courtroom 15 minutes after her husband had, he did not acknowledge her presence. Wearing a black mourning dress, she appeared to be quite nervous. She arrived just in time to hear the indictment about her husband being read aloud and Frank's plea of not guilty.

There were no women on the jury in those days - no mothers who would be sickened by the murder of a little girl - so it was made up of primarily middle-aged farmers and businessmen. Two of them claimed they knew absolutely nothing about the case, even though it had been front-page news.

Attorney General Willard Tanner opened the trial for the state, describing for the jury what had occurred on the day of the murder. He then began calling a string of witnesses to the stand, including doctors who had examined the body and those who were present at the park when the murder occurred, like Robert Quinn, who had accompanied Harrington to the scene. He told of what they'd found and about carrying Maggie's body to the park's theater.

Newell Belcher and Frank Holden told the jury what they had seen that day and about the defendant's strange behavior. Two employees of the Shore Dinner Hall described the odd way that Frank stared at the ceiling and gawked around the room instead of paying attention to his daughter, who was chatting excitedly.

Deputy Sheriff Michael Lynch testified about his conversations with Frank at the jail when the warrant was being served. More witnesses followed, but Tanner closed the prosecution's case in less than an hour.

Nathan Lewis opened for the defense, explaining that he wouldn't try to deny that a terrible murder had occurred that day at Rocky Point. However, he would provide testimony proving that Frank had absolutely no motive to kill his daughter.

"It takes something beyond the mere physical act of killing to produce murder," Lewis told the jury. "If Frank Sheffield were acquitted and cured today, he could never expect to enjoy life again. But to his relatives who sit in the shadows of a great grief, your verdict, gentlemen, means something. Will you add to this sorrow the tingle of shame by branding the husband and father a felon?"

Lewis spent over 20 minutes setting the stage for what he planned to offer the jury before he called Nancy to the stand. After she was placed under oath, she was asked to describe Frank's behavior before Maggie's death. She told the court that, in addition to his unannounced trip to Attleboro, he had inexplicably wandered away from home on two previous occasions.

A year earlier, he had left home on a cold winter day without knowing where he was going. When he came to his senses, he was in Mystic with no idea how he'd gotten there. A month later, he disappeared again and was found in Preston, Connecticut. Nancy said that when her husband talked later about these strange excursions, he said he didn't know what was happening until something snapped back in his head, making him rational again.

Frank's courtroom demeanor seemed to change by the minute as the trial went on. His look of sadness would shift to an expression that seemed to indicate that he had no interest in what was happening. This lack of interest was noticed by many observers, who thought it odd that he appeared so uncaring since his life was literally hanging in the balance. Seemingly bored and not hearing the crowd whispering behind him, he barely glanced up when witnesses walked past him to take the stand.

George Brightman was called as a witness and was asked to offer an opinion on the mental condition of his brother-in-law. George stated that he believed Frank was insane and told the court that Frank's father had once suggested having him placed in an asylum. He also testified that he had been shocked by Frank's appearance when he had shown up at his house on that August day. He described him as haggard, unshaven, unkempt, and having an unusual expression on his face.

George said he was also surprised - and worried by - Frank's demanding manner and the urgent need he seemed to have to take Maggie home with him. "There was a peculiar glitter in his eyes when he looked at her, so much so that she asked him why he was staring that way," the minister added.

Dr. George F. Keene of the Rhode Island State Hospital for the Insane - who had finally been able to examine Frank in jail - took the stand and stated that he believed the defendant was undoubtedly suffering from insanity.

He described in detail the tests that he had performed on Frank and then explained in a strangely confusing way how a truly insane person was likely to hurt not only people he disliked but also those he loved the most. A person pretending to be insane usually didn't have the same kind of violent manner and disheveled appearance as one who was truly mad.

Nathan Lewis posed a hypothetical question: "Do you think that a man who has shown such symptoms as those that have been described and attributed to Frank Sheffield would be responsible for such acts?"

"I would have grave doubts about such a man's responsibility," Dr. Keene answered.

Other witnesses followed the doctor on the stand. Most of them also offered opinions about Frank's appearance, saying, "He could hardly be recognized," adding that his face was "all distorted and care worn." His old friend Dennison Hinckley said Frank had looked so bad to him that he didn't think he'd live much longer. Even the boat's purser that Frank and Maggie had taken to Rocky Point commented on his appearance. He testified that his face was "neglected" and that he used aimless movements and stared strangely.

Lewis also received testimony from people Frank had worked with, and he talked about the jobs he'd lost because of his behavior. One witness testified that he had lost his job at the railroad station six months before the murder because he could not keep the freight accounts straight.

A man who had worked with Frank at the depot testified that he had told him several times that he feared his eventual death would be a "fearsome one." His co-worker said Frank always seemed despondent and scared of the future.

The most disturbing testimony of the day came from Dr. John Morgan, a physician Frank had been visiting regularly. Morgan admitted in court that Frank had told him that he'd had impulses to kill his daughter before he actually committed the act.

During his visits to his office, Frank told the physician that he was constantly worried about finding a job and his finances. He told him that he considered killing Maggie during his lowest points so that he could prevent her from suffering or becoming a burden on someone else.

Dr. Morgan called Frank's worries about money and providing for his family a "morbid fear," and when it occurred, he had to try very hard to keep his impulse to kill his daughter subdued. For this reason, he had instructed Nancy not to let Frank out of her sight. He had serious concerns about his patient and, yes, for some reason, had taken no other precautions to prevent him from acting on his murderous impulses.

Dr. Morgan had failed again a few days before the murders, too. Frank had tried to commit suicide with an overdose of laudanum, which lends some credence to the idea that Frank was an opium user or at least had it at his disposal.

After more than a dozen witnesses had appeared, Lewis told the jury that he'd planned to call more but did not expect the state's case to be presented so quickly, so he had not asked them to appear that day. Not wanting to prolong the trial, he had decided that the jury had already heard enough - they had been sufficiently convinced that his client was insane.

Or at least he hoped so.

In his closing argument, Lewis reiterated that even though his client had killed his daughter, he should not be held accountable for it. There were several things beyond Franks' control that Lewis felt caused his horrific actions that day, including the fact that he had contracted an illness called erysipelas in 1891. It is an infection caused by bacteria that originates in a person's nose and throat. Eventually, the disease spreads to the lymph nodes, causing swelling, chills, fever, distorted facial expression, and dry, scaly skin.

Erysipelas doesn't just form on its own. It needs a breeding ground in the nose and throat that is already damaged - damage caused perhaps by snorting cocaine.

Lewis maintained that Frank's painful bout with the disease had left him depressed and despondent, affecting his mental health.

This was obvious, the attorney said, because Frank was not the type of man who, in a normal state of mind, would have killed his own child. He was the son of a minister and a man of excellent character. He had held the position of school principal and was always kind to children, especially his own. After the tragic death of his wife just a few years earlier, he'd also suffered an injury when that school bell hit him. His mind had been further altered, which caused him to have memory lapses and other odd afflictions. His mental illness was the only reason that Frank would have to kill his daughter.

Once the case was turned over to the jury, they would have an important decision to make - was Frank temporarily insane or a cold-blooded killer?

The public would have its decision to make about Frank, too, which would decide his future reputation. Was he truly insane? Had the murder happened because a school bell hit Frank in the head? Or was he a dope fiend whose addiction caused him to murder?

Those who knew Frank were as divided as those who encountered him during the crime. Harrington, the manager at Rocky Point, told a newspaper reporter, "I think he is daft."

Officer Kettle disagreed. "I don't think the man is crazy. I can't get it into my head that he is. It seems to me there was too much deliberation. But for his own benefit, I hope he is."

Before the jury was sent to deliberate, the judge defined the crime of murder for them. He compared the murder of a person being committed by someone insane to that of a murder committed by a child. "There can be no criminal intent in either case," he said. "It is up to you, the jury, to decide if Frank Sheffield had criminal intent when he killed his daughter."

Just a few minutes before 3:00 p.m., the jury quietly exited the room. The prosecutor and defense attorney gathered papers together, and Nathan Lewis bent down to speak to his client. Frank would be returned to his cell. It would soon be supper time, and he advised Frank to eat and try and get some rest. It was likely that the jury would not return until at least the next day at the earliest.

But Lewis was wrong.

Just eight minutes after beginning their deliberations, the jury announced they had reached their verdict. A ripple of surprise went through the courtroom. Those who had not yet left the room scrambled back to their seats, and word was spread, causing a commotion in the hallway.

The verdict was handed to the judge, who read it aloud - not guilty, by reason of insanity.

The verdict in the case certainly did not allow Frank to go free. He was judged insane. He had murdered his daughter, whether or not he was responsible for it. The verdict didn't land him in a penitentiary cell or at the hangman's rope, but it did send him to the Rhode Island State Hospital for the Insane in Cranston.

Nancy Sheffield remained living at her house on Liberty Street for the rest of her life. In 1900, her widowed sister, Wealthy Sisson, moved in with her. Nancy continued to work as a dressmaker, visiting clients' homes who sought her skills. Her son, Amos, also lived with her and worked in a local lumberyard. In 1917, he was given an exemption from the wartime draft because he had an elderly mother who was dependent on him for support.

Wealthy Sisson died on April 19, 1925, and Nancy followed her to the grave just weeks later, on June 25. Amos sold the house on Liberty Street and mostly vanished from history.

Frank and Nancy's daughter, Sarah Elizabeth, went on to marry William Goff, a piano tuner, and they eventually settled in Westerly.

Maggie's maternal grandparents raised her brother, Mason, and he was raised a privileged young man. He applied to an engineering college and received four years of training as a shipbuilder. He graduated in 1902 and, in 1910, married Elsie Thorp, whose father was in the hardware business. They moved to New York City, where Mason worked as a draughtsman, then returned to Mystic, where he began building boats. The following years brought two children for the couple, numerous work opportunities, and moves from Connecticut to New York and New Jersey. Mason died on June 28, 1952.

As for Frank Sheffield, his stay at the asylum was not as long as most expected. On March 14, 1901, Frank died from epilepsy and tuberculosis. The latter illness was not a surprise. Tuberculosis spread easily through institutions like the asylum, and there had been a recent outbreak.

Epilepsy was usually a childhood disorder that is outgrown as an adult, but some believed the blow to the head by the school bell had caused brain damage that manifested as epileptic seizures. But that was only a guess based on medical science in the early 1900s.

There is no clear explanation for why Frank killed Maggie that day at Rocky Point. Worse, Maggie almost seemed to be forgotten after her death, her father's trial, and his time in the asylum. Her family, Frank's co-workers, doctors, friends, and even complete strangers seemed more concerned about Frank's well-being than what happened to the slain little girl.

Everyone questioned what had caused such a wonderful man to simply snap. He was raised by a minister; his early life had been perfectly normal and happy, with no tragedy or hardship. He fell in love, married, and had two beautiful children, including the one he would eventually kill.

Those friends and strangers picked apart Frank's life, knowing he'd been happy until something unexpected happened. The woman he loved was suddenly gone. She died bringing Maggie into the world. Frank loved Maggie, but perhaps he loved her tragically. It was never his infant son that he worried about. Never his son, he admitted to his doctor that he was afraid of being unable to support.

It was always Maggie - the little girl he loved but who took away his wife. It was Maggie who'd torn his life apart. It was Maggie that, deep down, he blamed for all the sadness that ruined his life.

In his madness, Frank thought about Maggie all the time. But once she was dead, he seemed to be the only one. In the sensational drama of the trial, everyone focused on, talked over, and wondered about Frank.

But what about Maggie?

Well, it seems that neither her story nor the story of Rocky Point Amusement Park was over just yet.

Rocky Point Amusement Park, of course, endured beyond the scandal of Maggie Sheffield's death in 1893. However, her death wouldn't be the last to occur on the grounds; there would be plenty of mishaps, tragedies, and trouble to come.

In the summer of 1905, a man named Fred Bruemel was found dead in a secluded section of the park. The New Jersey man had come to Rocky Point to take his own life. He succeeded.

Randall Harrington, who had been managing Rocky Point and nearby Crescent Park for years, bought Rocky Point outright in 1910. He began importing rides and attractions that had never been seen before in New England. New Ferris Wheels, roller coasters, and even a small railroad began drawing even bigger crowds to the resort. On top of vaudeville shows, band performances, and dance nights were the Gypsy's Cave, the Mystic Moorish Maze, the Parisian Carousel, a Japanese Garden, flying sleighs, an underground river, the electric parlor, and more.

By 1911, Rocky Point had far less competition along the Eastern Seaboard. It had outbuilt and outspent the competition, and one by one, other parks closed down, and the land was sold off to be used for other things.

Harrington managed to outlast them all, even when the cost of clams caused the price of seafood dinners to go up. He also battled with the religious residents of Rhode Island, who'd been fighting against baseball games at the park on Sundays. They also wanted to stop the Sunday dance nights, but Harrington managed to keep both going.

The ball field remained a favorite destination for visitors, but they were given quite a shock on July 16, 1911, when a man was killed there in front of hundreds of spectators. A driver named William Fort had driven his employer, William Hunter, and three of his friends down from Boston to see a game. Fort had parked the automobile with all the others in the grass not far from the entrance to the field. As the end of the game neared, Fort went to the car, started it up, and backed out of his parking spot.

It wasn't until a witness told him that he discovered he had just run over someone.

A Providence carpenter named Hiram Bangs had laid down to take a nap in the grass - right behind Fort's car. When he backed out, he ran over Bangs and crushed his chest under the wheels.

When the cry went out for a doctor, the game had to be stopped for the emergency. It was too late for Bangs, though. He died a few minutes later.

In June 1912, another death occurred at the park. A Massachusetts man named Thomas Martin, along with three friends, came to Rocky Point to catch a baseball game. Martin was driving a new car and wasn't completely familiar with its mechanisms. He turned into the parking lot near the dance hall and attempted to back into a spot along an iron fence.

Unknown to Martin and the others, the iron fence was also a protective barrier to keep anyone from falling off a steep, rocky cliff into the ocean.

Martin backed in and reached for the brake handle - but grabbed the reverse handle instead. The car shot backward through the fence, tipped backward, and did a complete somersault before landing at the bottom of the cliff.

All four men were thrown from the vehicle into the rocks. Martin walked away with bruises, and friends William Hartigan and Joseph Mahoney broke bones. His fourth friend, Thomas Brady, was pinned under the car.

People nearby who had seen the accident ran to the scene, and a group of them were able to lift the auto and pull Brady to safety. He was severely hurt, and an ambulance was summoned. He was rushed to Rhode Island Hospital but died a few hours later.

More attractions were added to the park - the Scenic Mountain Railway Ride, the Palm Garden, the Rivers of Venice, the Rattlesnake

Den, L.B. Walker's Diving Girls - and were joined by an $8,000 organ that reproduced the effect of a 60-piece band. The Shore Dinner Hall was expanded to provide comfortable seating for as many as 2,500 people.

By 1913, the era of the aviator had arrived, and air shows became popular up and down the Atlantic coast. That year, Harrington got into the act and hired the beautiful pioneer female aviator Ruth Bancroft Law to perform in the skies above Rocky Point for three consecutive days. According to the contract, Ruth was supposed to perform aerial stunts on May 30 and 31 and June 1, making two flights per day and flying 30 minutes each day. In return, she'd receive $1,200. Harrington was supposed to pay her $300 when she arrived at the park on May 30 with her biplane and an additional $300 on completion of her performances each day.

When Ruth arrived, she was paid $300. That afternoon, she went up for her first show, but after just three minutes of acrobatics, a heavy gust of wind blew the light airplane out of the sky, and she crashed into a parked automobile when she reached the ground. Obviously, the show was over, but when Harrington asked for her money back, Ruth refused. He took her to court over it, but they eventually settled the matter. Believe it or not, she wasn't the last aviator to perform at the park, but Harrington had certainly lost his taste for this latest fad.

Later in 1913, the park's ball field became the site of New England's first automobile polo game. It drew a crowd of over 2,500 people. The game featured four cars, each with a driver and a polo player leaning out of the auto with a mallet.

That same summer saw the addition of a new ride called the Scranton Coal Mine, which carried passengers through dark tunnels and down a deep shaft where "coal miners" could be seen in action.

The expensive ride used 27 burros that had been imported from Mexico to pull the cars through the mine.

The trip up from Mexico by the owner of the animals, W.A. "Snake" King, had taken three months and traveled through the middle of the Mexican Revolution. Snake had to go 35 miles out of the way to stay out of the line of fire. Even on this route, he had to pass through towns where the bodies of Mexican soldiers were lying in the streets. Food and water were nowhere to be found, and five of the burros died on the way.

When Snake finally made it to Rocky Point, he told Harrington that if he wanted more burros in the future, he would have to go and get them himself.

The park continued to attract visitors with new attractions and shows, like Torelli's Dog and Pony Circus, and with performances in the theater and bandstands by popular performers of the day like Beulah Ballas, comedian Frank Dobson, blackface comics Kelly and Davis, Nellie Fillimore, soprano Isabella Hackley and Clinton and Bernice, who exhibited fancy rifle shooting.

High-wire acts had also become all the rage. They always drew large audiences, especially a pair of trick-riding bicyclists known only as the "Two Demons." They performed on the wire in a pair of devilish costumes.

Another huge draw was Mademoiselle Emerie, a French trapeze artist. She began each performance in full evening garb, and then an assistant would bring her a glass of wine. Pretending to become inebriated, she would disrobe while sailing through the air. Her shows were said to have been hilarious and ended with her clad only in tights.

But the laughter and applause temporarily stopped on May 4, 1914, when another fire occurred at the park. It burned for hours, destroying the vaudeville theater, peanut stand, shooting gallery, and two unoccupied stands. But the show had to go on.

More attractions followed - and more accidents, too.

One of the biggest new attractions was the Motor Dome, a large motorcycle track set at a 40-degree angle. Stunt performers often referred to them as the "Wall of Death." During one thrilling show, an employee who wasn't aware a race was taking place - somehow missing the roar of several motorcycles right above his head - lifted a trapdoor beneath the track and collided with the front wheel of a bike driven by a performer named "Daredevil McFee." The motorcycle was moving at 70 miles per hour when it hit the door, throwing McFee onto the track. He didn't get up for several minutes, and the crowd watched in terror. But then, he got up and limped off the track, somehow walking away from the accident with only cuts and bruises.

It wasn't only motorcycles that raced at Rocky Point. In 1920, the Monkey Speedway was added. It was inside a circular tent near the park entrance and showcased six chimpanzees who drove tiny automobiles at breakneck speed. Children loved it - adults, not so much.

Circus, sideshow, comic, and musical performers continued to come to the park, but baseball remained one of the big draws. Even so, the games continued to be a thorn in the side of those who felt the games should be banned on Sundays. Finally, three Warwick residents and a local minister decided to visit the capital and appeal to the governor to stop the games being played on Sunday at the park. The governor assured them he'd put an end to it, but the legislature rejected his plan.

Baseball did finally end at Rocky Point later that year, but not because the busybodies had their way. Randall Harrington's health was failing, and not enough attention had been paid to the ball field during his illness. Most of the teams that had been playing there expressed displeasure at the state of the field and decided to look for a new venue. When the last game was played at the end of the 1917 season, it became the final baseball game at Rocky Point.

Randall Harrington died in 1918, and his widow, Amelia, decided to lease the park to some businessmen. They took over what seemed to be a risk-free business, only to have their first taste of misfortune when the Mansion House burned down in 1919.

Despite this eye-opening event, Rocky Point continued to revolve, renovate, and add attractions like the Witching Waves, new carousels, the Whip, the Circle Swing, and more. Admission to the park remained free, but the rides now all required the purchase of a ticket to get on board. Those who wanted the thrill of the new coasters and rides were happy to hand over a dime, in any case.

A new wooden Wildcat roller coaster was added in 1926, and a bobsled coaster called the Flying Turns was installed five years later. The Tunnel of Love was introduced for those who wanted a different kind of heart-pounding experience.

In the 1930s, Rocky Point was hit by two very different kinds of storms. The first was one of public opinion. A newspaper based in Maryland accused Rocky Point's owner and staff of racial discrimination, stating that African American guests were not allowed on the beach or in the swimming pools. Several young men from an outing with the Ebenezer Baptist Church were told by an attendant that management would not allow them to rent lockers to "colored people." Worse, it was alleged that the park's saltwater pool had been drained dry by the management to avoid having to refuse entrance to African Americans who wanted to swim in it.

If a reputation for racism wasn't enough, fate had more in store for Rocky Point.

The seaside location - incredible in fair weather - often fell victim to storms that blew in off the ocean. On September 21, 1938, a massive hurricane hit New England, wreaking havoc with wind speeds of up to 160 miles per hour. Over 600 deaths and over $300 million in damages were reported from the storm. The destruction of dunes and beaches and the obliteration of hundreds of buildings changed the landscape overnight. New England had never seen such death and destruction.

Most of the buildings and rides at Rocky Point were washed away or smashed to splinters by the ferocity of the wind and waves. The metal rails of the roller coasters were twisted, the carousels were simply gone, and the storm swept away the midway amusements and the dining hall.

Most of Rocky Point was gone.

Following the devastation, the park was returned to Amelia Harrington, who then leased the grounds to Thomas F. Wilson, who struggled to restore the park. He gave up a year later, so in 1941, Amelia tried to sell the park, but there was no interest in it. A few potential buyers approached her, planning to tear down the park's remains and use the land for oil tanks and other industrial uses, but Amelia couldn't bear to see it end up that way.

Finally, in 1945, a land company of several partners, including Vincent Ferla, bought the park. Along with family and friends, Vincent began a costly restoration of the amusement park. Aside from basic cleanup, they had to rebuild everything that had been destroyed. A new Shore Dinner Hall was the first on the agenda. The new structure was set farther back from the sea and used concreted piers that would withstand another storm. Vincent also purchased hurricane insurance - just in case.

The saltwater swimming pool was renovated, the dance hall was replaced with the new Palladium, and many rides were restarted. But even after all that, the park's re-opening didn't draw the public in the way it once had. The post-war economy forced people to rethink spending on rides and games of chance. Vincent was soon forced to shut down some of the rides to cover the park's expenses, and it became clear that the once-bright lights of Rocky Point were starting to dim.

To add insult to injury, Hurricane Carol crashed into the park on August 31, 1954. More of the rides were destroyed, as was the new Shore Dinner Hall, which wasn't stormproof after all. When the insurance company failed to pay out the way Vincent Ferla expected, he took them to court.

While dealing with the lawsuit, he also began cleaning things up again, repairing the storm damage, and rebuilding the dinner hall. This time, the construction crew used steel and cement to - hopefully - withstand the winds.

Vincent was determined to restore the park's reputation and poured money into exhibitions and events that would draw crowds. Bands were booked, dances scheduled, and even the College Queen Beauty Contest was held at Rocky Point. The Shore Dinner Hall was soon booming once again, and advertisements that called the park "100 Acres of Fun" reached their intended audience. Rocky Point veterans returned and brought new thrill-seekers with them. Things had started to brighten again - at least for a little while.

But tragedy was never far away from the park. In July 1967, Dale Kitchings of New York drowned one Saturday afternoon after diving into the park's saltwater pool.

Less than two years later, an exhausted Vincent Perla sold the park to Alvin H. Cohen, who continued to maintain the rides and shore dinners that had put Rocky Point on the map. These were the things that had made the place famous - well, those things and the deaths.

In September 1970, a former Navy veteran named Edwin Walker worked as a maintenance crew member in the park. While repairing a cable guard pulley on the Skyliner overhead tram ride, he stood on the large wheel that pulled the cable. Somehow, the ride started up, and he was pulled between the wheel and the base of the ride and was horrifically crushed to death. Walker had survived two tours of duty in Vietnam but couldn't survive one season at the possibly jinxed amusement park.

And the possibility of that jinx started to be talked about again in the fall of 1980 when another fire destroyed a row and game concession stands on the midway. Two park employees were later arrested and charged with setting the fire. One of them would later be convicted of arson.

In the 1980s, three more roller coasters were added to the park while some longtime rides and attractions were being shut down. The saltwater pool was one of them. It was closed and then filled in. One of the new rides, the Freefall, which gave riders the stomach-dropping sensation of falling 12 stories, had initially been in another amusement park, but after four teenagers were killed while riding it, the ride was quietly moved to Rocky Point. What could go wrong?

It wasn't fires or hurricanes that finally ended Rocky Point - it was cash, or really, the lack of it. The last ten years or so of the park's life saw various companies involved with it defaulting on loans, filing for bankruptcy, and being unable to scrape up enough money to keep things going. In 1996, auctions were held to sell off the rides and equipment from Rocky Point. Anything that couldn't be moved off the property was either torn down or left to collapse.

The former resort, with some of its many structures still standing, sat empty for years. It became a destination for urban explorers and vandals, and on October 16, 2006, a fire destroyed the Cliff House, where the park's seasonal staff once lodged.

That final fire served as the death knell for Rocky Point.

In 2014, the land where the amusement park once stood was turned into a state park. Despite this, some pieces of the past remain, like the upper and lower stations for the Skyliner ride, the stairs that led to the House of Horror, and a steel arch by the entrance that was originally built for the 1964 World's Fair New York and subsequently moved to Rocky Point.

But that's all. Almost nothing is left of the place once considered the greatest amusement park on the East Coast.

And that's really kind of a shame - although it's not as tragic as the memories that still linger here about the death of a little girl named Maggie Sheffield and her reported ghost.

As mentioned, Maggie's story is not quite finished. After her murder, the little girl was largely forgotten in the whirlwind of newspaper stories, insanity pleas, trials, and her father being locked away in an insane asylum. Some believe that's why Maggie's spirit continued to walk in the years that followed. She wanted to be remembered, and the place where she demanded attention was the place where she died - Rocky Point.

As people told and re-told Maggie's story, they often spoke of a haunting at the beach where she had died that August afternoon. Her father had crushed her head with a rock, and perhaps the suddenness of the crime prevented her spirit from moving on. Over the years, there were dozens of accounts of park guests seeing a young girl in an old-fashioned dress as she walked along the stretch of beach where the murder occurred.

As more time passed, most didn't remember Maggie's terrible murder and only knew that an ethereal figure had been spotted as she walked across the sand. Many of those witnesses likely wouldn't have known she was not a flesh and blood girl except for the fact that when she walked, she left no footprints behind in the sand. She simply passed over it, leaving no trail behind her but terrifying those who saw her slowly fade toward the trees at the beach's edge.

Maggie - although never identified as anyone other than a ghostly girl in an old dress - was also frequently spotted at the park's vaudeville theater, which was the place where she had breathed her last after the park manager and the house paint had carried her body up from the beach.

According to witnesses who reported her there, the girl roamed about, looking behind curtains, peering into shadowy doorways, and climbing staircases as if searching for someone. Once again, no one had any idea that she was a ghost until they approached her and tried to help her find whatever she was looking for. If they got too close, she either just vanished or ran away, leading the witness on a chase through the dark theater with tapping footsteps and child-like laughter as its soundtrack. The little girl would never be caught, though.

If this was Maggie - and I suspect it was - what was she looking for in the old theater? Once again, we can only guess, but I think there's a very good chance that her father was the subject of her search.

Even though his actions may have frightened her a little when they were together at the Brightman house the day before her death, Maggie loved her father. She was thrilled to be leaving with him the following day and excited that he had taken her to an amusement park. We will never know what was going through her mind at the moment he raised that rock above her head - and perhaps she doesn't remember either. Maybe the only memories her spirit has of her father were the last few good ones they made together that day.

Rocky Point -- and that old vaudeville theater - has been gone for a long time. Once a few pieces of rusted metal and broken rubble remain today.

But what about Maggie Sheffield's ghost?

Is she still out there, still looking for her father? Or did she finally find him waiting for her somewhere along her journey?

I don't suppose we're really ever going to know.

BIBLIOGRAPHY

1810 United States Census

Anderson, Jean - *The Haunting of America: Ghost Stories from Our Past*, New York, NY, Houghton Mifflin, 1973

Atteberry, T. "Too Good to be True, Mayhem on the Highway Turns into a Ghost Story from Old Charleston and the Legend of Lavinia Fisher." *Witchery Art: A Gothic Cabinet of Curiosities and Mysteries.* May 20, 2020

Baker, D. V. -- *Women and Capital Punishment in the United States: An Analytical History.* McFarland & Company, Inc., 2016

Baurick, T. -- *Olalla's 'starvation heights' still causes chills after a century.* Kitsap Sun, December 30, 2014

Battles, Kathleen – *Calling All Cars: Radio Dragnets and the Technology of Policing*, Minneapolis, MN, University of Minnesota Press, 2010

Belcher, Horace – "Old Rocky Point," *Rhode Island History*, April 1948

Bellamy, John Stark II – *The Corpse in the Cellar*, Cleveland, OH, Gray and Company Publishers, 1999

Bettencourt, David and Stephanie Chauvin – *Rocky Point Park*, Charleston, SC, Arcadia Publishing, 2009

Bollinger, G. A. – "Historical and Recent Seismic Activity in South Carolina." *Bulletin of the Seismological Society of America*, 1972

Bovsun, M. – "True Crime Story Behind Classic Comedy, Arsenic & Old Lace." *New York Daily News*, January 17, 2020

Bricklin, Julia – *Blonde Rattlesnake*, Guilford, CT, Rowan and Littlefield Publishing, 2029

------------------ - "How the 'Blonde Rattlesnake' Stirred Public Fascination With Female Accomplices," *Smithsonian* Magazine, July 2019

Bromfield, Louis – *Pleasant Valley*, New York, NY, Harper and Brothers Publishers, 1945

Browning, A. H. -- *The Panic of 1819: The First Great Depression*. University of Missouri Press, 2019

Clark, R. -- *American Female Hangings 1632 to 1937*. Capital Punishment UK, no date

Dalhart, V. (1928). *Little Marian Parker* (song).

Davis, Jefferson – *Weird Washington*, New York, NY, Sterling Publishing, 2008

Domanick, Joe – *To Protect and Serve: The LAPD's Century of War in the City of Dreams*, New York, NY, Pocket Books, 1994

Dennis Moore -- *Monty Python's Flying Circus*, 1973

The Dubliners -- *Whiskey in the Jar*, 1967

Edwards, Janet Zenke – *Diana of the Dunes*, Charlestown, SC, History Press, 2010

Enss, C. Wicked Women: *Notorious, Mischievous, and Wayward Ladies from the Old West*. TwoDot, 2015

Gillespie, L. K. -- *Executed Women of 20th and 21st Centuries.* University Press of America, 2009

Hatler, C. – "*The Starvation Doctor: Quack cure or murder?" Forgotten Minnesota*, November 25, 2020

Hoover, Stephanie – *Pretty Evil Pennsylvania*, Guilford, CT, Globe Pequot, 2021

Jones, J. -- *The Feminine Macabre.* (A. R. Woomer, Ed.) (Vol. 1). Spook-Eats Publishing, 2021

Jordan, Mark Sebastian _ *The Ceely Rose Murders at Malabar Farm,* Charleston, SC, History Press, 2021

Leuchter, F. A. (1989, November 27). *Execution by Electrocution* . Encyclopedia.com.

Levin, Peter – "Bizarre Mystery of Federal Man Who Disappeared," *Sunday News*, February 12, 1939

Lindgren, A. -- *Ronia, the Robber's Daughter.* Oxford University Press, 2010

Loreena McKennitt -- *The Highwayman*, 1997

Lovejoy, B. – "The doctor who starved her patients to death" *Smithsonian* Magazine, October 2014

McNicoll, Susan – *Gangster Women and Their Criminal World*, London, UK, Arcturus Publishing Limited, 2021

Meares, Hadley – "In the Summer of 1933, L.A. Had Its Own Bonnie Parker" *Los Angeles Magazine*, July 2019

Merriman, Mark – *Haunted Indiana*, Michigan, Thunder Bay Press, 1997

Morris, R. - *Lighting Out for the Territory: How Samuel Clemens Headed West and Became Mark Twain*, New York, NY Simon & Schuster Paperbacks, 2011

Morrow, Jason L. – *Vintage True Crime Stories, Volume II* / "The Spawn of Shoebox Annie, 1912-1929" by Courtney Riley Cooper, 1935, Historical Crime Detective Books, 2019

Nash, J. R. -- *World Encyclopedia of 20th Century Murder*. Marlowe & Company, 1994

O'Neil Spady, J. – "Power and Confession: On the Credibility of the Earliest Reports of the Denmark Vesey Slave Conspiracy." *The William and Mary Quarterly*, 2011

O'Shea, K. A. -- *Women and the Death Penalty in the United States*, 1900-1998. Praeger, 1999

Orr, Bruce – *Six Miles to Charleston: The True Story of John and Lavinia Fisher*, Charleston, SC, History Press, 2010

Oyer, K. – "Haunted Holy City: Some of Charleston's Famous Ghosts and Their Stories." *The Post and Courier*, October 26, 2022

Parsons, H. – "Charleston's Most Inhospitable Hosts: The Story of John and Lavinia Fisher." *Historical Crime Detective*, no date

Perper, J. A., & Cina, S. J. -- *When Doctors Kill: Who, Why, and How*. Scholars Portal, 2010

Pezz, Kelly Sullivan – *Murder at Rocky Point Park*, Charleston, SC, History Press, 2014

Pickering, M. (2019, November 29). "Toni Joe Henry: A Shocking Anniversary." *Leesville Daily Leader*.

Poulson, Ellen – *Don't Call us Molls*, Little Neck, NY, Clinton Cook Publishing, 2002

Reid, J.B., James. R.M. --*Uncovering Nevada's Past: a Primary Source History of the Silver State.* Reno: University of Nevada Press. (2004)

Renner, Joan and Christina Rice – *First with the Latest! Aggie Underwood, the Los Angeles Herald, and the Sordid Crimes of a City*, Los Angeles, CA, Friends of the Los Angeles Public Library, 2015

Scott, Beth and Michael Norman – *Haunted Heartland*, New York, NY, Dorset Press, 1985

Spraggs, G. -- *Outlaws and Highwaymen: the Cult of the Robber in England from the Middle Ages to the Nineteenth Century.* Pimlico, 2001

Taylor, Troy – *"I Want to Come Home Tonight: The Haunting Story of Marion Parker*, Jacksonville, IL, American Hauntings Ink, 2017

Twain, Mark – *Roughing It*, New York, NY, Chelsea House, 2021 edition

Tygiel, Jules – *The Great Los Angeles Swindle: Oil, Stocks, And Scandal During the Roaring Twenties*, Berkley, University of California Press, 1996

Wagar, M. (2005, May 7). "Owners say 'Starvation Heights' home is haunted." *Kitsap Sun.*

Willis, James – *Haunted Indiana*, Mechanicsburg, PA, Stackpole Books, 2012

Wise, W. L. – "Lavinia Fisher of Charleston: Nation's First Female Serial Killer or Wrongly Accused?" *The Post and Courier.* October 28, 2021

Woodyard, Chris – *Haunted Ohio*, Beavercreek, OH, Kestrel Publications, 1991

Woomer, Amanda R. – *Harlots and Hauntings*, Spook-Eats Publishing, 2022

Zierold, N. -- *Three Sisters in Black: The Bizarre True Case of the Bathtub Tragedy*, Open Road Media, 2018

Newspaper and Online References (Toni Jo Henry):

American Press Staff. (2020, February 28). *Toni Jo Henry.*
Anomalien.com. (2018, September 27). *A Courthouse Ghost: Toni Jo Henry.* Anomalien.com.
Blanco, J. I. (n.d.). *Toni Jo Henry: Photos.* Murderpedia, the Encyclopedia of Murderers.
The Daily Alaska Empire. (volume) (Juneau, Alaska), 30 Nov. 1942
The Daily Monitor Leader. (volume) (Mount Clemens, Mich.), 24 Nov. 1942.
Detroit Evening Times. (Detroit, Mich), 19 July 1942.
Detroit Evening Times. (Detroit, Mich), 24 Nov. 1942.
Detroit Evening Times. (Detroit, Mich), 29 Nov. 1942.
Evening Star. (volume) (Washington, D.C.), 30 March 1940.
Evening Star. (volume) (Washington, D.C.), 08 Feb. 1941.
Evening Star. (volume) (Washington, D.C.), 23 Jan. 1942.
Evening Star. (volume) (Washington, D.C.), 04 Aug. 1942.
Evening Star. (volume) (Washington, D.C.), 05 Aug. 1942.
Evening Star. (volume) (Washington, D.C.), 06 Aug. 1942.
Evening Star. (volume) (Washington, D.C.), 11 Nov. 1942.
Evening Star. (volume) (Washington, D.C.), 21 Nov. 1942.
Evening Star. (volume) (Washington, D.C.), 24 Nov. 1942.
Evening Star. (volume) (Washington, D.C.), 26 Nov. 1942.
Evening Star. (volume) (Washington, D.C.), 27 Nov. 1942.
Evening Star. (volume) (Washington, D.C.), 28 Nov. 1942.
Evening Star. (volume) (Washington, D.C.), 29 Nov. 1942.
Evening Star. (volume) (Washington, D.C.), 24 March 1943.
Imperial Valley Press. (El Centro, Calif.), 24 Nov. 1942.
Tacoma Times. (volume) (Tacoma, Wash.), 28 Nov. 1942.
Toni Jo Henry: A Love Worth Dying For? Capital Punishment UK. (n.d.).

Wilmington Morning Star. (volume) (Wilmington, N.C.), 31 March 1940.
Wilmington Morning Star. (volume) (Wilmington, N.C.), 13 Aug. 1942.
Wilmington Morning Star. (volume) (Wilmington, N.C.), 02 Dec. 1942.
Ypsilanti Daily Press. (Ypsilanti, Mich.), 21 Nov. 1942.
Ypsilanti Daily Press. (Ypsilanti, Mich.), 28 Nov. 1942.

Newspaper and Online References (Linda Burfield Hazzard)

Aberdeen Herald. (volume) (Aberdeen, Chehalis County, 09 June 1916.
Alaska Daily Empire. (volume) (Juneau, Alaska), 13 Aug. 1913.
Arizona Republican. (volume) (Phoenix, Ariz.), 24 Jan. 1912.
Barre Daily Times. (Barre, Vt.), 02 Feb. 1912.
Bismarck Daily Tribune. (volume) (Bismarck, Dakota (N.D.)), 02 Feb. 1912.
Blackfoot Optimist. (volume) (Blackfoot, Idaho), 12 Feb. 1912.
Cairo Bulletin. (Cairo, Ill.), 20 Jan. 1912.
Clearwater Republican. (volume) (Orofino, Idaho), 29 Aug. 1913.
Daily Capital Journal. (Salem, Oregon), 07 Feb. 1912.
Daily Capital Journal. (Salem, Oregon), 08 May 1912.
Daily Capital Journal. (Salem, Oregon), 27 Dec. 1913.
Daily Gate City. (volume) (Keokuk, Iowa), 21 Jan. 1912.
Daily Gate City. (volume) (Keokuk, Iowa), 09 May 1912.
Daily Missoulian. (volume) (Missoula, Mont.), 21 Jan. 1912.
Daily Missoulian. (volume) (Missoula, Mont.), 13 Aug. 1913.
Daily Missoulian. (volume) (Missoula, Mont.), 24 Dec. 1913.
Daily Star-Mirror. (Moscow, Idaho), 07 Feb. 1912.
Daily Star-Mirror. (Moscow, Idaho), 26 Dec. 1913.
Day Book. (volume) (Chicago, Ill.), 22 May 1912.
Day Book. (volume) (Chicago, Ill.), 27 Dec. 1912.
Day Book. (volume) (Chicago, Ill.), 28 March 1913.
Dillon, L. (2022, November 3). *The starvation doctor: Dr. Linda Hazzard's deadly cure.* Historic Mysteries
East Oregonian: E.O. (Pendleton, OR), 07 Aug. 1911
East Oregonian: E.O. (Pendleton, OR), 08 Aug. 1911.
East Oregonian: E.O. (Pendleton, OR), 07 Feb. 1912.
El Paso Herald. (El Paso, Tex.), 26 Oct. 1911.
Evening Standard. (volume) (Ogden City, Utah), 26 Jan. 1912.
Evening Standard. (volume) (Ogden City, Utah), 27 Jan. 1912.

Evening Standard. (volume) (Ogden City, Utah), 20 Jan. 1912.
Evening Star. (volume) (Washington, D.C.), 21 Jan. 1912.
Evening Star. (volume) (Washington, D.C.), 07 May 1936.
Greene County Herald. (Leakesville, Miss.), 26 Jan. 1912.
Hall, H. (2016, December 14). *Natural medicine, starvation, and murder: The story of Linda Hazzard.* Science-Based Medicine.
Hawaiian Star. (volume) (Honolulu (Oahu)), 07 Aug. 1911.
Hawaiian Star. (volume) (Honolulu (Oahu)), 08 Feb. 1912.
Hawaiian Star. (volume) (Honolulu (Oahu)), 16 Feb. 1912.
Iditarod Pioneer. (Iditarod, Alaska), 29 Jan. 1916.
Irish Standard. (volume) (Minneapolis, Minn. ;), 16 Aug. 1913.
Leavenworth Echo. (volume) (Leavenworth, Wash.), 06 May 1910.
Medford Mail Tribune. (Medford, Or.) 1909-1989. Oregon 05 Feb. 1912.
Meridian Times. (Meridian, Idaho), 09 Feb. 1912.
Minneapolis Journal. (volume) (Minneapolis, Minn.), 09 Nov. 1901.
Newport Miner. (volume) (Newport, Wash.), 19 May 1910.
Newport Miner. (volume) (Newport, Wash.), 18 Jan. 1912.
Nome Daily Nugget. (Nome, Alaska), 12 July 1912.
Nome Daily Nugget. (Nome, Alaska), 27 Dec. 1915.
Norwich Bulletin. (volume) (Norwich, Conn.), 24 Jan. 1912.
Omaha Daily Bee. (Omaha (Neb.)), 21 Jan. 1912.
Princeton Union. 22 Dec. 1915.
Roundup Record. (volume) (Roundup, Mont.), 26 Jan. 1912.
Salt Lake Tribune. (volume) (Salt Lake City, Utah), 07 Aug. 1911.
San Francisco Call. (volume) (San Francisco (Calif.)), 09 Aug. 1911.
San Francisco Call. (volume) (San Francisco (Calif.)), 13 Aug. 1911.
San Francisco Call. (volume) (San Francisco (Calif.)), 20 Jan. 1912.
San Francisco Call. (volume) (San Francisco (Calif.)), 24 Jan. 1912.
San Francisco Call. (volume) (San Francisco (Calif.)), 02 Feb. 1912.
San Juan Islander. (volume) (Friday Harbor, Wash.), 29 Aug. 1913.
Santa Fe New Mexican. (volume) (Santa Fe, N.M.), 24 Jan. 1912.
Santa Fe New Mexican. (volume) (Santa Fe, N.M.), 05 Feb. 1912.
Seattle Republican. (volume) (Seattle, Wash.), 26 Jan. 1912.
Seattle Star. (volume) (Seattle, Wash.), 19 April 1910.
Seattle Star. (volume) (Seattle, Wash.), 31 Jan. 1912. /
Seattle Star. (volume) (Seattle, Wash.), 13 Aug. 1913.
Seattle Star. (volume) (Seattle, Wash.), 02 Oct. 1919.

Seattle Star. (volume) (Seattle, Wash.), 25 July 1922.
Seattle Star. (volume) (Seattle, Wash.), 30 Jan. 1924.
Seattle Star. (volume) (Seattle, Wash.), 31 Jan. 1924.
Seattle Star. (volume) (Seattle, Wash.), 14 Feb. 1925.
Seattle Star. (volume) (Seattle, Wash.), 12 March 1925.
Seward Daily Gateway. (volume) (Seward, Alaska), 12 March 1925.
Spokane Press. (volume) (Spokane, Wash.), 01 Feb. 1908.
Spokesman Review. (1936, May 6).
Star Tribune. 17 Dec. 1914.
Tacoma Times. (volume) (Tacoma, Wash.), 30 April 1910.
Tacoma Times. (volume) (Tacoma, Wash.), 07 Aug. 1911.
Tacoma Times. (volume) (Tacoma, Wash.), 09 Aug. 1911
Tacoma Times. (volume) (Tacoma, Wash.), 18 Jan. 1912.
Tacoma Times. (volume) (Tacoma, Wash.), 20 Jan. 1912.
Tacoma Times. (volume) (Tacoma, Wash.), 26 Jan. 1912.
Tacoma Times. (volume) (Tacoma, Wash.), 29 Jan. 1912.
Tacoma Times. (volume) (Tacoma, Wash.), 03 Feb. 1912.
Tacoma Times. (volume) (Tacoma, Wash.), 06 Feb. 1912.
Tacoma Times. (volume) (Tacoma, Wash.), 07 Feb. 1912.
Tacoma Times. (volume) (Tacoma, Wash.), 03 July 1912.
Tacoma Times. (volume) (Tacoma, Wash.), 22 Oct. 1912.
Tacoma Times. (volume) (Tacoma, Wash.), 19 Feb. 1913.
Tacoma Times. (volume) (Tacoma, Wash.), 25 March 1913.
Tacoma Times. (volume) (Tacoma, Wash.), 13 Aug. 1913.
Tacoma Times. (volume) (Tacoma, Wash.), 15 Aug. 1913.
Tacoma Times. (volume) (Tacoma, Wash.), 04 Nov. 1913.
Tacoma Times. (volume) (Tacoma, Wash.), 24 Dec. 1913.
Tacoma Times. 24 Dec. 1913.
Tacoma Times. 24 Dec. 1913.
Tacoma Times. (volume) (Tacoma, Wash.), 06 Jan. 1914.
Tacoma Times. (volume) (Tacoma, Wash.), 18 Dec. 1915.
Tacoma Times. (volume) (Tacoma, Wash.), 03 June 1916. 4/
Topeka State Journal. (volume) (Topeka, Kansas), 26 Jan. 1912.
Twice-a-Week Plain Dealer. (Howard County, Iowa), 30 Jan. 1912
Washburn Leader. (Washburn, McLean County, N.D.), 26 Jan. 1912.
Washington Standard. (Olympia, Wash. Territory), 04 April 1913.
Washington Standard. (Olympia, Wash. Territory), 31 July 1914.

Wellington Daily News. 8 Aug. 1911.
Wibaux Pioneer. (volume) (Wibaux, Mont.), 09 Feb. 1912.

Newspapers and Online References (Lavinia Fisher)

Alexandria Gazette & Daily Advertiser. (Alexandria (Va.)), 23 Sept. 1819
Alexandria Gazette & Daily Advertiser. (Alexandria (Va.)), 26 Feb. 1820.
Charleston Daily Courier. (Charleston, S.C.). 22 Feb. 1819.
Charleston Daily Courier. (Charleston, S.C.). 20 Feb. 1820.
Charleston Daily Courier. (Charleston, S.C.). 25 March 1820.
Independent. (Wahoo, N.E.). 26 Sept. 1878.
Kelly, E. -- "The Controversial Story of America's First Female Serial Killer and Her Alleged House of Horrors." *All That's Interesting.*
"Lavinia Fisher: The Story of Charleston's Infamous Serial Killer." *Ghost City Tours*
Rhode-Island Republican. (volume) (Newport, R.I.), 02 Feb. 1820.
Rhode-Island Republican. (volume) (Newport, R.I.), 22 March 1820.
Schexnayder, B. "Lavinia Fisher." Southern Gothic. No date
Weiser-Alexander, K. (2021). "Lavinia Fisher." Legends of America.
Yorkville Enquirer. (York, S.C.), 8 August 1922.

Newspaper and Online References (Ocey Snead)

Birmingham Age-Herald. (volume) (Birmingham, Ala.), 17 Dec. 1909.
Bovsun, M. "The Sisters in Black: The Murder of Ocey Snead" *1909. New York Daily News.*
"Caroline B. Martin dies | Had Been Committed as Insane After Confessing to Killing Her Daughter" (1913, June 21). *The New York Times.*
Christiansburg News | Mr. Wardlaw Sheed Fatally Burned --Used Oil to Light Fire. (1906, March 3). *Evening News of Roanoke.*
Daily Sentinel. (volume) (Grand Junction, Colo.), 09 Dec. 1909.
Daily Sentinel. (volume) (Grand Junction, Colo.), 10 Dec. 1909.
Daily Sentinel. (volume) (Grand Junction, Colo.), 13 Dec. 1909.
Daily Sentinel. (volume) (Grand Junction, Colo.), 17 Dec. 1909.
Daily Sentinel. (volume) (Grand Junction, Colo.), 20 Dec. 1909.
Daily Sentinel. (volume) (Grand Junction, Colo.), 28 Dec. 1909
Detroit Times. (volume) (Detroit, Mich.), 06 May 1910.
El Paso Herald. (El Paso, Tex.), 11 Jan. 1911.

Evening Star. (volume) (Washington, D.C.), 17 Dec. 1909.
Evening Star. (volume) (Washington, D.C.), 23 Dec. 1909.
Farmer and Mechanic. (volume) (Raleigh, N.C.), 28 Dec. 1909.
Fletcher Snead Missing. Husband of Bath-Tub Murder Victim Disappeared. It Is Feared He May Have Suicided. (1910, January 11). *Urbana Daily Courier*
Mrs. Snead's Family Full of Fatalities | Family Apparently Pursued by a Strange Fatality for Many Years | Bathtub Victim Buried | Carried to the Grave Almost Unmourned, with Her Mother Still in Hiding . (1909, December 9). *The New York Times.*
New-York Tribune. (volume) (New York (N.Y.)), 22 Jan. 1911.
Newark Evening Star and Newark Advertiser. (volume) (Newark, N.J.), 03 Dec. 1909
Newark Evening Star and Newark Advertiser. (volume) (Newark, N.J.), 17 Dec. 1909.
Newark Evening Star and Newark Advertiser. (volume) (Newark, N.J.), 21 Dec. 1909.
Newark Evening Star and Newark Advertiser. (volume) (Newark, N.J.), 20 Sept. 1910.
Newark Evening Star and Newark Advertiser. (volume) (Newark, N.J.), 07 Feb. 1911.
Norwich Bulletin. (volume) (Norwich, Conn.), 03 Dec. 1909.
Norwich Bulletin. (volume) (Norwich, Conn.), 24 Jan. 1911.
Palestine Daily Herald. (volume) (Palestine, Tex.), 07 May 1910.
Palestine Daily Herald. (volume) (Palestine, Tex.), 21 Sept. 1910.
Perth Amboy Evening News. (Perth Amboy, N.J.), 02 Dec. 1909.
The Salt Lake Herald-Republican. (Salt Lake City, Utah), 15 May 1910.
Vilas County News. (Eagle River, Vilas County, Wis.), 08 Dec. 1909.
Virginia Gazette. (volume) (Williamsburg, Va.), 06 Jan. 1910.
West, M. (2017, October 26). "*Fearless confederate died mysteriously in NYC.*" *Murfreesboro Post.*

Newspaper and Online References (Marion Parker)

Albany Democrat-Herald. (1927, December 23). Alleged Child Murderer Got Gas in Albany.
Albany Democrat-Herald. (1927, December 23). Prepare to Send Hickman to California.

Chattanooga Daily Times. (1927, December 20). Auto Used by Man in Capture Found.
Chattanooga Daily Times. (1927, December 20). Check Fingerprints Against Records.
Chattanooga Daily Times. (1927, December 20). Mother Not Told How Daughter Died.
Douglas Daily Dispatch. (volume) (Douglas, Ariz.), 25 Dec. 1927.
Edmonton Journal. (1927, December 27). Hickman Lone Coyote Instead of 'The Fox'; Youth Confesses All.
El Paso Evening Post. (1928, October 19). Chronology of Hickman Crime.
El Paso Evening Post. (1928, October 19). Thinks Hickman Could Have Been Genius.
Hillman, W. G. (n.d.). *Edgar Rice Burroughs Reports on the Notorious 1928 Hickman Trial.* Erbzine 1767
Imperial Valley Press. (El Centro, Calif.), 19 Dec. 1927.
Imperial Valley Press. (El Centro, Calif.), 20 Dec. 1927.
Imperial Valley Press. (El Centro, Calif.), 21 Dec. 1927.
Imperial Valley Press. (El Centro, Calif.), 22 Dec. 1927.
Imperial Valley Press. (El Centro, Calif.), 23 Dec. 1927.
Imperial Valley Press. (El Centro, Calif.), 24 Dec. 1927.
Imperial Valley Press. (El Centro, Calif.), 27 Dec. 1927.
Imperial Valley Press. (El Centro, Calif.), 16 March 1928.
Indianapolis Times. (volume) (Indianapolis (Ind.)), 20 Dec. 1927.
Indianapolis Times. (volume) (Indianapolis (Ind.)), 23 Dec. 1927.
Indianapolis Times. (volume) (Indianapolis (Ind.)), 28 Dec. 1927.
Kusko Times. (volume) (McGrath, Alaska), 24 Dec. 1927.
Kusko Times. (volume) (McGrath, Alaska), 20 Oct. 1928.
Las Vegas Age. (volume) (Las Vegas, Nev.), 20 Oct. 1928.
Michaels, S. *The Incredibly Gruesome Murder of 12 Year Old Marion Parker.* (2020). *YouTube.*
Modesto News-Herald. (1927, December 23). Hickman Names "Pal" as Slayer.
Monroe, H. (2020, February 12). *The horrifying murder of Marion Parker.* Medium.
Morristown Gazette-Mail. (1927, December 21). Parker Girl's Slayer Still Eludes Captors.

News-Pilot. (1927, December 16). All Available Officers Aid Man-Hunt.
Oakland Tribune. (1927, December 19). Hickman Final Letter.
Oakland Tribune. (1927, December 28). Chemical Tests.
Pomona Progress Bulletin. (1927, December 20). How Police Link Youth With Crime.
Rasmussen, C. (2001, February 4). Girl's Grisly Killing had City Residents Up in Arms. *Los Angeles Times.*
Richmond Times-Dispatch. (1927, December 18). Kidnapper Returns Little Girl, Dead.
Salt Lake Tribune. (1927, December 23). Photographic Sidelights of Most Fiendish Crime of Century.
Santa Ana Register. (1927, December 16). Speed Away in Coupe.
Seward Daily Gateway. (volume) (Seward, Alaska), 19 Dec. 1927.
Seward Daily Gateway. (volume) (Seward, Alaska), 20 Dec. 1927.
Seward Daily Gateway. (volume) (Seward, Alaska), 22 Dec. 1927.
Seward Daily Gateway. (volume) (Seward, Alaska), 04 Jan. 1928.
St. Croix Avis. (volume) (Christiansted, St. Croix (V.I.)), 29 Dec. 1927.
St. Croix Avis. (volume) (Christiansted, St. Croix (V.I.)), 31 Dec. 1927.
St. Croix Avis. (volume) (Christiansted, St. Croix (V.I.)), 30 Jan. 1928.
St. Croix Avis. (volume) (Christiansted, St. Croix (V.I.)), 31 Jan. 1928.
Visalia Daily Times. (1927, December 17). Ransom is Demanded by Girl's Kidnapper.
Visalia Daily Times. (1927, December 19). Gory Clues are Found in House.
Washington Times. (volume) (Washington (D.C.)), 22 Dec. 1927.
Washington Times. (volume) (Washington (D.C.)), 23 Dec. 1927.
Washington Times. (volume) (Washington (D.C.)), 28 Dec. 1927.
Washington Times. (volume) (Washington (D.C.)), 29 Dec. 1927.
Washington Times. (volume) (Washington (D.C.)), 27 Jan. 1928.
Washington Times. (volume) (Washington (D.C.)), 08 Feb. 1928.

Newspaper and Online References (Julia Bulette)

1868: John Millian, Who Martyred a Madam. ExecutedToday.com. (2008)
Buergin, M. (2020). *Knowing Nevada: Killing the Queen of the Comstock.* KRNV.

Chan, A. (2017, August 15). *To The Miners of Virginia City, Julia Bulette was the Beloved Queen of the Comstock.* HistoryNet.
Dustman, K. (2018, August 2). *Julia Bulette... There's More to Her Story!* Clairitage Press.
Flinchum, R. (2017). *A Mysterious Murder on the Comstock.* Nevada Magazine.
Gold Hill Daily News. (volume) (Gold Hill, N.T. (Nev.)), 22 Jan. 1867.
Gold Hill Daily News. (volume) (Gold Hill, N.T. (Nev.)), 24 May 1867.
Gold Hill Daily News. (volume) (Gold Hill, N.T. (Nev.)), 25 May 1867.
Gold Hill Daily News. (volume) (Gold Hill, N.T. (Nev.)), 25 May 1867.
Gold Hill Daily News. (volume) (Gold Hill, N.T. (Nev.)), 31 May 1867.
Gold Hill Daily News. (volume) (Gold Hill, N.T. (Nev.)), 26 June 1867.
Gold Hill Daily News. (volume) (Gold Hill, N.T. (Nev.)), 27 Feb. 1868.
Gunn, J. (2022, January 6). *Who was Julia?* Julia C Bulette 1864.
Idaho Semi-Weekly World. (Idaho City, Boise County, Idaho Territory), 06 May 1868.
James, R. M. (2020, November 12). *Sex, Murder, and the Myth of the Wild West: How a Soiled Dove Earned a Heart of Gold.*
Layne, M. A. (2020, May 15). Pine Nuts: A short history of Julia Bulette. *Sierra Sun.*
Reno Gazette-Journal - From 1867: Julia Bulette is murdered.
Virginia City. (2018, August 4). *Cemeteries.* Virginia City.
Virginia Daily Union. January 21, 1867.

OTHER NEWSPAPERS AND PERIODICALS

Chesterton Tribune
Chicago Daily News
Chicago Daily Tribune
Chicago Examiner
Chicago Herald
Chicago Herald and Examiner
Cleveland Press
Columbus Dispatch
Fort Wayne Weekly Sentinel
Gary Evening Post
Gary Tribune

Lake County Times
Los Angeles Daily News
Los Angeles Herald Examiner
Los Angeles Times
Mansfield Daily Shield
Mansfield News Journal
Michigan City News
Porter County Vidette
Providence Journal
Radio Guide
Rhode Island Evening News
Santa Ana Register
St. Louis Star and Times
True Story

SPECIAL THANKS TO:

April Slaughter: Cover Design and Artwork
Becky Ray: Editing and Proofreading

FROM TROY:

Samantha Smith
Athena & the "Aunts" - Sue, Carmen & Rocky
Brianna Snow
Orrin and Rachel Taylor
Rene Kruse
Rachael Horath
Bethany Horath
Elyse and Thomas Reihner
Lisa Taylor and Lux
John Winterbauer
Kaylan Schardan
Maggie and Packy Lundholm
Cody Beck

Tom and Michelle Bonadurer
Lydia Rhoades
Susan Kelly and Amy Bouyear
Cheryl Stamp and Sheryel Williams-Staab
Joelle Leitschuh and Tonya Leitschuh
Jami Kennedy
Scott and Hannah Robl
Jake and Emily Fink
Dave and Donna Nunnally
And the entire crew of American Hauntings

FROM AMANDA:

The Traveling Museum of Memento Mori Patrons, particularly Kerri Collins, Brian Hogan, Jim Sturgill, and Carolyn Woomer.
My parents (Mark and Carolyn)
And husband, Adam.

ABOUT THE AUTHORS

Troy Taylor is the author of books on ghosts, hauntings, true crime, the unexplained, and the supernatural in America. He is also the founder of American Hauntings Ink, which offers books, ghost tours, events, and weekend excursions. He was born and raised in the Midwest and divides his time between Illinois and wherever the wind decides to take him. See Troy's other titles at:
www.americanhauntingsink.com

Writer, anthropologist, and paranormal researcher, Amanda R. Woomer was born and raised in Buffalo, NY. The owner of Spook-Eats, she is a featured writer for Haunted Magazine, creator of the all-female paranormal journal, *The Feminine Macabre*, and the founder of the Traveling Museum of Memento Mori, an interactive exhibit of mourning and death customs of the past. She is also the author of 10 books, and you can follow her spooky adventures at spookeats.com and on Facebook, Instagram, and Twitter.

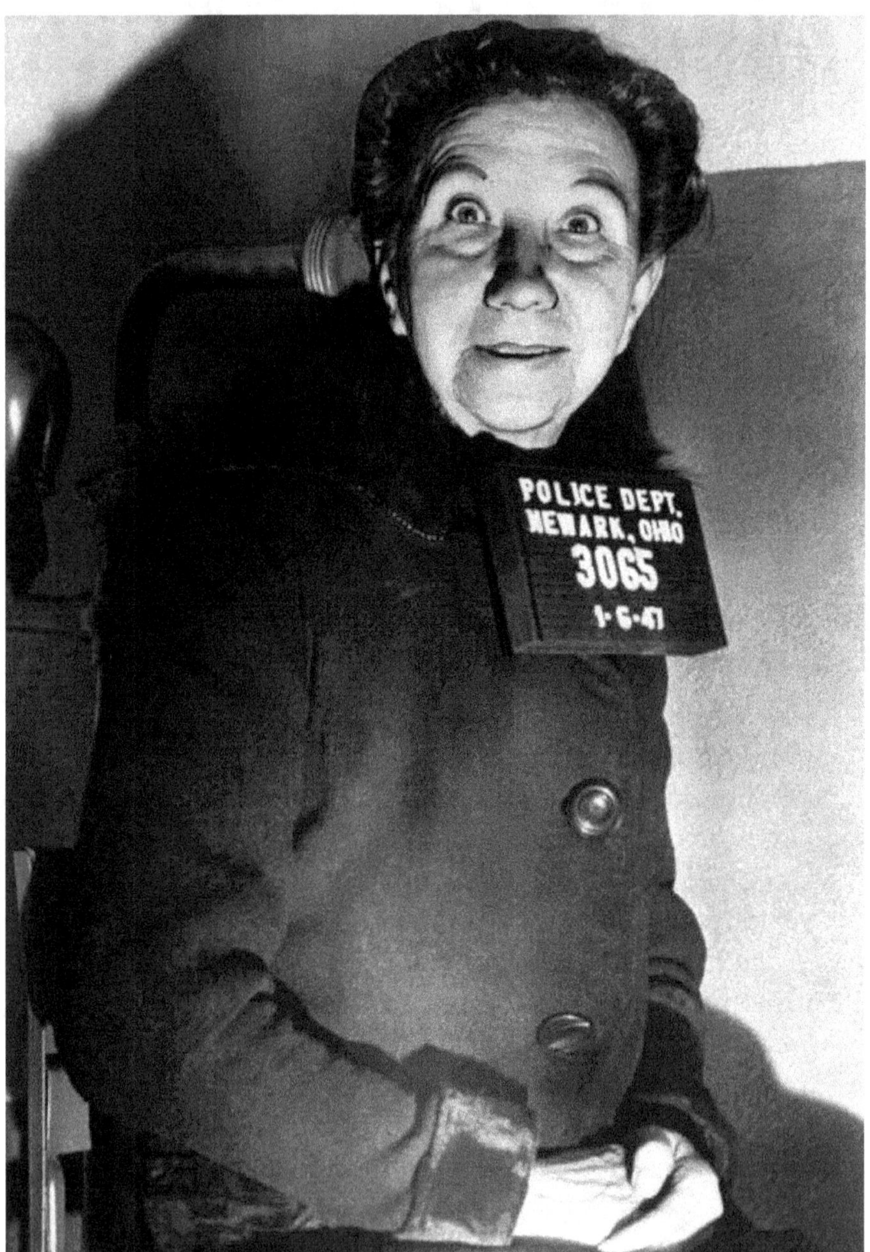
POLICE DEPT.
NEWARK, OHIO
3065
1-6-47

www.ingramcontent.com/pod-product-compliance
Lightning Source LLC
LaVergne TN
LVHW010853110826
845149LV00005B/1393

* 9 7 8 1 9 5 8 5 8 9 0 5 2 *